Competition Among the Few

WILLIAM FELLNER

PROFESSOR OF ECONOMICS, UNIVERSITY OF CALIFORNIA

Competition Among

the Few

OLIGOPOLY AND SIMILAR MARKET STRUCTURES

Reprints of Economic Classics
Augustus M. Kelley
New York 1960

PREFACE AND GUIDE
TO THE 1960 PRINTING

AN author is bound to feel apologetic when confronted
with a book he finished a decade or more ago, especially
if the book is concerned with a branch of economic theory
which is in flux. But some readers still seem to have an
interest in the book—readers to whom I would like to express
my gratitude for their willingness to see the good there may
be in a contribution and to overlook its shortcomings—and
I will make use of this opportunity to say a few words about
those parts of my presentation which I still like to emphasize
in my own thinking or in class-room discussions of oligopoly
and of bilateral monopoly.

I continue to believe that it is fruitful to regard oligopolistic relations as bargaining relations, in a somewhat extended
sense of the term, and to suggest that the *implicit* bargaining
of oligopolists tends to lead to *implicit* agreements. Furthermore, I continue to believe that the "content" of implicit
agreements deviates from joint-profit maximization because
of the existence of uncertainty which precludes dependable
forecasts of the available joint profits and of the relative
strength of the rival parties. For this reason the economist's
expectations concerning the extent and the character of the
deviations from joint-profit maximization should in each
specific situation be determined by his diagnosis concerning

v

the strength and the character of the factors that cause the uncertainty. The uncertainty which I have in mind here is in part uncertainty about future developments in the joint markets in which the participants do business, and it is in part uncertainty about the relative skills of the participants. An acceptable static theory of oligopoly would have to be a theory of joint maximization, very much like a theory of monopoly. Fortunately, we do not live in a static world.

It still seems reasonable to me to assume, as I did when I wrote this book, that in many oligopolistic markets the degree and the nature of the uncertainty are such as to make the individual firms exceedingly reluctant to trade any of their direct "market share" for higher joint profits which would be obtainable through pooling and inter-firm compensations. Thus, firms are much more likely to be engaged in implicit bargaining for individual market shares than for a share in the available maximum profits of a pooled aggregate of firms. Market sharing does of course confront each firm with a demand function—with a portion of the industry demand function or with whatever rough-and-ready equivalent this device has in the minds of business men—and in the first approximation it seems satisfactory to assume individual profit maximization along the resulting "demand functions" of the individual firm. But in the next analytical step the uncertainty characteristic of dynamic economies again influences the results, in that "implicit agreements" usually leave the individual firms quite a bit of leeway for improving their market shares (for shifting up their individual demand functions) *by specific methods* — mainly by the approved methods of product change and advertising. From the present point of view, the essential property of these "approved" methods is that, *in contrast to price-cutting*, they require *skill.* The use of this skill is not "signed away" readily in implicit agreements because its distribution among the rivals is subject to uncertainty. Moreover, the use of these approved methods takes time, and this makes it unlikely that these methods should generate a process of quick cumulative retaliation by which profits are wiped out, as could easily happen in the event of price-cutting. Therefore, the following seems a fruitful approximation in a great many instances: assume individual profit-maximization (with allowance for safety-margin considerations and some other qualifying factors) along market-sharing demand curves; and take account of the fact that firms do not violate the implicit agreements governing their relations with their rivals if, relative to these rivals, they shift up their individual market-sharing demand curves (their "iso-market-share-DD^1 curves") *by certain "approved methods."*

As for the policy problems connected with oligopoly, I continue to believe that, super-imposed upon "technologically justified" concentration, modern economies are exceedingly likely to experience further concentration which is profitable merely to narrow groups, and pays mostly, if not exclusively, by way of the market power which it conveys. Awareness of this should focus the efforts of policy makers on easing entry for technologically and organizationally efficient rivals or would-be rivals, not on futile efforts to make members of a small group behave as if they were unintelligent enough to overlook the obvious fact that they are indeed members of a small group. The position here developed does not favor the "atomization" of corporations; it merely favors broader market structures than those which develop when, in addition to the concentration resulting from the genuine cost-advantages of size, we get further concentration resulting from barriers to the entry of efficient competitors. In these matters the burden of proof rests, I feel, with those who succeed in keeping a market structure very highly concentrated. After all, we wish to preserve the economic ideology of the Western world as an ideology of effective competition.

Nor would I like to modify the statement that while the atomization of the labor supply is neither desirable nor possible, over-concentration on the supply side of the labor market is creating serious problems, particularly because it is giving rise to a conflict between the objective of the maximum utilization of resources and the objective of a reasonably stable general price level. This proposition was developed in detail in an earlier book (at that time, more as a forecast than as a statement of fact) but I think the proposition is repeated in the present volume with sufficient emphasis not to require further amplification.

Yet I would of course write much of this book differently if I were to write it for publication as a new book in 1960. In particular, I would make an effort to tie the argument in with contributions of the past decade which are too numerous to be considered here. To mention just a few examples, Thomas C. Schelling's brilliant work has given specific content to the concept of bargaining skill and bargaining advantages, by which results are determined within limits such as those discussed in this volume. The same author has thrown light also on the process by which people seem to guess at solutions acceptable to others, if they rightly assume that the others are also motivated by the desire to hit on solutions acceptable to those first mentioned. J. S. Bain has not only further developed his analysis concerning the significance of entry for oligopoly theory—a theme increasingly emphasized both in this country and abroad—but he has done valuable work on various aspects of the problem of economics of large-scale, and on the presumptive limits of these economies. George Stigler has continued to direct our attention to the high significance of the relationship between mergers and concentration, and Fritz Machlup has illuminated many sides of the competition-monopoly problem in two systematic treatises. Rudolf Richter in Germany, and more recently (in a somewhat different context) William Baumol of Princeton University, have developed the argument that in some cases maximization of gross revenue may give a better first approximation than does maximization of profits. As for bilateral monopoly, Lawrence Fouraker of Pennsylvania State University has conducted interesting experiments concerning the ability of parties to arrive at joint maximization with reliance on all-or-none clauses.

These are just a few illustrations of theoretical contributions toward which it would be tempting to build a bridge if the author of this volume were to formulate his analysis at the present date. As things stand, he will have to request his readers to put these and other bits and pieces together, hoping that one of these pieces—the piece in which Mr. Augustus Kelley is kindly placing his confidence here—will not be discarded altogether.

A few graphs in the book were redrawn and misprints were corrected. I have not reworked the book. The gist of the argument is found in Chapters I, V, VI, VIII and XI. But it is impossible to follow the reasoning in some of these chapters without occasionally turning back, with the aid of the index, to passages in earlier chapters. For example, the concise summary statement in Chapter VIII uses some concepts which are explained in Chapters III and VII. Furthermore, while Chapter I contains a general discussion of problems of

fewness—including problems of bilateral monopoly as well
as those of oligopoly, oligopsony, etc.—the technical extension of the reasoning to bilateral monopoly is contained not
in one of the five chapters which I have described as containing the "gist of the argument" but in Chapters IX and X.
I might add that my analysis of the relationship between
market structures and technological progress was further
developed in an article which has been reprinted as Chapter
16 in *Readings in Industrial Organization* (edited by Professor R. B. Heflebower and G. W. Stocking, 1958).

WILLIAM FELLNER

New Haven,
Connecticut.
October 1959.

INTRODUCTION

FEWNESS is an important characteristic of the contemporary economic scene. Many prices and wage rates are determined under conditions which are neither atomistic nor monopolistic. They are determined under conditions of fewness: a few decision-making units shape their policies in view of how they mutually react to each other's moves.

Fewness, however, is not a new phenomenon nor an all-pervading characteristic. In the past, even after the abolition of most mercantilistic restrictions, the spatial isolation of producers must have had a very significant restrictive effect on competition. In some fields of activity it still has this effect. Furthermore, economies of large scale as well as "artificial" methods of excluding competitors, have resulted in fewness even in broad and integrated market areas. But there are important economic relations which are not carried on in circumstances of fewness. Many markets operate under the more anonymous conditions prevailing when the single decision-making units are of negligible significance in relation to the market. This remains true in spite of the fact that, on these markets, attempts at organizing quasi-monopolistic groups with outside help are rather common.

A volume on fewness is not a value theory. But any value theory in which the economics of fewness receives merely cursory treatment is seriously incomplete.

The writer places no more than moderate confidence in some of his tentative answers to the specific questions raised in this book. He was mainly interested in helping to develop a general framework suitable for *asking* the questions with which realistic inquiries must be concerned.[1] He hopes that in the approach to practical problems a framework such as the one here developed will not prove entirely useless; or, at any rate, that *some* general framework developed with similar intentions will ultimately prove useful.

Over a period of many years, the author has had frequent discussions with Professor Howard S. Ellis on the limits of tolerance of private enterprise systems with respect to monopoly elements, and with Professor Joe S. Bain on special characteristics of oligopolistic markets. He is profoundly indebted to both, not merely for general suggestions but also for specific advice received after completion of the first draft of the manuscript. Valuable suggestions were made also by members of a faculty seminar at Stanford University which, under the chairmanship of Professor Bernard F. Haley, discussed some of the problems with which this book is concerned. Finally, the author's thanks must be expressed for the clerical help provided by the Bureau of Business and Economic Research of the University of California.

---

[1] For a discussion of the price-policy literature, cf. chap. iv of *A Survey of Contemporary Economics*, ed. Howard S. Ellis (Philadelphia, 1948); and for a discussion of the literature on labor problems, cf. chap. vii, ibid. Professor Joe S. Bain is the author of the first of these two chapters, Professor Lloyd G. Reynolds of the second.

CONTENTS

Competition Among the Few

CHAPTER ONE

Competition, Fewness, and Spontaneous Co-ordination

INDIVIDUAL DEMAND
AND SUPPLY FUNCTIONS:
THE POSSIBLE ABSENCE OF BOTH

VALUE theory, as it is usually presented, suffers from several limitations which are responsible for its failure to give a sufficiently realistic account of price formation in modern industrialized economies. In spite of considerable advance during the past two decades it is questionable whether, in the near future, it will be possible to bring value theory even to that level of realism and applicability that has gradually been reached in the field of monetary theory and the theory of employment. The main reason for this is that monetary theory and the theory of employment deal with broad aggregates with regard to which a greater wealth of factual material is available. More can be said with reasonable generality about magnitudes such as the ratio of money holdings to transactions for the public as a whole and for certain sections of the public, or the ratio of consumption expenditures to national income, than about relationships between certain measurable quantities on the one hand, and wages or prices in specific industries on the other. The relationships that are significant for value theory cannot be read from aggregative national balance sheets or from overall banking statistics. They can be derived only from intensive study of individual market behavior or the market behavior of comparatively narrow groups.

This, of course, follows from the definitions of the fields here considered. Value theory is concerned with relative prices, that is, with relationships between specific prices; the general price level, which is a broad aggregative concept, is defined to be a problem of monetary theory. Similarly, the output produced and the employment supplied by individual firms and industries are determined by precisely the same factors which determine individual prices, that is to say, the output and employment of specific firms and industries are problems of value theory. Aggregate output and employment are problems of the other type of theory, which by now has reached a more advanced stage of development. It follows almost directly from the definitions of these various fields that the difficulties standing in the way of collecting relevant material and of arriving at reasonably useful generalizations are greater for the one type of inquiry than for the other. For one of the two types of inquiry (monetary theory and the theory of employment) is mainly concerned with overall data and overall relationships, while the other (value theory) is, by definition, concerned with specific data and the relationships between them. Superficial information about a great many specific things adds up to general information which is by no means useless; yet the elements of which such general information consists may be quite inadequate for a detailed study of specific processes and their interrelations.

In fact, the main shortcomings of the aggregative theories stem from the circumstance that they do not take into account adequately the effect of "specific" changes (such as relative price and wage changes) on the "aggregate" magnitudes. These theories reason mainly from certain aggregate magnitudes to others, as though the world of aggregates were completely separated from that of the specific. This deficiency is very largely a consequence of the fact that too little is known about the world of the specific. Since, however, the world of the aggregates actually is *in part* distinct from that of the specific—that is, since it is possible to establish certain valid propositions for aggregates that are not drastically affected by shifts in the realm of the specific—this deficiency reduces, but does not destroy, the usefulness of the aggregative type of theory. The weaknesses of value theory, and of the theory of the relative allocation of resources, show fully in the fields covered by these theories themselves. The same weaknesses manifest themselves but partly and indirectly in the fields covered by the aggregative theories.

These weaknesses are not entirely avoidable, and the difficulties are inherently greater in value theory than in aggregative theory. But some of the weaknesses of value theory could perhaps be reduced by further developing an analytical framework into which the discussion of empirically established relationships might be fitted. The technique of analysis of certain obvious facts has not yet been fully developed and integrated with the main body of the theory. The shortcomings of value theory in this respect have been considerably reduced in the first fifteen years of the era of monopolistic-competition theory. But it will take some time to develop a framework which lends itself readily to a systematic discussion of accumulating empirical materials. Progress is gradual.

It is not suggested that these shortcomings will be remedied in this volume. That would indeed be a much too pretentious claim. But an attempt will be made to discuss certain rather elementary problems of value theory in a framework which takes into account some of the difficulties encountered in the usual approach. The theory to be here developed is "general" only in the sense that it defines a limited number of main properties with respect to which actual market situations may be "more or less so." However, in the analysis of actual problems of fewness it is *generally* fruitful to ask these questions of "more or less" in terms of the categories here established. In no other sense can a theory aim at generality if it includes an analysis of so-called imperfections. It can merely describe the scales in terms of which the observed phenomena may be "placed."

Let us examine the difficulties more specifically. We are not here concerned with the weaknesses stemming from the "specific" rather than "overall" character of the subject matter, that is, with the greater difficulty of obtaining material from which reasonably general empirical relationships could be established concerning the bearing of specific processes on one another. We are concerned with certain difficulties encountered in the attempts to interpret the accumulating factual materials in terms of the theory. Even these weaknesses are not purely "accidental" in the

sense of resting entirely on oversight or on undue tradi-
tionalism. They are very largely a consequence of the
fact that the adjustment of the analytical framework to
the interpretative requirements of present-day economic
processes would make it necessary to introduce certain elements into the analytical framework by which this framework would become different *in kind* from what it has
been. Such an analytical framework would be suitable for
"explaining" economic processes in a sense somewhat different from that in which traditional value theory is
capable of explaining the unfortunately narrow range of
facts on which it can be used at all. Furthermore, the
sense in which the modified framework provides an explanation of certain processes is a more "modest" sense than
that in which the traditional framework intends to explain. Consequently, it might be said that a lowering of
standards is involved in such a procedure. We believe that
the procedure will, nevertheless, prove fruitful because it
is inherently impossible to explain a substantial range of
economic processes in the stricter sense attempted by traditional theory. If we insist on these strict standards of
"explanation," so far as theoretical reasoning is concerned, then we shall continue to have a value theory of
narrow applicability plus an increasing amount of factual
material which will have to be discussed in purely "institutional" terms, that is, outside the framework of the
theoretical apparatus. A theoretical apparatus that "explains" certain processes in the sense here suggested is
preferable to one that does not explain them at all, especially if some of these processes are vitally important.
Moreover, the required modesty, or willingness to accept
reduced standards of rigor, is more limited than is sometimes assumed. As we shall soon see, the requirement essen-

tially is that we should be willing to include in our analysis certain further "determinants" of value, in addition to the usual technological functions and utility functions. The behavior of these determinants is frequently more erratic than that of the traditional ones.

The specific problem which best illustrates this dilemma is that of the determinateness of equilibrium. Traditional value theory explains how, on particular markets, determinate equilibria are reached for price, output, input, and so forth, in a variety of circumstances. The standards of determinateness applied by traditional value theory are very special and very strict. The reasoning implies that, from engineering data on the one hand and from utility functions on the other, certain functions must be definable from which it is possible to derive unique equilibrium quantities and prices. These functions must, of course, be definable *ex ante* to the equilibrium magnitudes because they determine the equilibria. In practice, this means postulating that each seller-firm sets up a supply function or faces a demand function or does both, and that each buyer-firm sets up a demand function or faces a supply function or does both, and that the demand and supply functions can be derived from utility functions and engineering data alone. A firm which faces a demand function, but does not establish an independent supply function, is a monopolistic firm (or, better, a firm possessing some degree of monopoly power). As is well known, the assumption of monopoly results in determinate equilibrium, given the cost functions on the supply side. It is then possible to select a point on the demand function which is optimal for the seller, and the equilibrium position is thus uniquely determined. On the other hand, facing a supply function, but not setting up an independent demand function, marks monopsony (or, better, some degree of monopsony power). The equilibrium again is determinate, provided it is possible to define utility functions (or their equivalents) for the demand side. This is true because in these circumstances a point can be selected on the supply function which is optimal for the buyer. Finally, the existence of both a supply function and a demand function for each firm marks atomistic competition.

Present-day value theory recognizes that the conditions of determinate equilibrium are not satisfied on all markets. But the main body of value theory is concerned with markets on which determinate equilibria in the foregoing sense can be established. Figuratively speaking, the discussion of markets not complying with these conditions is still frequently relegated to appendices, if not to footnotes. However, as will be seen later in this chapter, recent discussion has paid increasing attention to the problems here discussed.

In this book, considerable emphasis will be placed on the fact that a significant proportion of the markets with which value theory must be concerned cannot be analyzed in terms of demand functions or supply functions derived from technological data and utility functions alone. Determinate equilibria, in the usual sense, cannot be established for these markets analytically. It is, however, wrong to say that for this reason theory must necessarily "fail" in its discussion of these markets. To believe that theory "succeeds" whenever it formulates from technological data and utility functions assumptions leading to uniquely determinate price and output, and that it "fails" whenever such assumptions cannot be formulated without doing violence to obvious facts is a preconception—and not a very fruitful one. Theory may "succeed" in a different (and perhaps somewhat more modest) sense, even if it does not establish uniquely determinate prices and outputs from such data alone. For the implication of the statement that price and output are indeterminate in certain ranges is *not* that we should be agnostic about what is likely to happen within the ranges in question. The implications of such a statement are essentially methodological. The statement merely carries the suggestion that, after the establishment of a range of possible values, a different apparatus should be employed in the discussion of what is likely to happen within that range.

For markets such as the purely competitive, the monopolistic, and the monopsonistic, the analytical procedure of theory leads from demand functions (or the underlying indifference functions) and from cost functions (or the underlying production functions) directly to the unique prices and outputs which will be established on the markets in question. In the course of this analytical procedure, there is nowhere a methodological "break." Such an explanation is intellectually more satisfactory than are those to be considered in the present volume. But the procedure is inapplicable to a substantial number of significant markets. The attitude that we either are capable of applying some procedure such as this or should refrain from developing theoretical analysis with respect to a problem is an improperly pretentious attitude. In the analysis of markets not complying with the standards set by tradition we can combine traditional methods with different ones, evolving an apparatus which possesses certain inevitable weaknesses but which is far from useless.

The markets on which it is possible to define neither demand functions nor supply functions for the individual firms are those on which specific sellers or buyers sell or buy considerable fractions of the total market volume, so that the other sellers and buyers are affected materially by what single firms are doing. Markets on which a unique buyer faces a unique seller also fall in this category. In other words, the problem is that of oligopoly, oligopsony, and bilateral monopoly, and, of course, also of markets which are oligopsonistic on the demand side and oligopolistic on the supply side. All these markets are characterized by "fewness."

The oligopolist, instead of "setting up" a supply function, attempts to select a definite price to be charged and a definite quantity to be sold, which, in combination with one another, are optimal from his point of view. But the quantity he is capable of selling at any given price depends on the prices charged by his competitors, which, in turn, are appreciably affected by what price *he* sets. Consequently, not only does the oligopolist fail to set up a supply function, but also it is impossible to define for him a demand function from information pertaining to buyers' preferences alone. Similarly, the oligopsonist, instead of setting up a demand function, attempts to select a definite price to be paid for the materials and services he buys and a definite quantity to be purchased, which, in combination with one another, are optimal from his point of view. But the quantity he is capable of buying at any given price depends on the prices paid by his competitors, which, in turn, are appreciably affected by what price *he* pays. Consequently, he not only fails to set up a demand function, but also is not faced with a supply function such as could be calculated from technological data and utility functions alone. Finally, in bilateral monopoly, the buyer, instead of setting up a demand function, tries to select a price to be paid and a quantity to be purchased which, among all price-quantity combinations acceptable to the seller, are optimal from his (the buyer's) point of view;

and, at the same time, the seller, instead of setting up a
supply function, attempts to select a price to be charged
and a quantity to be sold which, among all price-quantity
combinations acceptable to the buyer, are optimal from
his (the seller's) point of view. This, of course, means that
in bilateral monopoly it is impossible to define a demand
function or a supply function for the individual firm from
utility functions and from technological data (as is also
impossible in oligopoly or in oligopsony, although for
different reasons). Determinate equilibrium, in the usual
sense, does not exist if, for the individual firm, it is impossible to define either a demand function or a supply function (or both). Yet, oligopolists, oligopsonists, and producers operating in bilateral monopoly usually have cost
functions and utility functions (or their equivalents), and
these set limits to what is acceptable to them, that is, to
what from their point of view is preferable to going out
of business. The problem of these limits can be approached
with the tools of traditional value theory. These limits
always are in the nature of (long-run) zero-profit points.
They exclude the possibility of outcomes by which any one
party suffers a loss (negative profit) in relation to the
zero line determined by not concluding the deal in question.

For the range lying between such limits, the outcome
will be "indeterminate," if by "determinate" we mean
"uniquely determined by the type of functions used in
traditional value theory." On the traditional assumptions
of value theory, demand functions and supply functions
determine the outcome between these limits, and these
functions can be derived from utility functions and technological data. In the absence of either a demand function
or a supply function, we are at first left empty-handed.

The range between the limits appears to be a blank space.

The range between the (long-run) zero-profit lines appears to be a blank space *methodologically,* but obviously it is not *really* a blank space. In reality, price-quantity solutions *are* reached, and these are unique solutions at any moment of time. Methodologically, there is a "break" at this point because, within the relevant range, the behavior of all parties concerned depends on the assumed reaction of the other parties. The traditional tools remain adequate (or sufficient) if "what I am willing to do" depends on "what I assume the other party's response will be," as long as the reverse is not also true. But these tools become insufficient if what I am willing to do depends on what I assume the other party's response will be, and if, at the same time, what the other party is willing to do depends on what he thinks my response will be. On such an assumption, the traditional tools will not lead to determinate results. This, however, is precisely the assumption on which the theory of oligopoly, oligopsony, and bilateral monopoly must rest. In simple monopoly, what I (the seller) am willing to do depends on what I think the other party's (the competitive buyer's) reaction will be. But what the other party is willing to do depends on his given utility functions, or their equivalent, from which his demand functions are determined; he reacts along a demand function, which is determined by considerations lying outside the circle. In simple monopsony, what I (the buyer) am willing to do depends on what I think the other party's (the competitive seller's) reaction will be. But what the other party is willing to do depends on his cost functions, or their equivalents, on which he bases his supply function; he reacts along a supply function, which again is determined by considerations lying outside this circle. In

oligopoly, oligopsony, and bilateral monopoly, the *limit*
of what I can accept depends on my cost functions, or on
my utility functions, or on their equivalents rather than on
the assumed reactions of the other party. But given the
(long-run) zero-profit limits and the range between them,
further analysis must resort to some different method because, from there on, what I am willing to do depends on
the assumed reaction of the other party, *and vice versa.*
Neither reacts along a function given by considerations
lying outside the circle. Both react in view of how they
think the other will react.

It is now possible to indicate in what sense a "reduction
of standards" is involved in the acceptance of theoretical
explanations which take cognizance of the dependence of
each party's behavior on that of the other. Such conjectural interdependence, as it may be called, increases
the amount of information necessary for understanding
or predicting the outcome of specific processes. The additional necessary information cannot be obtained by the
methods by which production functions, cost functions, or
consumer habits may be studied. Part of the relevant information can be obtained only by observing the behavior
of persons in a range in which their behavior depends on
the assumed behavior of others and in which the actual
behavior of others depends on the assumed behavior of the
first group. Now, it is by no means impossible to make
reasonable statements about what may happen in such
circumstances, that is, about how things become determinate in so-called ranges of indeterminateness. But
proper understanding must rest partly on the kind of
judgment one would prefer *not* to rely on in a search for
dependable answers, namely on judgment concerning the
toughness, or the popularity, or the political advantages

of certain persons and institutions in relation to others. The proposition that under fewness we are faced with ranges of indeterminateness merely means that within the ranges in question we obtain determinate results by "using this kind of material." This is not the most desirable kind of material with which to work, but an attempt to avoid it leads to disregarding some of the most important problems of contemporary economic systems.

CONJECTURAL INTERDEPENDENCE, BARGAINING, AND QUASI-BARGAINING

The situation in which the behavior of all parties concerned depends on the assumed reactions of the other parties is typically that leading to "bargaining." In all cases in which bargaining (in the everyday sense of the word) takes place we are faced with conjectural interdependence. Bargaining in the usual sense presupposes conjectural interdependence, but bargaining *in the usual sense* does not take place in all cases in which conjectural interdependence exists. Bargaining in the usual sense requires direct contact and negotiations between the parties concerned, in addition to conjectural interdependence. But, it will be argued in this volume that there is no fundamental difference between those instances of conjectural interdependence which lead to explicit bargaining and those which do not. In the one case, explicit negotiations are carried on, and, in the course of these, the parties concerned attempt to find out by direct observation what the most favorable agreement is which they can reach with the others. In the other case, each party tries to find out from the responses of the other parties what the ultimate consequences of its own patterns of behavior are; and each party tries to discover which of the alternative patterns of behavior results in mutual reactions that are in the nature of a tacit agreement (or convention), and are more favorable from his point of view than any other tacit agreement acceptable to the others. Such processes may be termed implicit bargaining or quasi-bargaining and the resulting state of affairs may be termed quasi-agreement. The difference between "true" agreement and quasi-agreement is that the former requires direct contact while the latter does not. This difference is not always insignificant. But from the economic point of view the difference between true agreement and quasi-agreement is one affecting fine points more than the fundamental characteristics of the problem. The distinction is analogous to that between "collusion" and what we will call *spontaneous co-ordination*. We may say that all problems of conjectural interdependence are essentially problems of bargaining—provided we interpret bargaining in the broader sense, including the "implicit" variety, that is, quasi-bargaining. Actually, when dealing with the main characteristics of these problems on the level of "first approximations," we shall take this attitude. In a more detailed discussion of market processes, various distinctions will have to be drawn, and the distinction between true bargaining, on the one hand, and merely implicit (or quasi) bargaining on the other will be one of them. In the real world, quasi-agreement may shade over into true agreement by gradations.

Conjectural interdependence (or bargaining in the broader sense) is an outstanding feature of contemporary capitalistic communities. Conjectural interdependence has been an important phenomenon all along in history. But, in the more rigidly organized communities of the past, the "market" played a much less significant role, and consequently the bearing of exchange value on the everyday lives of the population also was much less significant. We are here concerned with conjectural interdependence in relation to value in exchange, and the social significance of this problem is, of course, very much greater in the modern industrial world than it was in the pre-capitalistic era. But even in the contemporary scene, there are important communities in which this phenomenon is of no consequence. This is true not only because a very considerable proportion of mankind lives more or less outside the realm of industrialism, but also because the more "totalitarian" a country is, the less room there is in it for the determination of economic magnitudes by the mutual agreement of sellers and buyers. Economically, conjectural interdependence is a phenomenon of monopolistic competition.

Conjectural interdependence, then, is significant for value theory in areas such as bilateral monopoly, on the one hand, and oligopoly, on the other. More precisely, the phenomenon is significant for markets on which one buyer faces one seller, and for markets on which there are sellers or buyers (or both) who are sufficiently important to warrant the assumption that the effect of their individual actions on their competitors will not be disregarded. The number of such important sellers or buyers must be small —they must be *few*—in a sense defined in relation to the term "important"; individual members of a very large group are not important in this sense. Such important sellers or buyers are called oligopolists or oligopsonists. They may or may not coexist with an atomistic group of sellers or buyers in the same industry. Fewness in this sense covers a wide range of markets: labor-management relations clearly contain an element of bilateral monopoly; and, on a great many commodity markets, there is a small number of sellers (or buyers, or both) who are important in the sense that the effects of their individual policies on rival firms can definitely not be disregarded.

About one-third of the American national income originates in manufacturing and mining, and in these areas fewness is very common. In manufacturing, prior to the Second World War, 57 per cent of the value of the output was produced under conditions where the four largest producers of each product produced more than one-half of the output. It is unlikely that there has been a significant change in this respect during the last decade.[1] Figures of

---

[1] For illustration, the following data are taken from *Economic Concentration and World War II: Report of the Smaller War Plants Corporation* (Washington, 1946). In the steel industry, in 1945, U. S. Steel owned 35 per cent of the ingot capacity, Bethlehem 13 per cent, Republic 10 per cent. The two leading tin-can producers (American Can and Continental Can) sold about 80 per cent of the total value of tin cans (1939). Before the war all the primary aluminum and the bulk of fabricated products were made by the Aluminum Co. of America, which is still the largest producer, although its estimated share in primary aluminum has declined to 50 per cent and its share in sheet, strip, and plate to about the same percentage. This is due mainly to the competition of Reynolds Metal Co. and of Kaiser. The falling share of Alcoa is at least partly a consequence of court action. Before the war Dow Chemical was the only producer of magnesium and it will continue to be the dominant producer. During the war, when the value of output rose more than twentyfold, its share fell to 30 per cent. Kennecott Copper, Phelps Dodge, and Anaconda are mining about 80 per cent of the copper (1944). American Smelting and Refining (which belongs in the same sphere of interest as Kennecott) refines almost 40 per cent of the copper; the rest is refined by Anaconda, Phelps Dodge, and American Metal. American Smelting also refines more than 50 per cent of the lead (of which St. Joseph Lead is the most important miner), and Anaconda refines almost two-thirds of the zinc. In incandescent lamps, General Electric and Westinghouse share the bulk of the market. International Harvester, Deere, and Allis Chalmers produce about two-thirds of the agricultural machinery (1940). In 1940 Singer alone sold about one-half of the value of sewing machines and

this kind are indicative, even though they convey the impression of greater precision than is justified. High concentration in the manufacture of a product may mean different things depending on the closeness of the available

---

White another 30 per cent. About one-half of the value of washing machines and of vacuum cleaners and somewhat less than one-half of that of refrigerators were sold by the four largest producers. In 1945 more than 60 per cent of the value of electron tubes was produced by the four largest producers. General Motors and SKF account for more than 60 per cent of the output of ball bearings. In 1940 the Big Three sold about 90 per cent of the automobiles (roughly: General Motors, 50 per cent; Ford, 20 per cent; Chrysler, 20 per cent). In 1938 eight oil producers, including three Standard Oil companies and one other member of the Rockefeller group, produced about one-third of the crude oil and more than one-half of the refined oil. They owned about 50 per cent of the pipe-line mileage. Goodrich, Firestone, Goodyear, and U. S. Rubber (which belongs to the Du Pont group) produced 80 per cent of the rubber tires and tubes. Allied Chemical and Du Pont produced about 60 per cent of the dyestuffs and they also were the largest producers of fixed-nitrogen fertilizers. Procter & Gamble, Lever Brothers, and Colgate-Palmolive-Peet accounted for 80 per cent of the pre-war soap output. Five companies produced 90 per cent of the industrial alcohol. American Viscose and Du Pont own about 50 per cent of the rayon capacity, with the Celanese Corporation as the third largest producer. Swift, Armour, Wilson, and Cudahy accounted for somewhat less than one-half of the output of the meat-packing industry (1939). National Dairy, Borden, Carnation, and Beatrice sold almost one-third of the value of dairy products (1944). The three largest flour-milling firms handle about 40 per cent of the commercial wheat. About one-third of the beet sugar is produced by Great Western, with Holly Sugar and Utah-Idaho as the next largest producers. About 50 per cent of the cane sugar is refined by American Sugar Refining, National Sugar Refining, and California & Hawaiian. Seagram, Schenley, National Distillers, and Hiram Walker account for about 50 per cent of the whisky production. American Tobacco (Luckies), Reynolds (Camels), Liggett-Myers (Chesterfields), Philip Morris, and Lorillard (Old Gold) account for between 80 and 90 per cent of the cigarette production. The United Shoe Machinery Co. controls 95 per cent of the output of shoe machinery and it leases its machines to the shoe manufacturers. In the glass-container industry the basic patents are owned by two firms, Owens-Illinois and Hartford-Empire; the first also produces glass containers, while the other merely licenses machinery to other manufacturers. It should be added that some of the industries of much lower concentration (leather, textiles, printing and publishing,

substitutes and on the existence or the absence of competition with foreign producers. On the other hand, although the four largest producers turn out considerably less than 50 per cent of the output in many manufacturing industries, a very small group of firms produces a percentage high enough to enable it to influence the policies of the others. Moreover, in some cases more than one firm belongs in the same family of concerns.

Trade (representing somewhat less than one-fifth of national income), the service industries (about 10 per cent

---

stone and clay, lumber and products, etc.) manufacture special products for which concentration is high.

It is known from other sources that prior to the war the five largest producers of motion pictures—Paramount, Loew (MGM), Warner Brothers, Twentieth Century Fox, and RKO—accounted for 50 per cent of the pictures produced and that this proportion rises to two-thirds if Columbia and Universal are added. They also had a controlling influence on film distribution and owned a considerable proportion of the theaters. Cf. TNEC monograph 43; also M. D. Huettig, *Economic Control of the Motion Picture Industry* (Philadelphia, 1944).

High concentration in industries buying their materials from agriculture implies oligopsony power in the purchase of raw materials as well as oligopoly power in the sale of finished goods unless the materials in question have "equally good" alternative uses of sufficient importance. Obviously, the leading tobacco firms or meat packers, as a group, are capable of influencing the prices of the materials they buy. The same is true of the leading dairy firms, although in this case the buyer-seller relationship contains an element of bilateral monopoly (rather than merely of oligopsony) wherever the buyers are faced with farmers' co-operatives which can be organized under state laws. An element of bilateral monopoly enters indirectly also into the relationship between the tobacco firms and the farmers (and, to some extent, into that between the leading flour millers and farmers) because certain crops, including tobacco and wheat, can be restricted, under federal law, for the purpose of price maintenance, and the federal government sets lower limits to the prices of these materials by direct purchases. Elements of bilateral monopoly are present also within the manufacturing sector, wherever an oligopolistic group is a sufficiently important buyer of goods produced by other oligopolistic groups. This is true, e.g., of the tin-can producers as buyers of tin plate from the steel industry, or even of the automobile manufacturers as buyers of steel, etc.

of national income), finance, insurance, and real estate (about 8 per cent), and contract construction (about 4 per cent) are much less highly concentrated. However, partly through outside regulation which has been made legal in spite of the anti-trust laws, and partly through the spatial separation of competitors, these activities are not free from elements of fewness. As for trade, resale-price maintenance [2] extends the effectiveness of oligopolistic organization well into this branch of activity. Furthermore, the share of chain stores in retail trading is estimated at more than 20 per cent. In the retailing of foodstuffs the share of chain stores approximates 40 per cent and that of the five leading grocery chains [3] alone, 25 per cent. Hence in many areas a very limited number of firms is capable of exerting a strong influence on prices, individually. State laws made minimum-price regulation possible, and violation punishable, in several service industries (barbering and laundering, for example). The results of collusive oligopoly may hence be obtained even though the numbers of potential competitors are large. In finance and real estate as well as in contract construction, concentration is high in many specific geographical areas; this is far more significant than the national figures which show low concentration for these activities. In agriculture (about 10 per cent of national income, if forestry and fisheries are included), federal and state laws make it possible to organize many activities so as to maintain prices in the interest of the existing producers, and to set production quotas in accordance with such price objectives. Here again the results of collusive oligopoly may be obtained

---

[2] This applies to the retail prices set by the manufacturers of branded products and it possesses legal force.

[3] The Great Atlantic & Pacific, Safeway, Kroger, American Stores, First National Stores.

even though the number of producers is large. In transportation (about 5 per cent of national income), as well
as in communication and public utilities (7 per cent),
government-supervised monopoly or oligopoly are the
prevalent forms of organization.

It is, of course, possible to exaggerate the significance
of fewness in the contemporary economy. There exists no
basis for quantitative appraisal and none for categoric
statements concerning the rise or fall of concentration
during recent decades.[4] Perhaps one gets nearest to a bal-

---

[4] Measured by the percentage of assets held by the largest corporations concentration rose considerably during (and before) the inter-war
period. Some rearrangement of the available data makes it appear very
likely (almost certain) that concentration in this sense has risen considerably not only within the universe of all corporations but also
within that of manufacturing corporations alone. But concentration
does not seem to have risen appreciably in the period 1914–37 if measured by the percentage of manufacturing establishments employing
one-half of the labor force in different industries. Cf. Willard L. Thorp,
The Structure of Industry, TNEC monograph No. 27, Washington,
D. C., 1941. This may mean that the largest corporations have come
to own a higher share of the total assets without employing an appreciably higher share of the labor force and perhaps without producing an
appreciably higher share of the output. It may also mean that they
have come to control a higher percentage of the existing establishments and therefore account for a higher share of employment and
output. The implications of these two possibilities are of course different, when trends in concentration are considered. Cf. the present
writer's *Monetary Policies and Full Employment* (Berkeley, 1946 and
1947), pp. 91–94. The discussion in connection with Harrison F. Houghton's paper before the annual meeting of the American Economic As-
sociation may give the reader the impression that concentration has
clearly risen since the late nineteen-thirties, owing to the post-war
disposal of war-time facilities. But the information submitted by Mr.
Houghton indicates that it has risen in some industries and fallen in
others and that it may not have risen in overall terms (cf. *American
Economic Review, Papers and Proceedings*, May 1947). It is obvious
that unionism has grown considerably since the early part of the nineteen-thirties and this also is a significant aspect of the concentration of
economic power. Union power and producers' monopoly power are
partly of a mutually neutralizing character but partly they are addi-
tive, in relation to other groups.

anced statement by saying that fewness is very common although not ubiquitous in manufacturing and in mining; and that the other segments of the economy are not free from its manifestations, even if transportation, communication, and the utilities are disregarded as constituting a specific type of problem. In addition, it should be remembered that collective bargaining introduces or strengthens the element of fewness (bilateral monopoly) in labor-management relations. About one-half of the labor force, other than proprietors and professionals and clerical workers, is believed to work on the basis of agreements reached by collective bargaining, and the terms so reached undoubtedly affect the working conditions of the remaining part of the labor force. Any value theory which neglects the phenomenon of fewness is sufficiently incomplete to be highly misleading.

The problem of bilateral monopoly is obviously one of negotiating and bargaining in order to reach an agreement between certain limits of feasibility. The oligopoly (and the oligopsony) problem is perhaps not "obviously" of this character, but it is useful to consider it as being "essentially" of this character. In most cases, it appears to be realistic and, at the same time, convenient to view the behavior of oligopolists as aimed at testing the reactions of their competitors to alternative price-output policies; or as being based on completed tests. This is very much like "making offers" and seeing whether they are accepted or rejected. When a certain pattern of behavior becomes established in an oligopolistic industry, it is *as though* some such "offer" had been accepted. This is true even in the cases in which no explicit agreement is reached. The process is one of bargaining without negotiating (that is, of bargaining in an extended sense) and the result may be termed spontaneous co-ordination. Therefore, the kind of approach suitable for analyzing the problems of conjectural interdependence between the bargaining limits in bilateral monopoly may also be used in the analysis of oligopoly problems.

FOUR FACTORS PERTAINING TO THE OUTCOME WITHIN THE BARGAINING RANGE

As was stated before, the limits of the bargaining ranges are zero-profit limits and they are determined by the traditional functions of value theory. Here we are concerned with the factors entering into the determination of the outcome *within* the bargaining ranges. These factors will be considered the determinants of bargaining power, or of relative strength. It will be assumed throughout this section that the joint gain, which is being divided by bargaining, is a given magnitude, and that it depends exclusively on cost functions and on the demand functions for the products of entire industries. A participant reaches the upper limit of the bargaining range if he receives the total joint gain. At the lower limit he receives zero profits. The determinants of the outcome within the bargaining range may be grouped in the following categories.

(a) *Long-run consequences of violating accepted value judgments* (*that is, of faring too well*): In any going society, certain ideas of right and wrong limit the extent to which a person or an institution may benefit at the expense of others without being regarded as "taking advantage" of them. In the long run, it is unwise to "take advantage" of others, because this is apt to result in

organized social action on behalf of the victims. The point
at which "exploitation" or unfair treatment starts depends, of course, very much on the nature of the society
in question and on the position of the group in that society. But given the value judgments of a society, persons
and institutions will make a strong effort to convince the
public that they do not take advantage of others. The
social esteem of long-established institutions rests largely
on the feeling that it is impossible to survive long without
observing certain limits set by quasi-ethical considerations. By calling these considerations *quasi*-ethical, we
mean to express the fact that the "ethics" of social communities are always somewhat different (and sometimes
they are far removed) from the standards developed in
ethical systems of religious or philosophical character.
The interest of ethically oriented schools and institutions
in economic matters derives partly from the conviction
that economic processes can be influenced by making these
quasi-ethical considerations more genuinely ethical, as the
term is interpreted by the schools or institutions in question. The strength of quasi-ethical factors has been different in different societies, and it also has varied within
any society with the stage of its development. However,
factors of this character have always played an important
role in shaping social and economic relations. Compliance
with these postulates does not always result from con-
scious thought processes.

(b) *The immediate political consequences of a stalemate in the relations between the parties concerned*: In
important industries, failure of the parties to arrive at an
agreement (in bilateral monopoly) or at a quasi-agreement (in oligopoly) affects the public interest. Popular

discussion stresses the harm done to the public interest by explicit agreement in oligopoly, and points, though with less emphasis to the fact that quasi-agreement may be harmful. But, in most instances, general discussion is concerned with "agreements" (in the broader sense) *already reached;* it focusses on what usually happens rather than on what might happen. Failure to develop established patterns of behavior in oligopolistic industries would not typically be desirable. In the absence of such patterns of behavior, these industries would not typically produce the "ideal" results of perfect competition. On the contrary, they would be involved in a process in which the various firms would be trying to force each other into accepting some pattern of behavior. Such warfare creates a great deal of instability, and it does not tend to lead to a socially desirable allocation of resources. In bilateral-monopoly relations, the situation is even more obvious. Failure to arrive at agreements is harmful to the public interest because it results directly in a reduction of output (work stoppage). This, of course, is not to deny that in both bilateral monopoly and oligopoly the parties may arrive at agreements (or quasi-agreements) that are distinctly objectionable from the social point of view. In fact, on these markets, there undoubtedly is a tendency to produce such results, and this amply justifies the public-policy emphasis on the dangers of collusion. But work stoppages or cutthroat competition that affect significant industries over an extended period of time are practically certain to lead to regulation by political authorities. Any single party may be influenced importantly in its decision to accept or to reject certain patterns by guesses as to how it would fare under administrative regulation, as compared with receiving its "share" under freely accepted patterns of behavior.

(c) *The ability of the parties to take and to inflict losses during stalemates*: This factor affects the outcome through the direct economic consequences (or assumed consequences) of failure to establish stable relations between the parties. In bilateral monopoly, such failure typically results in the inability of the parties to conclude a sales agreement. Under oligopoly or oligopsony, "failure" means a significant degree of instability, and it means losses (or foregone profits) which could be avoided if one of several patterns of behavior were followed by which all parties concerned would realize better results. Failure to arrive at an agreement in bilateral monopoly, or at a quasi-agreement in oligopoly, is, of course, always a consequence of the fact that the different possible agreements or quasi-agreements divide the aggregate gains in different proportions. In bilateral monopoly, one of the two parties may turn down an offer for agreement, hoping that a more favorable one will be obtained. In oligopoly, a condition may develop which is much worse for all parties concerned than certain available alternatives would be, because one party may try to force a definite alternative while another tries to force a solution more favorable to himself and less favorable to his rivals. Failure to arrive at an agreement (or quasi-agreement) is always "costly" in the short run, that is, in the instantaneous sense, and the ability of the different parties to take losses obviously is one of the determinants of the outcome of the struggle. This ability depends on wealth in general and on liquid wealth in particular; and it may depend importantly on the internal organization of firms, that is, on the distribution of power within firms. However, firms may differ not only in their ability to take losses but also in their ability to inflict losses. Therefore, cost advantages, superiority of product, and superiority of sales techniques bring increased relative strength. They always bring increased relative strength in connection with factor (c). In addition, factors (a) and (b) *may* also be affected by such superiority because it testifies of fitness. (In exceptional cases, however, certain manifestations of superiority may be interpreted as signs of "ruthlessness.")

(d) *Toughness in the sense of unwillingness to yield in a range in which the other party is expected to yield if one fails to do so*: Of the factors so far considered, the first (a) may in many instances prevent a party from realizing immediate "advantages" which otherwise would be available in the short run. The second and the third—(b) and (c)—relate to the consequences of *temporary* stalemates, and they provide criteria by which it is possible to judge the advisability or inadvisability of avoiding *temporary* stalemates at certain costs. If these three factors are correctly appraised, and are known to be correctly appraised by all parties, their effect is to reduce the range of indeterminateness lying between the limits determined by the usual kind of cost (or zero-profit) considerations. With mutually correct appraisal of the first three factors and of the zero-profit limits, the outcome in the remaining range depends exclusively on each party's appraisal of the other party's psychological properties as compared with its own. The degree of toughness—factor (d)— evinced by each party depends upon the lack of toughness attributed to the others. However, if mutually correct appraisal of factors (a), (b), and (c) and of the zero-profit limits is not postulated, there develops an interrelation between toughness and the assumptions of each party concerning factors (a), (b), and (c) and concerning the zero-profit limits. Toughness now depends on the appraisal of these as well as on the appraisal of the other party's psychological properties, or the other party's lack of toughness. If the mutual appraisal of either the zero-profit level *or* of factors (a), (b), and (c), *or* of the other party's psychological properties is incorrect, then a stalemate may develop. Errors of appraisal that lead to the assumption that the other party will yield, when he will not, produce a stalemate. Under bilateral monopoly, a stalemate means failure to conclude a deal. Under oligopoly it means cutthroat competition, that is, attempts at hurting one's rivals even at the cost of a short-run sacrifice.

In the event of a stalemate a reappraisal of the relative properties of the parties is likely to occur. Concessions ultimately resulting in agreement of quasi-agreement presuppose, of course, reappraisal. *But if factors (a), (b), and (c), and the zero-profit limits are appraised correctly for all parties from the outset, a permanent stalemate would have to rest on a series of mutual errors.* Incorrect appraisal of factor (d) coupled with correct appraisal of the other factors cannot rest on bad judgment of a single party. At least two parties must be *mutually* underestimating each other's toughness. It is unlikely that this would persist.

It is less safe to conclude that the zero-profit limits and factors (a), (b), and (c) will "in due time" *always* be correctly appraised. Incorrect appraisal of these factors is less unlikely to result in a permanent stalemate, because a stalemate of this character may be produced by an error in judgment committed by a *single party*. Factor (c) may lead to a permanent stalemate if one party *believes* itself to be financially much stronger than the other, while the other *knows* (that is, believes correctly) of itself that it *is* stronger. The stalemate will then result in a change in the institutional setting, by which one party may become eliminated. The same is true, *mutatis mutandis*, of factor (b). Any party may believe *incorrectly* that a stalemate will result in political interference in its favor, while the other side may know (or believe correctly) that the political forces unleashed by a stalemate would change the institutional setting in its own favor. A single (although substantial) error of a single party may result in a permanent stalemate, and indirectly in institutional changes. As for factor (a), this operates not via stalemates, but, on the contrary, by preparing the ground for organized action against the parties which succeed in taking unfair advantage of their power over others. Yet unilateral incorrect appraisal of factor (a) may also lead to a permanent stalemate because a party may believe erroneously that the other—for fear of factor (a)—will not press its claims beyond certain limits, while the other may appraise factor (a) correctly when it *does* press its claims. Needless to say, unilateral incorrect appraisal of the zero-cost limits may also result in permanent stalemate.

In the event of more than two participants, analysis in terms of factors (a) through (d) must be applied to groups of participants as well as to individual participants. For, the bargaining strength of a group of n participants need not be the same as that of the sum of the participants when these bargain individually. Any feasible grouping and any feasible division of the gains between groups and within the groups must satisfy the condition that no participant should find it profitable and possible to increase his gains by regrouping. This usually implies not only that the existing groups must be strong enough to satisfy their members but, in a sense, also that they must not fare "too well" because no group must reduce non-members to a level at which they find it profitable to attract a member into a new group by offering him a sufficiently high share in it. Detailed discussion of the mathematical theory of coalitions is beyond the scope of this volume and beyond the competence of the author.[5] But it should be pointed out that these considerations do not invalidate the statement that the outcome of the bargain is decided by factors such as those discussed under (a) through (d), within ranges which otherwise would be "ranges of indeterminateness." However, the considerations applying to coalitions tend to change the range of possible (or "permissible") outcomes. Patterns of division that under individual bargaining would not be excluded by factors (a) through (d) may become excluded by the fact that certain divisions based on group formation satisfy the condition that no regrouping will occur, while a universe in which each "group" consists of merely one participant may not satisfy this condition. This will be the case if, for example, two participants can increase the sum of their shares by getting together against a third, and the third is in no position to offer the first or the second more than these now get. Possibilities such as these exclude outcomes which otherwise would be consistent with the four factors previously considered. On the other hand, outcomes which are not possible under individual bargaining may be established between coalitions.

No general conclusion is suggested as to whether this changing of the range of possible outcomes changes the probability of stalemates. No sufficiently clear-cut relationship exists between the magnitude of the range and

---

[5] Cf. John von Neumann and Oskar Morgenstern, *Theory of Games and Economic Behavior* (Princeton, 1944). Among several excellent preview articles, see, in the present context, particularly that by Professor J. Marschak in the April, 1946, issue of the *Journal of Political Economy*.

the *a priori* probability of arriving at a bargain. The relative role of factors (a), (b), and (c) as against factor (d), and the correctness of the appraisal of the first three factors in alternative situations appear to be more significant in this respect because mutual or unilateral incorrect appraisal of these factors may be the most important source of permanent stalemates. Moreover, the formation of coalitions may not merely change the range of possible outcomes. It may also increase the number of bargains that must be reached, for actual and potential relations exist between alternative groups as well as between individuals and groups.

On the whole, it may be said that "equilibria" will usually be reached unless at least *"one side"* misjudges the working of factors (a), (b), and (c) or of the zero-profit limits *badly enough*, or unless at least two participants simultaneously misjudge the working of factor (d). This latter possibility, pertaining to factor (d) in isolation, is distinctly unlikely because it assumes that at least two parties involved in an economic conflict simultaneously persist in a definite attitude in spite of the fact that the attitude rests on presumptions about the behavior of others which prove to be wrong, and in spite of the fact that there would be opportunities for changing this attitude. The possibility of lasting stalemates from the first three factors or from the misjudgment of the zero-profit limits is small in societies with stable standards. Given reasonably stable standards, experienced persons do not frequently misjudge these factors very badly. The danger of persistent misjudgment and of stalemates is greater in strongly dynamic societies with changing standards. It is greater for disputes arising in the "world society" of nations than for disputes arising in national communities, because the standards of the world society are especially vague and especially unstable. Yet, even in the world society, most disputes are "settled" (which, in this particular case, may be weak consolation, because it is quite bad enough if *some* are not).

QUALIFIED JOINT MAXIMIZATION

The main suggestions of this volume may now be expressed as follows: In markets of the oligopolistic and of the bilaterally monopolistic kind, there is a tendency toward the maximization of the joint profits of the group and toward division of these profits in accordance with factors (a) through (d). This proposition follows directly from the assumption (and from the observed fact) that bargaining "normally" leads to an agreement. When it does, the parties will surely not be indifferent to the size of the pie they are now dividing. Jointly they have the size of the pie under control. They are, of course, subject to limitations imposed by cost functions and by buyers' preferences, but these need not be stressed because they are taken for granted when we speak of the maximization of the joint profit. The maximization of the joint profit means that the bargaining ranges are determined by the traditional functions of value theory in such a way that for each firm the upper limit is set by the possibility of obtaining for itself the entire (maximized) joint profit, while the lower limit is at the zero-profit level. The division of the maximized joint profit is governed by factors (a) through (d) for individuals and possible coalitions of individuals. Given the quasi-agreement—or a true agreement—with respect to the division of gains, it becomes possible to describe individual market functions (demand and supply functions) for the participating firms. But these are not derived from utility functions and technological functions alone. They are derived from these functions plus the interaction of factors (a) through (d).

Quasi-agreements established to regulate the relations between rivals must be changed, sometimes because of far-reaching changes in relative strength, sometimes because changes in the market functions make it necessary to test the views of rivals by tentative price-setting. Consequently, the periods of established quasi-agreement will be interrupted by intervals of strength-testing (aggressive) competition; and also by periods of tentative price-setting aimed at testing the market views of rivals. Effective price-leadership may eliminate interruptions of the second kind.

Furthermore, even under quasi-agreements, the tendency toward joint-profit maximization is in many cases counteracted by the circumstance that the requirements set by factors (a) through (d) are better satisfied at price levels and levels of output *other* than those maximizing joint profits. In other words, it may in many cases be impossible to accomplish an acceptable distribution of the joint profit at the values of the relevant variables which would maximize the joint profit, while some pattern of distribution relating to a smaller joint profit may prove acceptable to all parties concerned. Agreements or quasi-agreements do not usually handle *all* economic variables entering into the determination of aggregate gains. This may be partly a consequence of institutional and purely administrative circumstances but it is largely a consequence also of uncertainty due to which various persons and organizations discount their own future possibilities

in different ways and are unable to find a mutually acceptable method of discounting these possibilities. The
greater the number of firms involved in the oligopoly relation, the more likely is this to be the case. Therefore,
placing all relevant variables under joint control would
imply a commitment with respect to the distribution of the
joint gain such as would not be acceptable *a priori* to all
parties. This is especially true of those variables that require skill and ingenuity in handling (such as those directly connected with advertising, product variation,
technological change, and so forth). Yet it is impossible
to maximize joint gains without the collusive handling of
all relevant variables. Nor is it possible to accomplish this
without pooling all resources and their earnings. This implies complete disarmament of the firms in relation to each
other and hence it also implies discounting the future possibilities of all participating firms. Consequently, the tendency towards joint-profit maximization and division of the
gains in accordance with factors (a) through (d) is counteracted by the circumstance that agreement on the basis
of factors (a) through (d) may be feasible for a non-
maximized joint profit, while it may not be feasible for the
maximized joint profit.

In consequence of conflicts between joint-profit maximization and acceptable distribution, deviations from joint-
profit maximization are quite common in oligopoly as well
as in bilateral monopoly. Economic behavior under fewness is *imperfectly co-ordinated; it remains competitive in
a limited sense.* The competitive element stays significant;
it applies mainly to the dynamic aspects of the problem
which are connected with ingenuity and inventiveness and
on the discounting of which it is difficult to reach agreement. Later in the volume this will be developed at some

length. The profit-maximization principle is subject also
to certain general qualifications which are unrelated to the
problem of distributing the profit among bargaining units.
In other words, certain qualifications apply not only to
oligopolists and to parties involved in the bilateral-
monopoly type of relationship but also to monopolists.
These qualifications will also be discussed later in the book,
but they too should be mentioned briefly at this point.

In the first place, entrepreneurs do not usually wish to
maximize "today's" profits if thereby they diminish those
of tomorrow to such an extent that the profits of the two
periods are smaller than if they had not maximized today's
profits. They usually are interested in long-run profits. If
they maximize short-run profits it is usually because they
believe that in the particular case in question they cannot
maximize long-run profits without so doing. This may
happen if, because of differences between their own judgment and that of outsiders, or because of institutional
obstacles, they are unable to bridge gaps in time by borrowing. In this event, short-run profit maximization may
be the only method for the achievement of long-run
maximization. But aside from differences in judgment between various individuals and organizations, and aside
from possible institutional obstacles, it is preferable to
take the long-run point of view even if one plans to go out
of business before long, because long-run profit prospects
express themselves in the valuation of assets. While differences in judgment and institutional obstacles are
significant in many cases, they do not technically create
a conflict between the short-run and the long-run points
of view, since whenever they acquire decisive significance,
the short- and the long-run point of view coincide for the
problem at hand. It is, of course, possible to argue that

this does not qualify the profit-maximization principle but merely calls for the appropriate interpretation (in this case, long-run interpretation) of the principle. This can always be argued in connection with qualifications of profit maximization. They all can be "taken care of" by interpretation instead of qualification. But if this is done, too many things may become hidden behind concepts. This may be illustrated with reference to the problem just considered. While it may be possible to postulate that profit maximization *means* long-run maximization and that therefore the long-run point of view does not introduce a "qualification," it is certainly not fruitful to postulate that marginal-revenue and marginal-cost functions of value theory *mean* long-run functions. It will not do to express the long-run character of the profit-maximization axiom by simply interpreting the usual marginal-cost and marginal-revenue functions as functions applying to these longer periods and by postulating that these functions will be equated. Such a simple solution of the dilemma would obscure the fact that the shape of the *functions* of tomorrow depends on the *price* which rules today. Consequently, it is impossible to put together the *ex ante* short-run functions of two successive periods into an *ex ante* long-run function for the double period without first knowing or estimating the *ex post* data for the first period. If profit maximization is defined by the equality of marginal cost and marginal revenue, then long-run considerations *must* be said to introduce a "qualification." The data of a short period will not be determined by the marginal intersection if this would reduce long-run profits.

Secondly, we must also keep in mind that the tendency is toward the maximization of *expected* profits. Since the probability calculus, in its usual form, is not properly ap-

plicable to the kind of "universe" with which entrepreneurs are faced, this raises problems which are incapable
of being resolved in any neat or clear-cut fashion. The assumption that appears to be most realistic is that entrepreneurs maximize "most probable profits," [6] roughly
derived from a universe of experiences which is *not* a
homogeneous universe, but which, in the mind of the
entrepreneur, is transformed into a hypothetical homogeneous universe. This transformation is carried out by
"allowing" in a rough way (pretty much by instinct) for
the differences between the special characteristics of the
diverse situations in which these various "experiences" occurred. When this transformation is made, the entrepreneur may derive something in the nature of a rough
probability judgment from a universe which was made
hypothetically homogeneous by these allowances, and
which, by the same token, can be viewed as being "such as"
the universe in which the present instance belongs. Entrepreneurs try to maximize "best guesses" of profits
(some vague concept of the most likely) in this sense, but
they also try to take into account the possibility of outcomes other than those appearing most probable. No insurance can be based on these probability judgments
because the subjective "allowances" of a person are not
shared by a sufficient number of others. The presumption
is strong that the possibility of less favorable outcomes is
taken into account with a higher weight than the possi-

---

[6] Whether we assume that some vague concept of the most probable
or some vague concept of the mean serves as a basis for these decisions
is arbitrary once we recognize that the possibility of deviations enters
significantly into decision-making. Of course, the meaning of the deviations becomes different, depending on whether we start from modes
or from means. In connection with these essentially unique instances
it seems psychologically more realistic to start from the most probable.

bility of more favorable outcomes, because the cumulative adverse consequences (losses) produced by unfavorable surprise are typically more serious than the profitable direct and indirect consequences of favorable surprise. It is, therefore, likely that the scale of operations will in general be smaller—and liquidity provisions greater—than would be required for the maximization of what to the entrepreneur seem best-guess profits (although his best guess may of course be an unduly optimistic guess).

Thirdly, it should not be overlooked that the interests of corporate managements are not, strictly speaking, identical with those of the stockholders, even though managements usually are interested in earning high profits for the stockholders. This leads to no qualification of the profit-maximization principle as long as the policies resulting in profit maximization are also those which maximize the "income" (pecuniary and other) of the management. But this is not always true, especially if we take into account the problem of uncertainty. The attitude of managements to uncertainty is likely to be different from the attitudes of the various groups of stockholders, and the attitudes of these groups are also likely to be different from each other. The significant decisions are usually made either by managements plus certain groups of stockholders or by managements more or less alone. Profit maximization for these groups need not be the same thing as profit maximization for others. In view of these circumstances the profit-maximization principle needs to be qualified not merely in the analysis of fewness but also more generally.

The characteristic feature of the present analysis is the attempt to provide a framework for the discussion of business coordination resulting in qualified joint maximization and in limited competition. Such a framework is different from that developed by the nineteenth-century (classical) oligopoly theories which postulated individual profit maximization on specific but arbitrary assumptions concerning rival behavior. While the discussion of the first three decades of the present century was concerned mainly with extensions of the classical theories, some authors observed during this period that more attention should be paid to joint maximization (e.g. Schumpeter [7] and A. A. Young [8]). As is well known, Professor Chamberlin included oligopoly in the concept of monopolistic competition. He developed the position that the possibility of joint maximization was underrated by most previous writers and that oligopolistic firms do not disregard the indirect consequences of their individual policies. In fact, these are the main conclusions of his oligopoly analysis which was first published in an article [9] in 1929 and then was included in the *Theory of Monopolistic Competition* (1933). Chamberlin also pointed out, however, that uncertainty sets limits to oligopolistic co-operation and this idea was further developed by Moses Abramovitz.[10] In his treatise on *Monopoly*, which seems to have been completed in the late nineteen-thirties but, owing to the outbreak of war, was not published until 1941, E. A. G. Robinson discussed oligopolistic combinations in the framework of monopoly theory, recognizing, however, that collusion is likely to be incomplete under oligopoly. This general trend of thought has continued also in the American literature.

---

[7] Cf. our footnote 1, p. 55, *Economic Journal*, 1928.

[8] Cf. ibid.

[9] Edward H. Chamberlin, "Duopoly: Value When Sellers Are Few," *Quarterly Journal of Economics*, November 1929.

[10] Moses Abramovitz, "Monopolistic Selling in a Changing Economy," *Quarterly Journal of Economics*, February 1938.

William H. Nicholls, in his *Imperfect Competition Within Agricultural Industries* (1941), discusses a variety of oligopoly equilibria which rest on correct anticipations of rival behavior and which go some way, but not all the way, toward joint maximization. The treatment of oligopoly in George J. Stigler's *Theory of Price* (1946) points directly to a theory of limited joint maximization. The same is true of Joe S. Bain's *Pricing, Distribution and Employment* (1948) and the focus becomes even sharper in a recent note by the same author.[11] These are examples. Recent economic thought points in the direction of the kind of analysis which will be attempted here.[12]

THE FUNDAMENTAL CONDITIONS OF FEWNESS

Pure competition and Chamberlinian monopolistic competition *in the "large group"* require that no firm be large enough in relation to the market to be able to affect the value of the relevant market variables to the extent that any other firm could be influenced by the effect. In such "atomistic" circumstances concerted action without outside aid is usually impossible. Each firm knows that

[11] Joe S. Bain, "Output Quotas in Imperfect Cartels," *Quarterly Journal of Economics*, August 1948.

[12] The theory developed by John von Neumann and Oskar Morgenstern for "games" resembling oligopoly also leads to joint maximization. The "solutions" established in their *Theory of Games and Economic Behavior* maximize the joint gains of the participants, and they also postulate that the division of the gains as well as the number of parties allowed to participate with positive gains depends on the relative strength of the parties individually and on their ability to form coalitions of various kinds. However, the von Neumann-Morgenstern analysis has not so far been presented in a form in which economists could find it directly applicable to their problems. For comments on an interesting paper by H. Gregg Lewis, cf. footnote 4, p. 239.

whether *another firm* violates an agreement or quasi-agreement does not depend on whether *it* violates, and this means that each firm has an interest in violating. Consequently, collusion usually is impossible. This is subject to the qualification that even in very large communities the *esprit de corps* is such in certain respects as to preclude the violation on a major scale of certain unwritten rules which serve the joint interest. The behavior of political communities shows this clearly. But this assumes that the constituents of that community consider it repulsive to benefit at the expense of others and that they are highly confident that the great majority of other constituents share this feeling. Such a spirit is then indirectly rewarded by the advantage of sharing in the joint benefit. But there is no short cut to this advantage. It can be obtained only if genuine, subjective utility attaches to making a "sacrifice" for the group. Anybody will violate—will have a short-run as well as a long-run interest in violating—unless he is confident that the others will not; and in an atomistic group he cannot be confident *unless he knows of himself and believes of the others that he and they consider it repulsive to benefit at each other's expense*. Such *esprit de corps* may be "enforced" against a small minority by stigmatizing a few violators. But this does not explain the functioning of the mechanism. What requires explanation is the fact that the stigmatizing community does not disintegrate; and this leads back to the proposition that concerted action without outside aid in an atomistic group presupposes a spirit of "sacrifice" to which there is no short cut. The great majority of the individual members must be so constituted or so conditioned as to feel unhappy if they do not make this sacrifice. The individual knows that whether others violate does not depend on whether *he* violates; and yet he does not violate because he places above individual advantage good standing in the group, or the interests of the group. Large groups of small producers do not typically satisfy this condition, although attempts to develop such spirit in trade associations and similar organizations are rather common. They usually are incapable of co-ordination except by getting the government (or possibly some outside economic institution on which they depend) to penalize the violators.[13] Hence, in the absence of outside interference, effective co-ordination will not tend to develop in the event of all-round smallness in relation to market.

Spontaneous co-ordination will tend to develop if more than one firm is of appreciable size in relation to the market. Effective co-ordination requires, of course, ability to reach quasi-agreement on the basis of factors (a) through (d).[14] If the big firms (those of appreciable size in relation to the market) coëxist with atomistic firms, as is frequently the case, this sets limits to the effectiveness of co-ordination, but co-ordinated action among the big firms usually remains profitable. In the first place, the big firms may be capable of forcing the small ones into oligopolistic price behavior by punishing violators economically. Even aside from this, co-ordination is profitable for the big firms whenever competition among themselves would lower prices below the level established by small-firm competition. It pays to avoid this. Spontaneous co-ordination

---

[13] Labor groups, groups of farmers and of retailers, and members of certain service industries and certain "professions" have succeeded in accomplishing this.

[14] Cf. pp. 24–9.

among big firms does not require the kind of *esprit de corps* which would be required in an all-round atomistic industry because each firm knows that the question of whether the other firm violates does depend on whether *it* violates. Therefore, the problem of fewness and co-ordinated action acquires significance as soon as certain firms grow to such size in relation to the market that they affect one another to a noticeable extent by their individual policies.

In what circumstances is it profitable and possible to grow to appreciable size in relation to the market? It is *profitable and possible* to do so whenever big firms possess real-cost advantages, that is, cost advantages not derived from oligopsony power, over smaller firms. Let us call this Case 1; and let us distinguish under Case 1 two subcases, namely, that in which the real-cost advantage of large size expresses itself in lower production costs (Case 1*a*) and that in which it expresses itself in a more profitable relationship between sales cost and revenue (Case 1*b*). In pure instances of Case 1 oligopoly, these cost-advantages alone account for the absence of atomistic competition. Aside from Case 1 (real-cost advantage), it is *profitable* to grow to appreciable size if the real (social) cost *disadvantage* of large size is outweighed by other advantages, namely, by the cost advantage derived from oligopsony power, *or* by the price-policy advantage associated with oligopoly power, *or* (from the standpoint of influential inside groups) by gains derived from financing mergers and managing bigger units. Let us call this Case 2. However, while in Case 2 bigness is profitable for owners in general and for controlling groups in particular, bigness will be *possible* only if smaller entrants can be kept out by aggressive use of short-run financial superiority or by the acquisition of certain *exclusive rights*. Otherwise, smaller entrants could compete effectively with the would-be big firms, since they possess a real-cost advantage. Even in the event of real-cost indifference (neither advantage nor disadvantage of size) potential smaller entrants must be kept out by artificial means, and it therefore seems advisable to include real-cost indifference in the concept of Case 2 (not Case 1) oligopoly. The exclusive (discriminatory) rights which may exclude rivals and thereby render Case 2 oligopoly possible may stem from the exclusive possession of natural resources; *or* from patents or licenses or contracts with persons possessing some specific know-how; *or* from such Case 1 oligopoly power as vertically integrated big firms may possess in the industries from which the industry in question buys its materials or in the industries to which the industry in question sells its products; *or* from discriminatory arrangements between non-integrated big firms of an industry and the firms of the preceding or succeeding stages in the structure of production; or from discriminatory arrangements between the firms of an industry and the unions of the same industry. In pure instances of Case 2 oligopoly, these exclusive rights or the aggressive uses of short-run financial superiority account for the absence of atomistic competition. Exclusive rights of course always apply to resources or to sales outlets.

The problems raised by Case 1 oligopoly (real-cost advantage) are different from those raised by the Case 2 variety (real-cost disadvantage or indifference). In Case 1, oligopoly could be prevented only by forcing the firms onto cost-of-production functions which are more expensive than the best cost functions available; or (in Case 1b) by interfering with certain sales techniques. By including selling cost in social cost (real cost) we don't imply that interference with sales techniques is always undesirable. This will become clear in Chapter XI. Here it is sufficient to state that prevention of Case 1 oligopoly requires direct interference with permissible methods of production or marketing. In Case 2, oligopoly could be prevented by increasing the short-run financial strength of small firms in relation to the big ones or by forcing the big firms to abandon certain exclusive (discriminatory) rights. It will be argued later that many real cases should be interpreted as hybrids of Case 1 and Case 2. In these intermediate cases it would require a significant sacrifice in *real cost* to make the industry atomistic, *i.e.*, to eliminate oligopoly. This is the Case 1 element of the problem. At the same time the superior financial strength and (or) the possession of exclusive rights by certain big units result in concentration exceeding that which is explainable in terms of real-cost consideration. In other words, the Case 2 element of the problem tends to produce narrower oligopoly, or monopoly, instead of the broader oligopoly which would exist if we were faced with Case 1 in its pure form. The existing oligopoly is Case 2 oligopoly but its elimination *as such* would result in (broader) Case 1 oligopoly rather than in atomistic competition. These hybrid cases pose the most interesting problems to policy.

The cases so far discussed may become blended also in another way: historically, so to speak. Firms may grow big as Case 1*a* oligopolists (e.g., on a geographically isolated market) or as Case 2 oligopolists (e.g., under patent protection) and later, when these sources of oligopoly power cease to be effective, they may continue more or less automatically as Case 1*b* oligopolists. They are established as big firms and the relationship of sales costs to revenue is very much more favorable for them than for any small entrant. This is the way in which goodwill may become a source of oligopoly power.

In addition to Case 1 and Case 2 oligopoly, we shall distinguish Case 3 restriction. This will be said to exist if an *atomistic* group gets organized quasi-monopolistically or quasi-oligopolistically in such a fashion that the "agreement"—the scheme adopted in the interest of the existing producers—is enforced by an outside agency. The organizing agency may consist of other producers on whom the producers in question depend for raw materials or for sales outlets; or it may consist of the government itself which is called upon to intervene in favor of the economically weak or the politically powerful. Prices may be "maintained" in this fashion and the price policy may be implemented by quota allotments or by a buffer-stock policy or by both. Resale-price maintenance, farm-price maintenance, the enforcement of trade agreements reached by collective bargaining, and the limitation of numbers in certain professions—all are examples of Case 3 restriction. It is preferable not to call Case 3 restriction a case of "oligopoly" because the number of producers is large, and —in contrast to Case 1 oligopoly and to Case 2 oligopoly —they all are atomistic. However, the results may be very similar to those obtained in oligopolistic industries. The existing producers will usually try to get the organization to operate along lines similar to those which would be adopted by oligopolistic industries. It must be remembered, however, that Case 3 restriction requires the active aid of an outside agency, which in turn means that some compromise must be reached between the interests of the atomistic group in question and the organizing agency. If the outside agency is a group of private producers, the profit objectives of the two groups must be reconciled by compromise. If the organizing agency is the government itself, compromise will be necessary because the government cannot disregard the interests of all groups other than the one it is organizing. The organized atomistic group may stand in the bilateral-monopoly type of relationship with other groups in the economy.

With an outside private group as the organizer, the public-policy question posed is that of tolerating (sanctioning) or of preventing such organizing activity. With the government as the organizer, the question is that of extending or of narrowing the area in which the government itself is willing to restrict competition. The argument put forward to secure the co-operation of the government usually underlines the inequity of a purely competitive position in the midst of a partly monopolistic or oligopolistic economy and also the adverse general consequences of the excessive uncertainty which may be produced by atomistic competition with highly imperfect foresight and with imperfect mobility. Such arguments cannot be dismissed as always invalid or unjustified. But obviously they will be put forward in many more instances than those in which they are justified. For the existing producers of an atomistic group usually have an interest in Case 3 restriction regardless of how justified this kind of argument is.

In summary, we may state that the conditions of fewness proper are those of Case 1 oligopoly (real-cost advantage of size in production costs or in sale costs, that is, variety 1a or 1b); or those of Case 2 oligopoly in which real-cost disadvantage of size is outweighed by other (monopolistic or institutional) advantages and in which small entrants are kept out by cutthroat tactics or discriminatory rights enjoyed by the big firms. Case 3 restriction also introduces

an element of fewness into economic relations. It presupposes the quasi-monopolistic or quasi-oligopolistic organization of an atomistic group by an outside agency.

In none of these Cases can the price, in the long run,
rise beyond the level which induces further entry, and the
profit-maximizing price may lie considerably below this
upper limit. Potential entrants may be small firms which
disregard their individual effect on other firms, or they
may be big firms which believe they have sufficient bargaining power to secure themselves a place in the oligopolistic industry. However, unless the "big" entrants
merely displace an existing firm, their entry should be
interpreted as the entry of *smaller* firms because the average size of the firms is reduced, although they do not become atomistic. In pure Case 1 instances, entry is certain
to be forthcoming at the cost-of-production price of atomistic firms and hence the price cannot, in the long run, rise
beyond a level determined by technological factors and
consumer preferences. The oligopolistic power cannot be
exploited beyond a limit set by the real-cost advantage of
the oligopolists. In the other Cases, and in the hybrid
instances, technological functions and consumer preferences alone do not determine a price at which entry is certain to be forthcoming. Entry depends on who is capable
of overriding the existing institutional obstacles. Destroy-
ing the institutional ("artificial") obstacles and the misuse of short-run financial superiority for cutthroat policies means eliminating all oligopoly except the pure Case
1 instances or the Case 1 element in the previously hybrid
instances. All oligopolistic structures would be transformed into atomistic structures or into pure instances of
Case 1 oligopoly. Big firms could not stay alone in the
market unless they possessed real advantages over smaller

firms, in production cost or in selling cost. If they possessed such advantages, they could not exploit their oligopoly power beyond the limits set by these.[15]

APPENDIX

The Theory of Market Structures and the Industry Concept

The distinction between the different market-structures discussed in Chapter 1 can also be drawn in terms of cross-elasticities. This was recognized by Robert Triffin in his *Monopolistic Competition and General Equilibrium Theory* (Cambridge, 1940, p. 104).

---

[15] The real-cost advantages and disadvantages of size which are crucial for this classification may stem from the following circumstances. (*1*) Plant that is too small or too big does not give optimum technological yields for reasons which can be explained by laws of physics and chemistry. (*2*) Plant that is too big may overtax the capacity of the available unit of "government" (top-management). (*3*) Plant that is too big may have to withdraw increasingly valuable factors from competing uses. (*4*) If the optimum plant-size determined by (1) is not subject to downward correction because of (2) or (3), then multiplant-expansion may go with further real-cost advantages over some range because the available unit of "government" may be underutilized. Beyond this range it becomes overtaxed. Also, beyond some range increasingly valuable factors may have to be acquired. (*5*) Plant that is too small or a firm that consists of too few plants may not create the optimum relationship between selling cost and demand because the overhead required to overcome initial resistances may be high. These are economies of large-scale selling. Product-differentiation probably makes it possible to avoid important diseconomies of large-scale selling.

Real-cost advantages may give rise to vertical as well as to horizontal multiplant growth. This is mainly a consequence of (4). But while horizontal growth which is induced by real-cost advantages may create Case 1 oligopoly, vertical growth cannot. Both can become instruments of establishing Case 2 oligopoly.

In connection with these problems cf. D. H. Robertson, *The Control of Industry* (Cambridge, 1923); J. M. Clark, *Studies in the Economics of Overhead Cost* (New York, 1923). Edward H. Chamberlin, "Proportionality, Divisibility and Economies of Scale," *Quarterly Journal of Economics*, February 1948.

However, we feel that Triffin did not distinguish clearly between the effect of another *single firm's* price changes on a firm and the effect of another *group's* price changes on a firm. In other words, he did not distinguish clearly between cases where, for the cross-elasticities in question, the "other group" may contain any number of firms and cases where 't should be defined as a "one-firm group." This distinction seems crucial to us and, hence, we will develop the required categories here. Such a theory is essentially an extension of the Chamberlinian way of looking at market relations.

We define the following conditions.

(1) The elasticity of the quantity demanded from a single firm with respect to the price charged by *some definable group of firms* is infinite. In symbols $\frac{p_j}{q_i}\frac{\delta q_i}{\delta p_j} = \infty$, where p_i and q_i stand for the price charged by firm i and for the quantity demanded from firm i, respectively, while p_j and q_j stand for "the" price (average price) charged by group j and for the total quantity demanded from group j. The group in question (j) may be of any size whatsoever. In the limiting case it may consist of one firm.

(2) The foregoing expression, $\frac{p_j}{q_i}\frac{\delta q_i}{\delta p_j}$, is finite, with all terms defined as above (i.e., i standing for a firm, j for *some* group).

(3) The expression $\frac{p_j}{q_i}\frac{\delta q_i}{\delta p_j} = \infty$, if i stands for a single firm and j stands for *some* other single firm or single firms. Condition (3) cannot be satisfied if condition (1) is not but condition (1) may be satisfied without condition (3).

(4) Condition (3) is satisfied and holds also *vice versa* for the same pair of firms, that is to say, the corresponding cross elasticity of q_j with respect to p_i is also infinite. In symbols: $\frac{p_j}{q_i}\frac{\delta q_i}{\delta p_j} = \frac{p_i}{q_j}\frac{\delta q_j}{\delta p_i} = \infty$

(5) The expression $\frac{p_j}{q_i}\frac{\delta q_i}{\delta p_j}$ is finite if i stands for a single firm and j for *some* other single firm or single firms. Condition (5) cannot be satisfied if condition (2) is not but condition (2) can be satisfied without condition (5).

(6) Condition (5) is satisfied and holds also *vice versa* for the same pair of firms, that is to say, the cross-elasticity of q_j with respect to p_i also is finite.

(7 through 12) These conditions are defined in the following way: Define q as expressing the quantity purchased *by* a firm or a group—*i.e.*, sold *to* a firm or a group—rather than demanded *from* a firm or a group, and define p as the price paid *by* a firm or a group rather than the price which they charge. The meaning of *i* and of *j* remains the same as in conditions (1) through (6). This way we obtain conditions for the effect of buyers on other buyers, just as the previous conditions relate to the effect of sellers on other sellers. Condition (7) becomes the precise analogy of (1), (8) of (2), (9) of (3), (10) of (4), (11) of (5) and (12) of (6).

We now proceed to the definition of market-structures.

Pure competition is approached as condition (1) is approached for some firm, provided that conditions (3) and (5) are not met. This implies that condition (1) is satisfied for many firms: for a sufficient number to eliminate (3) and (5), practically speaking. While condition (3) is not met, it would be satisfied if reformulated in such a way as to have δp_j mean *merely* a price reduction, and not a price raise, by a single firm. Such a reformulated condition (3) is satisfied in the large group without product differentiation but neither this reformulated condition (3) nor an analogously reformulated condition (5) is satisfied in monopolistic competition in the large group. δp_j, if not "reformulated," means of course a price change, regardless of sign.

Monopolistic competition in the large group exists if condition (2) is satisfied for some firm, provided that conditions (1), (3), and (5) are not satisfied; and monopolistic competition in the large group also requires that the cross-elasticity defined in condition (2) should be numerically high and positive. It is *implied* that condition (2) should be satisfied for many firms: for a sufficient number to eliminate (3) and (5).

There exists no simple name for market-structures resulting if condition (2) is satisfied (without conditions (1), (3), and (5)) but if the cross-elasticity in question does not possess a high positive value. These market-structures are "structures" merely in the sense that the products of groups of firms are complementary or rival products. (It is possible to define the complementary relationship by negative and the rival relationship by positive cross-elasticities. Such a definition does not, however, eliminate the income effect from these concepts. As Professor Hicks has shown, eliminating the income effect requires basing the distinction between complementary and the rival relationship on indifference maps rather than on cross-elasticities.)

Pure monopoly exists if *neither* condition (1) nor condition (2) is satisfied for a firm. This implies that the cross-elasticity in question is zero regardless of what group is defined as j (including *any* "one-firm group"). This, like pure competition, is a limiting case.

Full oligopoly without product-differentiation (undifferentiated oligopoly) exists if condition (4) is satisfied for some pair of firms, regardless of what other conditions are met. Condition (1) must, of course, be met if (4) is.

Full oligopoly with product-differentiation (differentiated oligopoly) exists if condition (6) is satisfied for some pair of firms, regardless of what other conditions are met. (Conditions (4) and (6) are not mutually exclusive nor are the corresponding market-structures. Condition (2) must be satisfied if (6) is.)

Partial monopoly without product differentiation exists if condition (3) is satisfied for some firm defined as i, but condition (4) is met for no pair of firms. At the same time condition (1) is met for *certain* firms. By partial monopoly we mean the coexistence of a firm possessing monopoly power with a competitive sector.

Partial monopoly with product differentiation exists if condition (5) is satisfied for some firm defined as i, but condition (6) is met for no pair of firms. At the same time condition (2) is satisfied for certain firms.

Partial oligopoly without product-differentiation requires that condition (4) should be satisfied for one pair of firms defined as i and j or for several pairs; and that condition (3), but not condition (4) should be satisfied if any of *these* firms is defined as i and some other firm is defined as j. At the same time condition (1) must be satisfied for certain firms. Partial oligopoly means the coexistence of an oligopoly group with a competitive sector.

Partial oligopoly with product-differentiation requires that condition (6) should be satisfied for one pair of firms defined as i and j or for several pairs; and that condition (5), but not condition (6), should be satisfied if any of *these* firms is defined as i and some other firm is defined as j. At the same time, condition (2) must be satisfied for certain firms. (Undifferentiated and differentiated partial monopoly are not mutually exclusive. Nor are undifferentiated and differentiated partial oligopoly.)

So far we were concerned with relationships between sellers. The corresponding logical categories for buyer-buyer relationships are purely competitive buying, the buying of close substitutes by large groups, pure monopsony, oligopsony, etc. They can be defined by analogy, if condition (7) is substituted for (1), (8) for (2), (9) for (3), (10) for (4), (11) for (5) and (12) for (6).

It follows from the foregoing that, analytically, significant groups of firms consist of the aggregate of firms defined as $i + j$ in the foregoing pages. More specifically, in a market-structure satisfying condition (1), the significant group consists of any firm i satisfying the condition, *plus* of group j in relation to which the condition is satisfied. Precisely the same statement should be repeated for the market-structures satisfying conditions (2) through (12). For each "condition" and for each market-structure, it is possible to define aggregates consisting of the $i + j$ firms. These are the analytically significant groupings.

The institutional "industry" concept is never strictly coextensive with relevant $i + j$ groups. This was rightly emphasized by Triffin. In fact, the logical purist would have to insist that full discussion of any economic problem requires considering all $i + j$ groups connected by cross-elasticities other than zero. Moreover, the logical way of making concessions is that of limiting oneself to groups of firms which are especially closely interrelated in these terms and not that of limiting oneself to industries in the conventional sense. For obvious reasons, it is difficult to "rationalize" conventional industry classifications. Fortunately, in most cases industry classifications define groups which are significantly interrelated by cross-elasticities and which for certain analytical purposes constitute the most significant $i + j$ group that should be "formed." But this will never be true of *all* analytical purposes with which an investigator may go to work. Needless to say, data are more readily available for industries in the conventional sense than for most other $i + j$ groups.

In the present volume the family of oligopolistic market-structures will be interpreted as consisting of the $i + j$ groups corresponding to conditions (3) through (6); and of those corresponding to the analogous conditions (9) through (12) for markets in which the firms in question *buy* rather than sell.

CHAPTER TWO

Classical Oligopoly Theory
and Its Extensions

Before we apply the considerations of the preceding chapter more specifically to the theory of oligopoly, it seems desirable to discuss briefly some of the older oligopoly models. Many of these relate to special cases, characterized by drastically simplified assumptions. Yet we believe that the models discussed in the present and the subsequent chapter have contributed significantly to the understanding of the oligopoly problem. The contribution of the analysis is frequently indirect because in most cases the underlying assumptions are clearly unrealistic. But unrealistic models sometimes isolate in pure form difficulties that are encountered—and have to be dealt with—in any analysis pertaining to the problem at hand.[1]

---

[1] In connection with the problems discussed in this chapter and the next, cf. the following: Augustin Cournot, *Researches into the Mathematical Principles of the Theory of Wealth* (1838), trans. Nathaniel T.

COURNOT'S PROBLEM

It was Augustin Cournot's great achievement to have discovered the distinctive feature of the oligopoly problem. He also showed in 1838 that on certain assumptions a determinate equilibrium solution is obtained for the duopoly problem and that this solution can be extended from duopoly to oligopoly (cf. chap. vii of Cournot's *Researches*).[2] It seems to us that the determinateness of Cournot's solution is the least significant feature of his analysis. In fact, it may be argued that the truly significant problems arise in connection with legitimate criticisms of the Cournot solution. But this is another way of saying that we have to start by considering how the deter-

Bacon (2nd ed.; New York, 1927); review of Cournot's *Researches* by Joseph Bertrand in *Journal des Savants*, September 1883; F. Y. Edgeworth, "The Pure Theory of Monopoly," translated and reprinted from the 1897 volume of the *Giornale degli Economisti* in *Papers Relating to Political Economy* (London, 1925), Vol. I, Sec. II; Joseph A. Schumpeter, *Wesen und Hauptinhalt der Nationaloekonomie* (Leipzig, 1908); idem, "The Instability of Capitalism," *Economic Journal*, September 1928; A. C. Pigou, *The Economics of Welfare* (4th ed. London; 1932), chap. xv; A. L. Bowley, *Mathematical Groundwork of Economics* (Oxford, 1924); G. C. Evans, *Mathematical Introduction to Economics* (New York and London, 1930), chap. iii; Edward Chamberlin, *The Theory of Monopolistic Competition* (5th ed.; Cambridge, Mass., 1946), chap. iii and Appendix; Robert Triffin, *Monopolistic Competition and General Equilibrium Theory* (Cambridge, 1940); Heinrich von Stackelberg, *Marktform und Gleichgewicht* (Wien and Berlin, 1934); Wassily Leontief, "Stackelberg on Monopolistic Competition," *Journal of Political Economy*, August 1936; Erich Schneider, *Reine Theorie Monopolistischer Wirtschaftsformen* (Tuebingen, 1932); J. R. Hicks, "Annual Survey of Economic Theory: The Theory of Monopoly," *Econometrica*, January 1935; George J. Stigler, "Notes on the Theory of Duopoly," *Journal of Political Economy*, August 1940; R. G. D. Allen, *Mathematical Analysis for Economists* (London, 1942), pp. 200–204, 345–47; F. Zeuthen, *Problems of Monopoly and Economic Warfare* (London, 1930).

[2] A related problem is discussed in chap. ix of Cournot's *Researches*. Cf. our footnote 13, p. 113.

minate solution is obtained. A realistic approach to oligopoly problems cannot be based on Cournot's theory. Yet now, after more than a century, it still is difficult to see what is involved in an oligopoly theory without showing how the theory is related to Cournot's basic construction.

As is well known, the Cournot solution is based on the assumption that (in undifferentiated duopoly) each duopolist believes that his rival will go on producing a definite quantity irrespective of the quantity *he* produces. Obviously in these circumstances each duopolist believes that he can calculate the quantity he should produce in order to maximize his profits. For, by deducting the fixed quantity of the rival's output from the total quantity indicated by the market demand function for each price, he can obtain his own assumed individual demand function; and he may then proceed to equate his individual marginal revenue to his marginal cost. Yet this is not the reason why the solution is regarded as determinate. Neither duopolist is likely to make a correct guess of the quantity his rival will produce, because the rival produces the quantity which maximizes his profits on the same assumption with respect to *his* rival's behavior, and hence does not generally keep his output constant. Consequently, the "position" (pair of outputs) obtained at first does not last; each firm will change its output.

The characteristic feature of the Cournot model is that if each duopolist continues to assume that the other will not change his rate of output, then ultimately they will prove to be correct although during the approach to the equilibrium, for a limited period of time, they will be wrong. *A* produces a quantity which maximizes his profits on the assumption that *B* will go on producing his present output, whereupon *B* adjusts his output so as to maximize his profits on the assumption that *A* will go on producing his present output, which induces *A* to adjust his output, etc. What Cournot proved is that these adjustments ultimately result in an output for *A* which he can actually *go on* producing on the assumption that *B* will continue to produce his "present" output because *B* will ultimately produce an output which truly justifies *A's* output on the assumption he makes. This statement must clearly be symmetrical: *B* must in this equilibrium position also be producing an output which is truly justified (that is, need not be further adjusted) on the assumption he makes about *A's* behavior.

This, of course, means that ultimately they prove to be "right" for the wrong reasons. Each *assumes* that his rival follows a policy of fixed output while *in reality* each follows a policy of adjusting his own output to the requirement of profit maximization, on the assumption that the other follows a policy of fixed output. But, if, on this incorrect assumption, they both have actually adjusted their output to the simultaneous output of the other, then (from there on) the assumption they make with respect to one another is "quasi-correct," as we might say. It has become true that the other producer goes on producing a fixed output, although the reason is *not* (as is mutually assumed) that he follows a policy of producing a fixed output disregarding his rival's behavior. This is what we meant by saying that they are right for the wrong reason.

The geometrical proof is essentially as follows: Measure along the abscissa the output of *A*, and along the ordinate that of *B*. Label the curve indicating *A's* output as a function of *B's* output F_1, and the curve expressing *B's* output as a function of *A's* output F_2. The shape of these reaction functions is given by the postulate that each duo-polist maximizes his individual profits on the assumption that the other will go on producing his "present" output. Let us first assume that the market demand function is linear (which Cournot did not assume) and that the producers have constant costs at the identical level (which Cournot did assume in the first exposition of his theory).

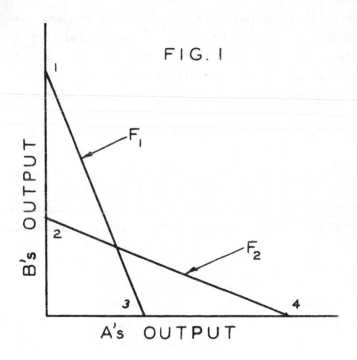

FIG. I

Both functions decline monotonically, as indicated in the figure.[3] The main proposition is established by the fact that the two curves intersect and that the intersection marks stable equilibrium. In other words, to the right of

---

[3] The more the one produces, the less will the other produce because the more to the left will his assumed individual demand function lie.

the intersection, *A's* output tends to fall and *B's* to rise, while to the left of the intersection *A's* output tends to rise and *B's* to fall, so that the equilibrium becomes restored in the event of disturbances. This must be so because F_1 must intersect with the ordinate above F_2, while it must intersect with the abscissa *to the left of* F_2. For point *1* shows that output of *B* which would induce *A* to produce nothing, while point *2* shows the output which *B* produces if *A* produces nothing. The first of these two quantities is the competitive output for the industry in question.[4] The second quantity is *B's* monopoly output. The competitive output exceeds the monopoly output. For the analogous reason *A's* output in point *3* must be smaller than in point *4*. Point *4* marks the competitive output and point *3* marks *A's* monopoly output.

The reaction functions (F_1 and F_2) are linear if we assume—as we did—linear demand functions and constant costs. Consequently, the stable intersection point just described is the only intersection point. Furthermore, given identical cost functions in undifferentiated duopoly, the individual outputs of the duopolists will be the same. It also is easy to show that on these assumptions the aggregate duopoly output is two-thirds of the competitive output, while the monopoly output would be one-half of output under pure competition. On analogous assumptions for undifferentiated oligopoly (instead of duopoly), the aggregate oligopoly output would be $\dfrac{r}{r+1}$ times the competitive output, where r stands for the number of producers.[5]

---

[4] Assuming that the *industry* cost functions would be the same under pure competition as those actually existing under duopoly.

[5] Taking at first linear demand functions and zero costs to clarify the nature of the problem, let the market demand function be $y =$

Reaction functions may be linear even if the demand and cost functions are not quite as simple as was assumed above. But linear reaction functions do require significant simplifying assumptions which are economically meaning-

---

$a - nx = a - n(x_1 + x_2)$ where y is the price, x the total output of the two duopolists, and x_1 and x_2 the two individual outputs, respectively. Both a and n are positive constants. The duopolist to whom the subscript 1 applies treats x_2 as a constant. His aggregate revenue is $ax_1 - nx_1^2 - nx_1x_2$. Since he equates his marginal revenue to zero:

$$a - 2nx_1 - nx_2 = 0 \qquad (1)$$

The second derivative of aggregate revenue $(-2n)$ is negative as required. From Equation (1):

$$x_1 = \frac{a - nx_2}{2n} \qquad (2)$$

This is the reaction function of the first producer. For analogous reasons,

$$x_2 = \frac{a - nx_1}{2n}. \qquad (3)$$

This is the reaction function of the second producer.

$$x_1 + x_2 = x = \frac{2a}{3n} \qquad (4)$$

where

$$x_1 = x_2 = \frac{a}{3n}$$

If the number of producers were r instead of two, then

$$x = \frac{ra}{(r + 1)n}$$

The monopoly output is found from (1) by setting $x_2 = 0$, and it amounts to

$$x = \frac{a}{2n} \qquad (5)$$

The competitive output is found by setting $a - nx = 0$, and it amounts to

$$x = \frac{a}{n} \qquad (6)$$

If instead of zero costs we take constant costs (c), then the right-hand term of equation 1 becomes c instead of 0. In all subsequent equations (2 through 6) we have to write $a - c$ instead of a.

Taking, instead of linear demand functions, demand functions of

less. Let us now drop these simplifying assumptions with respect to the market demand function and the cost functions, *except* that we require that the monopoly output of each firm should be smaller than the output which, if taken as given by the other producer, will induce the other producer to go off the market (that is, to produce zero). If this assumption is not made, the Cournot problem is obviously meaningless because monopoly would be established. However, on the assumption now made points *1*, *2*, *3*, and, *4* are still arranged as in Figure 1 because these points stand precisely for the outputs which have to be arranged in this fashion according to our assumption. The reaction functions will not be linear, but they will still be monotonically downward sloping because, on Cournot's premise concerning assumed rival behavior, a higher rival

---

the general form $y = \psi(x) = \psi(x_1 + x_2)$, and again assuming that each producer treats the output of the other producer as a constant, the first producer maximizes his profit by making

$$\frac{d[x_1\psi(x_1 + x_2)]}{dx_1} = \psi(x_1 + x_2) + x_1\psi'(x_1 + x_2) = 0 \quad (7)$$

(of which equation 1 is a special case), and the second producer by making

$$\frac{d[x_2\psi(x_1 + x_2)]}{dx_2} = \psi(x_1 + x_2) + x_2\psi'(x_1 + x_2) = 0 \quad (8)$$

Seven and 8 are two equations with two unknowns. They are the reaction functions. They determine x_1 and x_2.

By adding these two equations we get $2\psi(x) + x\psi'(x) = 0$ (of which equation 4 is a special case).

For r producers we would get $r\psi(x) + x\psi'(x) = 0$.

The duopoly output again is greater than the monopoly output and smaller than the competitive output. Monopoly output is determined by the equation $\psi(x) + x\psi'(x) = 0$ (of which equation 5 is a special case), and competitive output by $\psi(x) = 0$ (of which 6 is a special case). The oligopoly output rises with rising r.

On general assumptions with respect to costs, the right-hand side of equation 7 becomes the marginal cost of the first producer (instead of being zero), and the right-hand side of equation 8 the marginal cost of the second producer. We still have two equations with two unknowns.

output essentially means the lowering of one's assumed individual demand function.[6] Consequently, the reaction
functions will intersect, and at least one intersection will
have to be stable, although there *may* be several intersections including unstable ones. Cournot, of course, actually
implied that points *1*, *2*, *3*, and *4* were arranged in this
manner.[7] He also implied a unique and therefore stable
intersection, but the uniqueness of the intersection is not
a significant assumption.

It is essential to realize that, as long as the firms make
the Cournot assumptions concerning their rivals' behavior,
the analysis cannot be adjusted in such a way as to make
the firms be right for the right reasons, instead of describing a situation in which they turn out to be right for the
wrong reasons. This, as will be seen presently, raises the
problem of "leadership."

If producer *A* knows that his rival is reacting along the
function F_2, then he would not be reacting along F_1. Instead, he would try to select the point along F_2 which is
optimal from his own (*A's*) point of view. This point will
ordinarily correspond to a higher output for *A* and a
smaller output for *B* than those marked by the intersection
point in Figure 1 (and to a higher total output).[8] Similarly, if *B* knows that *A* is reacting along F_1, then, instead
of reacting along F_2, he would select the point along F_1
which is optimal from his own point of view. This would
ordinarily be to the left of the intersection point. Such be-

---

[6] Therefore, rising rival output reduces one's own output and *vice
versa*.

[7] In the first presentation of the theory (but not later) he even
implied identical constant costs (at the zero level). But the foregoing
arrangement of the four points is implied throughout his analysis. His
reaction functions are not linear.

[8] Cf. footnote 9, p. 64.

havior does not result in equilibrium because by postulating that they knew each other's reactions we also had to postulate that they abandoned the pattern of behavior which was postulated. In other words, the assumption that they know of each other that each reacts *à la* Cournot is an inconsistent assumption. Consequently, they cannot be right for the right reasons.

It is conceivable, however, that *one* producer should act on the assumption that the other reacts along his Cournot function and that the other should actually so react. This would result in a "leadership" equilibrium. If A knows that B reacts along F_2 (*à la* Cournot) but B, instead of anticipating reactions along F_1, believes that A will go on producing whatever output he actually produces at the moment, then A will be able to select the point along F_2 which is optimal from his point of view, and this point will mark equilibrium. For the very same reason, if B anticipates reactions along F_1, but A behaves *à la* Cournot (that is, actually reacts along F_1), then B's optimum point along F_1 will mark equilibrium. In the first case A, in the second case B is the leader.[9] These leadership equilibria

---

[9] With reference to footnote 5, p. 60, leadership equilibrium, with linear demand functions and with the first producer as the leader, is determined by postulating for the demand function $y = a - n(x_1 + x_2)$ that $x_2 = \dfrac{a - nx_1}{2n}$ (cf. equation 3). The marginal revenue from this demand function is then made equal to zero; that is, the first producer maximizes his profits, given the reaction function of the second. The first equation of footnote 5 then assumes the specific form $\dfrac{a}{2} - nx_1 = 0$.

From this we obtain $x_1 = \dfrac{a}{2n}$ and from equation 3 we get $x_2 = \dfrac{a}{4n}$, there-are, of course, different from Cournot's intersection-point equilibrium.

In essential respects, the Cournot model may be treated as the parent model for oligopoly analysis. But this is not a consequence of the equilibrium propositions wihch Cournot derived from his model. The intersection point in Figure 1 obviously does not express equilibrium unless the firms in question react in the manner reflected by F_1 and F_2, and it is quite unreasonable to assume that they would react in this manner. To be sure, that firms should assume of one another that the other follows a policy of fixed output is conceivable, but on the way to the Cournot equilibrium [10] they would necessarily realize that their assumptions were incorrect and they would change their assumptions. This would, of course, destroy the validity of the Cournot reaction functions and of any analysis based on them. Moreover, such approaches to the equilibrium —during which the Cournot assumptions concerning rival behavior are patently incorrect—would have to take place more or less "all the time" because, in consequence of shifting demand and cost functions in the actual world, no single equilibrium position would stay established for long.

---

fore $x = x_1 + x_2 = \dfrac{3a}{4n}$, which is in excess of the x determined by equation 4, but, of course, falls short of the competitive output.

Taking demand functions of the general form $y = \psi(x) = \psi(x_1 + x_2)$, the leadership equilibrium, with the first producer as the leader, is obtained by expressing x_2 in terms of x_1, from equation 8 and substituting this expression for x_2 in the demand function. For the proposition that on "normal" assumptions x will be greater under leadership than at the intersection-point equilibrium, cf. R. G. D. Allen, *Mathematical Analysis*, pp. 345–47.

[10] That is, on the way to the intersection point, starting from any section of the graph.

It should be borne in mind that Cournot's stability proposition relates to disturbances which carry the system out of the intersection point without affecting the reaction functions themselves. In the event of such disturbances the equilibrium will become restored. But there are compelling reasons to believe that the producers will become doubtful concerning the realism of their assumptions about rival behavior, and these doubts constitute a disturbance against which the system is thoroughly unstable. Such a disturbance invalidates the functions themselves because it is easy enough to find out that they rest on incorrect assumptions. Generally speaking, if these firms, in any phase of their relations, and for any reason whatsoever, change their (arbitrary and incorrect) assumptions about each other's pattern of behavior, then there will develop no tendency for the restoration of the Cournot pattern of behavior. This is true even if the original change in assumptions is small, for example, if they anticipate small output adjustments by their rival instead of anticipating a policy of fixed output. Surely to exclude such changes is unrealistic. After all, the Cournot assumption is at best one of a great many assumptions a firm can make about rival behavior.

At first sight, the objection seems possible that similar criticism could be voiced against equilibrium theories in general, not merely against Cournot's theory of duopoly equilibrium. The basic functions of conventional equilibrium theory also shift in the course of dynamic development. While sooner or later the shifts are reversed, it could scarcely be maintained that in the course of "cyclical" fluctuations some definite equilibrium level of these functions becomes automatically restored. But the analogy would be unconvincing. Equilibrium theories in

general abstract certain properties of the real world and
their fruitfulness depends on how convenient it is to *iso-late* these properties and to treat them separately as
problems of disequilibrium. It has proved fruitful to
treat in this fashion problems such as the immobility of
resources, uncertainty, and—if the equilibrium is sta-tionary—all problems of growth. A person might be
opposed to these admittedly arbitrary methodological
distinctions. But at any rate he would have to admit that
they are not meaningless distinctions because the problems
separated in this fashion—that is, the problems of "dis-equilibrium"—are articulate and significant. However,
the methodological proposition that the problems excluded
from the Cournot duopoly analysis should be treated
separately from those included in the model would be a
meaningless proposition. This would imply that it is
fruitful to develop, in addition to the Cournot theory, a
separate kind of "disequilibrium" analysis concerned
with the "disturbances" arising from the fact that firms
do not in reality assume that their rivals follow a fixed-output policy. The problem so "isolated" would have no
raison d'être. This is another way of saying that it is not
fruitful to consider the Cournot intersection as a point
of equilibrium in the sense of "pure theory," and to com-bine such "pure theory" with a "dynamic" theory of
imperfections. But clearly this is the only purpose such
a theory could serve.

Other analytical problems are raised if, instead of
considering the Cournot equilibrium, marked by the inter-section of F_1 with F_2, we turn our attention to the leader-ship equilibria that may be developed from the Cournot
model. In these cases no firm acts on incorrect and arbi-trary assumptions. The follower believes correctly that

the leader has adopted a policy of fixed output, at a level which he selects in full knowledge of the follower's reaction function. The leader actually behaves in this fashion. In other words, the leader has both the desire and the power to exercise the privilege of indicating the quantity he will produce and of keeping on producing this quantity; and the follower maximizes his profits in full knowledge of this. The leader, on the other hand, selects the quantity of his output in full knowledge of the fact that the follower will maximize his profits, given that output. The output of the leader is chosen in view of this behavior of the follower, and it is the maximum-profit output of the leader, given this behavior of the follower. Neither firm acts on incorrect assumptions about rival behavior. As long as the leader has both the desire and the power to make his own output a parameter from the follower's point of view, any change in the leader's assumptions about what the follower will do in these circumstances [11] will prove erroneous; and so will any change in the follower's assumptions about how the leader will set his own output.[12] The leadership equilibrium does satisfy this test, which is not satisfied by the intersection-point equilibrium.

Yet, unless further assumptions are introduced, even the leadership equilibrium fails to satisfy another test. Why should the leader have the desire and the power to act in this fashion? If he is more powerful than the follower, why should he be "more powerful" in this completely arbitrary sense of the term? His rival's reaction

---

[11] That is, any change in the assumption that the follower will move along his Cournot function.

[12] That is, any change in the assumption that the leader will set the output corresponding to the leadership equilibrium.

to some other behavior might result in higher profits to both firms. Why should he not try to test this? If he does try to do so, this theory again is neither "realistic," nor a fruitful "pure" theory.

The discussion of the last question will be taken up later. Meanwhile we shall examine the question whether the conclusions so far reached lend themselves to being extended to conditions other than those assumed in the Cournot model.

MORE PRODUCERS— PRODUCT DIFFERENTIATION

On Cournot's assumptions the equilibrium is determinate not merely for duopoly but for oligopoly with any number of sellers. Moreover, it is determinate not merely for producers selling perfect substitutes for one another's product but also for producers selling a differentiated product. In the event of product differentiation the boundaries of an oligopolistic industry may simply be defined as the boundaries of a group to which conjectural interdependence applies. Cournot did not discuss differentiated oligopoly but the reaction functions will have to be downward sloping for substitute products too; and the argument of page 60 with respect to the arrangements of points *1, 2, 3,* and *4* of Figure 1 applies to substitute products as well as to a homogeneous product (of course, with no general assumption concerning linearity of reaction functions).

However, all intersection points of Cournot reaction functions share the weaknesses of the Cournot intersection for undifferentiated duopoly. If conditions are varied by the introduction of more producers and by product differentiation, the "Cournot equilibrium" will still express a position in which each producer believes that his rivals are determined to produce a definite, invariable output (which is unaffected by what their rivals do), while in reality no producer acts in this fashion. Consequently, such an "equilibrium" will not be maintained, even if accidentally it should become "established." The reasons are the same as under undifferentiated duopoly.

Furthermore, the "superiority" of the leadership equilibria over the Cournot equilibrium proper (that is, over the intersection of Cournot reaction functions) disappears if more than two producers are included in the model. The Cournot reaction function of *each* follower is based on the assumption that *all* his rivals produce a definite quantity, irrespective of what he does. This assumption is correct only with respect to the leader. It is incorrect with respect to the followers. Therefore, if the number of producers exceeds two, the objection against the leadership equilibria is identical with the objection raised against the Cournot ("intersection") equilibria. If each follower sets up Cournot reaction functions and lets the leader choose his output in view of these, then each follower acts on incorrect and arbitrary assumptions about the other followers. Any change in these assumptions will prove that they were erroneous, and the pattern originally postulated will never be restored.

However, if the Cournot model is "extended" not as concerns the number of producers but as concerns the relationship between the products of two producers—so that product differentiation is admitted but the number of producers stays two—then the leadership equilibrium retains its superiority. The Cournot intersection remains subject to the criticism discussed before, but the leadership equilibria have the same properties as under undifferentiated duopoly. As long as it is postulated that the leader has the desire and the power to keep on producing a definite quantity of his own choosing, and thereby to make his output a parameter from the follower's point of view, the leadership equilibrium rests on *correct* assumptions of each producer. Any testing of this by the duopolists will confirm rather than destroy faith in these assumptions. Yet, here again the solution is subject to the criticism that it is quite arbitrary to postulate that the leader has the desire and the power to act this way. Why should he not test the reaction of his rival to other methods of asserting his will?

CONJECTURAL VARIATION (OUTPUT)

A further extension of the Cournot model is obtained if Cournot-type reaction functions are defined on an assumption more general than the Cournot assumption proper. It is assumed that the producers do not believe that the output of their rivals is fixed and independent of their own output. Instead, they believe that the output of their rivals depends on their own output *in some fashion*. Rival output is believed to be linked to the "own" output by *some* function and consequently any changes in the "own" output is believed to result in a definite change of rival output.[13] The assumed change in the output of a

---

[13] With reference to footnote 5, p. 60, we introduce two further functions, $x_2 = f(x_1)$ and $x_1 = g(x_2)$, which give us the first producer's idea of how x_2 depends on his own output, and the second producer's idea of

rival per (small) unit change of the "own" output is usually termed conjectural variation. The Cournot model is represented as a species of the genus of models thus defined. The characteristic of the Cournot species is that the conjectural variation is zero. As long as a producer believes he knows what changes in rival output will be undertaken under the influence of his own output changes, he will be able to set up a reaction function *such as* the F functions of Figure 1. The shape of the reaction function depends, of course, on the magnitude of the conjectural variation for all values of the variables. The F functions proper, as defined by Cournot, relate to zero conjectural variation.

This extension of the Cournot model and analogous extensions of the Bertrand model to be considered subsequently have received attention mainly in the stage pre-

---

how x_1 depends on his. Consequently, in equation 7, x_2 ceases to be a constant, and the derivative of the first producer's aggregate revenue with respect to his own output ceases to be $\psi(x_1 + x_2) + x_1\psi'(x_1 + x_2)$. Since x_2 now is a function of x_1, the expression $x_1 + x_2$ will have a derivative with respect to x_1, whose value will not be one—as would be the case with $x_2 = $ constant—but $1 + \dfrac{df(x_1)}{dx_1}$. To find the derivative of $\psi(x_1 + x_2)$ with respect to x_1 we have to multiply $\psi'(x_1 + x_2)$ by the derivative expressed in the preceding sentence, which was not necessary in equation 7 because there the value of this derivative was one.

Now we get in the place of equations 7 and 8

$$\psi(x_1 + x_2) + x_1\psi'(x_1 + x_2)\left(1 + \frac{df(x_1)}{dx_1}\right) = 0 \qquad (7a)$$

$$\psi(x_1 + x_2) + x_2\psi'(x_1 + x_2)\left(1 - \frac{dg(x_2)}{dx_2}\right) = 0 \qquad (8a)$$

The expressions $\dfrac{df(x_1)}{dx_1} = \dfrac{dx_2}{dx_1}$ and $\dfrac{dg(x_2)}{dx_2} = \dfrac{dx_1}{dx_2}$ are the conjectural variations of the two producers.

ceding the recent emphasis on collusive arrangements (p. 40). It is generally realized, of course, that the F functions in this extended sense need not intersect for positive outputs, and that if they intersect, the point of intersection *need not* be stable even in the sense in which the Cournot intersection *is* stable.[14] The conditions of stable equilibrium lend themselves to mathematical discussion. However, this extension of the Cournot model has pitfalls which, it seems to us, have not received sufficient attention.

In the first place, the likelihood that the intersection point will be reached at all is small because here again it is true by definition that for all points other than the intersection point the producers' assumptions about each other's behavior are arbitrary and incorrect. If in any region of a diagram such as Figure 1 the two reaction functions are apart (that is, do not coincide), this means that one producer produces an output on the assumption that the other will adjust his output in a certain way,[15] while the actual adjustment undertaken by the other producer induces the first producer to make a new adjustment. *This means that the original assumptions were incorrect.* It means this regardless of whether the original conjectural variation, expressing itself in the functions, is zero (as in the Cournot model proper) or other than zero. Whatever the original assumptions were, they are likely

---

[14] That is to say the intersection need not be stable even if the assumptions about rival behavior continue to be maintained indefinitely and the functions stay "put." Furthermore, Professor Bowley, in his *Mathematical Groundwork*, points out that both producers may be aiming at leadership, in which case equilibrium cannot be established.

[15] In the limiting case of zero conjectural variation (Cournot model) the assumed "adjustment" would be zero.

to be changed and the functions based on these assumptions are likely to shift because during the assumed approach to the intersection-point equilibrium the incorrectness of the assumption is revealed. Functions that shift as soon as a movement occurs along them are, of course, useless as tools of analysis. Moreover, even in the intersection point, the assumptions of the producers are merely "quasi-correct" (as we said in connection with the Cournot model proper).[16] They are correct in the sense that the rival produces the quantity which appears to justify the first producer's present output, and, at the same time, his present output appears to justify that of the rival. But these outputs are "justified" on the basis of entirely arbitrary notions of what a producer would do if the other producer changed his output. Any testing of these notions would show immediately that the rival does not behave in the fashion assumed. If the reaction functions in such a "generalized" model [17] possess a "stable" intersection point,[18] then the producers will move back to the intersection point, in the event of accidental disturbances, provided the reaction functions themselves remain unchanged. Yet any doubt about the correctness of these assumptions expresses itself in shifts of the functions, and these are not self-correcting because the functions as a whole rest on incorrect notions of rival behavior. Even in the intersection point the "correctness" of the assumptions is limited to one aspect: each firm actually produces the quantity the other expects him to produce on incorrect notions of how he acts if his rival varies his output. The equilibrium is stable only as long as nobody realizes that

---

[16] See p. 58.

[17] "Generalized" in the sense of conjectural variation other than zero.

[18] For which there exists no general presumption.

their notions are incorrect, and it is extremely unlikely
that no one should ever test them.

So far as "intersection point" equilibria *à la* Cournot
are concerned, these extended models are not superior
to the Cournot model proper. Perhaps they may be said
to be inferior rather than superior, for there is no presumption whatsoever for a "stable" intersection point
at positive outputs, unless specific assumptions are introduced. But we argued that this is not a significant point.
The kind of stability which exists in the Cournot equilibrium proper is of no significance because the equilibrium
proves unstable as soon as a producer becomes doubtful
concerning his assumptions about rival behavior. This is
true of the "extended" Cournot models as well as of the
Cournot model proper; if conjectural variation is included in the model, the incorrectness of mutual assumptions will still be revealed as soon as these assumptions are
tested.

Turning now to the leadership equilibria, we see that
these bring us back to the Cournot model proper, with
zero conjectural variation, provided the follower knows
that he is facing a leader. The leader selects a point along
the reaction function of the follower, and this means by
definition that the follower should set up a reaction
function expressing his own profit maximization for given
outputs of his rival, that is, with *zero* conjectural variation.[19] *The models with conjectural variation do not possess a leadership problem of their own.* They merely point

---

[19] If the follower does not know what is going on, then he may set
up a reaction function with conjectural variation, and the leader may
select a point. But in this event the solution is, of course, subject to
the same criticism as the intersection-point equilibria. The follower's
assumption is arbitrary and incorrect. He should find it very easy to
discover this.

back to the leadership equilibrium which can be developed from the Cournot model proper in which the reaction functions are defined with zero conjectural variation.

It may be argued that the leader—in contrast to the follower—does operate with "conjectural variation," and with correct conjectures, when he selects a point along the reaction function of the follower. He knows how the follower reacts to changes in his own (the leader's) output. But while this is true, the leader can, of course, not be said to set up a reaction function at all. He merely selects a point, and he does this on the basis of correct conjectures about the followers' behavior. The leader acts with "conjectural variation" *in this sense*, at any event, that is, by virtue of being a leader. This concept of "conjectural variation" does not introduce anything new beyond what is involved in the leadership equilibrium derived from the Cournot problem proper in which all reaction functions are defined with zero conjectural variation. "*Reaction functions* with conjectural variation" do not acquire significance by virtue of the leadership problem. They acquire significance only if we attach importance to their intersection points. It was argued on pages 73–4 that this should not be done.

It is necessary to emphasize that so far all reaction functions have been defined in relation to output. In the Cournot model proper (conjectural variation equals zero) each producer assumes that his rival produces a constant output, and he sets his own output on this assumption. In the extended models (conjectural variation other than zero), each producer makes some assumption concerning the output adjustments which his rival will undertake if he changes his own output. These output reaction functions are *not* freely convertible into reaction functions defined in terms of other variables. For example, let us consider price. Any assumption of a producer concerning the output which his rival (or rivals) will produce if he himself produces a certain output, *implies* an assumption concerning the price which will rule in these circumstances. But the same price could rule with a different distribution of the aggregate output between the individual producers. The problem of price reaction functions is distinct from that of output reaction functions. Price and the quantity of output are, of course, not the only significant variables in the contemporary world. Product variation and advertising introduce further problems. But we shall now turn to price. Other variables will be considered later.

PRICE REACTION FUNCTIONS: THE BERTRAND-EDGEWORTH PROBLEM

During the first forty-five years of its life, Cournot's book received no attention. In 1883 it was reviewed in the *Journal des Savants* by the French mathematician Joseph Bertrand who—though not expressing himself in these words—essentially objected that Cournot had used output reaction functions instead of price reaction functions. More specifically, Bertrand suggested that each duopolist assumes that the other will keep his price (not output) unchanged and pointed out that on this assumption prices will actually be reduced to the zero-profit level. Each producer will undercut his rival by a very small margin because, on the assumption he makes about his rival, he will obtain maximum profits by undercutting infinitesimally (or by the smallest observable margin). Edgeworth amended this analysis by pointing out that in reality price oscillations are likely to occur in a range lying between the monopoly price or a somewhat lower price, on the one hand, and a price higher than the zero-profit price, on the other. We shall now try to develop three possible sets of assumptions and examine the conclusions to which they lead. The Bertrand-Edgeworth analysis has not distinguished these cases clearly, and it has therefore remained somewhat vague.

For all three cases we shall assume that a producer who takes a price as given will try to sell at that price any quantity up to that which equates his marginal cost to the price, provided average cost is recovered. For all three cases we assume that nothing will be produced and sold at prices falling short of average cost. This implies that the producers sell quantities simultaneously produced rather than a fixed supply previously accumulated. Price policies concerning such supplies, and inventory-production policies, are matters of long-range price expectations. The Bertrand-Edgeworth problem is not a problem relating to the size of inventories.

Case 1: Each producer believes that his rival will stick to his present price for any quantity the market will want to buy from him; and the producers have identical cost functions. In this case at every stage of the competitive process each producer believes he has the choice between (a) eliminating his rival by undercutting slightly and (b) sharing the market at 50:50 with his rival at the rival's price. Consequently, the price will be beaten down to the level at which alternative (a) ceases to be preferable to (b). This price is that at which "one-half" of the market demand curve for the product [20] intersects with

---

[20] That is, a function indicating for each price one-half of the quantity indicated by the demand curve for the product.

the marginal-cost curve of a producer, provided this price is no lower than average cost for the quantity in question. At this price neither producer will want to increase his sales by undercutting because each producer is equating price to marginal cost. They will cease to undercut. The price will be stable; it will also not be increased because neither producer believes that he can sell any quantity at all at a higher price. During the slide of the price toward the equilibrium level, negligible quantities will be sold at each price because each price rules just long enough to be observable to the rival producer. If, however, the price cannot, without falling below average cost, reach the equilibrium level just described, the equilibrium level will be set by average cost (that is, by that intersection of the half-demand curve with the average-cost curve where the half-demand curve starts falling below average cost). This also is a stable equilibrium price. If average and marginal costs coincide (constant costs), then the equilibrium price can of course be described as that corresponding to average cost *or* to marginal cost.

Case 2:   Each producer believes that his rival will stick to his present price for any quantity the market will want to buy from him; and the producers have different cost functions. In this case the price will be beaten down to the marginal-cost intersection of the half-demand curve *for the low-cost producer*, provided that this price is no lower than average cost for either producer. Once the price is lower than that corresponding to the marginal-cost intersection of the half-demand curve for the high-cost producer, the high-cost producer will cease to undercut. He will just follow suit, but the low-cost producer will continue to undercut until his intersection is reached. This price, however, is not stable because the two producers jointly do not supply the entire quantity demanded. The low-cost producer supplies one-half of the quantity demanded, and the high-cost producer supplies less. Consequently, before the "day" is over the price will be raised to a "prohibitive level"—no goods will be available—and as soon as this is observed by a producer, he will set his monopoly price (assuming that the other will stick to the prohibitive price). There will be constant fluctuations between the lower limit here described and the monopoly price,[21] with just negligible quantities sold at any single price before it changes. If, however, the price, during its slide toward the lower limit, cannot reach the intersection of the half-demand curve with the marginal-cost curve of the low-cost producer without falling below the average cost of the high-cost producer, then the lower limit is set by the average cost of the high-cost producer. This price will also not be stable because the low-cost producer will drive out the high-cost producer by an infinitesimal price reduction. This establishes a "prohibitive price" for the high-cost producer and it will induce the low-cost producer to set his monopoly price. Subsequently the high-cost producer comes back and the price falls to the lower limit.

Case 3:   Each producer believes that his rival will stick to his price for the quantity per period which he (the rival) will want to sell in order to maximize his profit *at that price* and that the rival will be out of business for any quantity per period which might be demanded in excess of the quantity in question. In this case the price might not

---

[21] This is presumably the monopoly price of the low-cost producer because the high-cost producer wants to sell less at the lower limit and *he* should be expected to go off the market before the "day" is over.

decline as far as it would in Cases 1 and 2. At a higher price it may begin to be preferable to each producer to let his rival sell out and to get the monopoly price for the remainder of the market. The policy of letting the rival sell out begins to be profitable where the price is just low enough to make the additional profit obtainable at that price by *not* letting the rival sell all he wants (that is, by not withdrawing temporarily) weigh less heavily than the additional profit obtainable by increasing the price on a smaller quantity after the rival has sold out. Consequently, there may be constant fluctuations between this lower limit and an upper limit which equals the monopoly price *in the narrower market* existing after one producer has sold out. This latter price—"narrow-market" monopoly price—will be beaten down in the next market period when the rival comes back and again considers the ruling price "given" *à la* Bertrand. (It is possible to argue that the upper limit will be the *full* monopoly price rather than the narrow-market monopoly price because at the lower limit *both* producers might try to wait until the other sells out, and since in this case both set a prohibitive price, their rival might assume that he will remain without competition. This is a subtle and unrewarding question in the interpretation of the first sentence under Case 3.)

Bertrand had our Case 1 in mind, and he assumed in addition constant costs at the zero level (zero cost), so that his stable equilibrium price—cost-of-production price—was zero. Edgeworth had something in the nature of Case 3 in mind, but he did not make all assumptions explicit. He argued that in the case of fixed capacity for both producers at ¾ commodity units each, with zero costs up to this quantity, and assuming that all buyers have identical linear demand curves with a industry demand curve expressible by $y = 1 - \frac{x}{2}$,[22] the lower limit of the price fluctuations will be higher than $y = \frac{1}{4}$ (which would correspond to the full sale of the $\frac{3}{4}$ units by each producer) and that it *might* be lower than $y = \frac{1}{2}$ (which is the full monopoly price). The explanation suggests strongly that he thought of a situation such as is characterized in our preceding paragraph (Case 3). But he does not say at what price the undercutting will cease and give way to a price increase. Nor is his statement on the upper limit unequivocal.

The assumptions of our Case 3 constitute a hybrid. *A* believes that he cannot influence *B's* price by undercutting him but that he can influence it by refraining from sales for a while because in this event *B* will sell out and subsequently *B* will have to set a prohibitive price (that is, will have to go out of the market) for some time. However, on such assumptions oscillations of the Edgeworth type will occur, and since they will also take place in Case 2 (which was discussed neither by Bertrand nor by Edgeworth), we may conclude that certain modifications of the Bertrand assumption do lead to a theory of oscillating prices. The limits will, of course, not be the same in Cases 2 and 3 respectively.[23]

---

[22] With y standing for the price and x for the quantity demanded. Edgeworth gives the demand curve which each producer *would be* facing if he dealt with one-half of the customers in isolation from the other half as $y = 1 - x$, if the number of customers on this half-market is defined as 1.

[23] In Edgeworth's example (with the symbols used in the preceding paragraph and in footnote 22), the profit obtainable by each producer through undercutting price y is $\pi_1 = \frac{3}{4}y$ minus an infinitesimal magnitude due to the undercutting. The market available if the rival is allowed to sell out is $x = 2 - 2y - \frac{3}{4}$; therefore, the demand curve for such a "narrow market" is $y = \frac{5}{8} - \frac{x}{2}$, the corresponding aggregate

The question now arises as to what this means in terms of reaction functions, such as were used by Cournot but with prices rather than outputs as the variables. Geometrical representation of the problem becomes clumsy because the argument rests on infinitesimal differences. Waiving this difficulty, that is, exaggerating the price differentials, Case 1—the straight Bertrand case (no oscillations)—may be represented as follows:

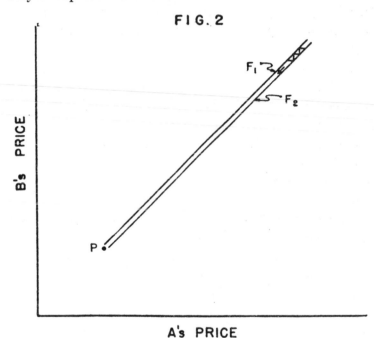

FIG. 2

revenue is $xy = \frac{5}{8}x - \frac{x^2}{2}$, and the quantity produced if $\frac{d(xy)}{dx} = 0$, is $x = \frac{5}{8}$. The corresponding price $y = \frac{5}{16}$, and the corresponding maximized profit $\pi_2 = \frac{25}{128}$. Therefore, the lower limit of the price fluctuations should be where $\pi_1 = \pi_2$, that is, $y = \frac{122}{384}$. The upper limit should be $y = \frac{5}{16}$. However, this is by inference. Edgeworth does not indicate this. It is possible to argue that the upper limit will be the full monopoly price, $y = \frac{1}{2}$ (cf. p. 81). The "recontracting" problem is disregarded in this argument.

Along the axes we measure the prices charged by the two duopolists respectively. F_1 and F_2 are the reaction functions, and the co-ordinates of point P express the price corresponding to the intersection of the "half-market demand curve" with the average or the marginal-cost curve of the individual producers (cf. page 79). The starting-point of the lines (up northeast) is the monopoly price. Equilibrium is established at point P. This is Case 1. In all other cases considered, fluctuations occur. In the cases in which fluctuations occur, the lower limit may be higher than point P on the diagram, and the upper limit may be lower than the highest point expressed in the diagram. There is no neat way of representing these oscillations because, while the slide of the price toward P occurs along a diagram such as the foregoing, the rise takes place discontinuously. The price first jumps up to a "prohibitive" level for the producer who has sold out and to the upper limit of the oscillations for the other producer (who now is a monopolist on his market); from this level it slides down continuously as shown in the graph (to the lower limit wherever this may be).[24]

In the straight Bertrand case (no oscillations), the equilibrium is subject to the same criticism as the Cournot equilibrium. The stability of the equilibrium rests on the assumption that the arbitrary and incorrect notions of the firms about each other's reactions are never tested. The equilibrium could probably never be reached because on the way to it both producers discover that their assumptions are incorrect. In actual circumstances they would almost always have to be "on the way" to the equilibrium because specific equilibrium positions shift during the cycle. Consequently, they would almost always be discov-

---

[24] Depending on the considerations discussed on pp. 80ff.

ering that their assumptions are incorrect: their rivals do not keep their prices constant. Moreover, even if we postulate that the equilibrium position has been reached and that it does not shift, we would still have to realize that each producer *knows* that he is maximizing his profits *only if* his assumptions about rival behavior are correct. Any testing of these assumptions will reveal their incorrectness. In all other cases (Bertrand-Edgeworth cases) which were considered in the preceding paragraphs—that is, in the cases other than the straight Bertrand case—fluctuations of a specific kind are represented as continuing indefinitely, on the assumption that the notions of the producers about each other's behavior are maintained indefinitely in spite of the fact that these notions prove wrong all the time. The objection is the same as against the straight Bertrand case.

In the Cournot framework, the leadership equilibria were not subject to this criticism. The leadership points discernible in the Cournot model may be interpreted as corresponding to positions in which the producers make correct assumptions about each other's behavior. We argued that these "equilibria," too, were arbitrary because they implied an arbitrary definition of the kind of superiority with which one producer is endowed in relation to the other and also of the use which he wants to make of this superiority. But this is a different question. The leadership positions discernible in the Cournot model express correct assumptions of the producers about each other. Is it possible to deduce leadership equilibria from the Bertrand-type model?

Something in the nature of the leadership equilibrium can be deduced only in one set of circumstances for which, however, the outcome can be adequately characterized in much simpler terms. If one firm can make profits at a price at which the other has to go out of business and if the first firm (that is, the low-cost firm) knows that the other acts along a Bertrand reaction function (in that it assumes that the first firm keeps its selling price unchanged) then the first firm might set the highest price which is low enough to drive the other out of business. It will do so unless in the range of price oscillations the profit on one-half of the market demand is greater on the average than is the profit on the entire market demand at the low price at which the competitor goes out of business. The low-cost firm may find it preferable to get rid of the competitor by setting the price which drives his competitor out, provided it can do so and still make a profit. This is perhaps in the nature of a "leadership equilibrium," [25] but it obviously is unduly complicated and pedantic to call it that. Essentially the leader establishes a monopoly which, however, he prefers not to exploit fully for fear that the dead competitor would revive. Aside from this, leadership positions cannot be deduced from Bertrand-type functions because as long as it is taken for granted that a firm reacting along such a function actually is in business, the other firm will not select a price and stick to it. Undercutting would always pay, except when it is even more profitable to let the rival sell out and then to raise the price.

MORE PRODUCERS—
PRODUCT DIFFERENTIATION

Introducing more than two producers does not change the nature of the Bertrand problem. We still get the

---

[25] Because a point is selected along the reaction function of the rival.

straight Bertrand result or oscillation depending on whether we are faced with conditions such as were assumed for two producers under Case 1, or Case 2, or Case 3, respectively (cf. pages 78–81). In other words, these results can be extended from duopoly to oligopoly with modifications which are sufficiently obvious not to require explicit treatment.

While introducing more firms does not change the character of the Bertrand problem, introducing product differentiation does. Product differentiation eliminates an element of discontinuity inherent in the Bertrand problem in undifferentiated oligopoly. If the product is homogeneous, a producer can sell nothing at prices exceeding that of his competitors and he can take the whole market at prices falling short of that price. Infinitesimal price differences are sufficient to produce these results, assuming that the market is perfect. The Bertrand-Edgeworth theory is based on this assumption. However, if the product is differentiated, the sales of any one producer may be expected to change gradually as he varies his price, given the prices of the other producers. Professor Hotelling has shown that another type of market imperfection—which is brought about by differences in location and the existence of transportation costs—has very similar consequences. In many respects these differences are like product differentiation.[26]

---

[26] Harold Hotelling, "Stability in Competition," *Economic Journal*, March 1929. Hotelling's problem is characterized by the assumption that two producers are located at two different points of a straight line which expresses the market and which in both directions extends by definite stretches beyond the points at which the producers are located. The assumptions are made that at each unit of distance one unit of the commodity is demanded (with zero price elasticity), that each buyer pays the price charged by the producer from whom he buys plus a fixed transportation cost per unit of distance, that there

If the product is differentiated, reaction functions may be defined, and the problem acquires characteristics similar to those of the Cournot problem. The main differences between the Cournot reaction functions proper and the functions applying to the Bertrand problem for differentiated products are these: (1) the reaction functions of the producers will be upward sloping because the higher the

---

is no cost of production, and that each producer assumes that the price of the other producer at his (the other producer's) plant is given regardless of the price *he* charges. The market of any producer is defined by the postulate that he sells to all buyers who can buy more cheaply from him than from his rival, taking the transportation cost into account. Hotelling obtains what essentially are price reaction functions. These intersect at a level securing profits for both firms. The difference between Hotelling's problem and Bertrand's is that in Hotelling's problem an infinitesimal price reduction does not give the undercutting firm the whole market but results merely in a slight increase of his market. A small reduction of the price at the plant overcomes the additional transportation cost over a small additional distance. Consequently, undercutting is less profitable and ceases at a higher price even though the rival's price at his plant is assumed to be unaffected by one's own. The Hotelling model shares this feature with a model in which *product differentiation* rather than *spatial differentiation* marks the deviation from the Bertrand assumptions. In this respect the introduction of product differentiation into the Bertrand model leads to the same gradualness. Yet only on highly schematic assumptions would product differentiation be *strictly* analogous to Hotelling's spatial competition. Product differentiation would have to be in one dimension, and it would have to relate to a property with respect to which the commodity can be "more or less so," with one producer on the "more so" side and the other on the "less so" side but not at the extremes of the range. Consumer preferences would have to be distributed over the range, with perfectly inelastic demands for the genus (that is, for the "commodity" in the usual sense) but with preferences for the one rather than the other brand that are overcome by definite price advantages (analogous to transportation costs).

It should be added that Hotelling's discussion takes it for granted that each producer competes with the other for the market lying between them but that he always supplies that stretch of the market line which lies beyond him (i.e., not toward the rival but in the other direction). Consequently, Hotelling's solution is correct only if it satisfies the test that no producer can increase his profit by setting a low price by which he could reach over to the other side of his rival.

price one's competitor charges (and keeps invariable regardless of one's own policies), the higher the price one will charge oneself; (2) it may not be taken for granted that the reaction functions intersect for positive prices, and, if they do intersect, it may not be taken for granted that an intersection point is stable in the sense in which the Cournot intersection point *is* stable.[27]

However, if the reaction functions intersect and if the intersection point is stable, then the objection to the ensuing determinate equilibrium is the same as that which

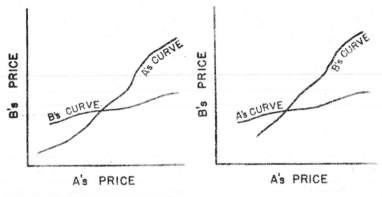

[27] Both pairs of price reaction functions appearing above are drawn with a single intersection point. The first pair intersects with "stability"; the other has an unstable intersection point. In other words, it is true of the first but not of the second pair of curves that to the right of their intersection prices tend to fall, while to the left of the intersection prices tend to rise. It is true of the first but not of the second situation that equilibrium will be restored in the event of disturbances. Both pairs of curves happen to be drawn on the assumption that for moderately low prices of *B*, his rival (*A*) finds it best to set *very* low prices. Yet the assumption that I sell at ten cents if I believe that my rival will sell at one dollar is compatible with the assumption that he sells at more than one dollar if he thinks that I will sell at ten cents (stable case), and also with the assumption that in this event he will sell at less than one dollar (unstable case). The answer depends on the cost functions of the two producers and also on consumer preferences at alternative price levels. These factors determine the shapes of the functions.

was expressed on pages 65ff. in relation to the Cournot equilibrium: it is unlikely that the intersection point would ever be reached because the assumptions prove to be incorrect on the way to the equilibrium. Moreover, if reached, the equilibrium would not be maintained. The reaction functions rest on the incorrect assumption that the rival keeps his price constant regardless of one's own policies. Any testing of this assumption would reveal its incorrectness, even if the intersection point should accidentally have been reached.

The corresponding duopoly leadership equilibria again are logically "superior" in the sense that they rest on mutually correct assumptions about rival behavior. One producer assumes correctly that the other—namely the leader—sets his own price and will stick to it regardless of the follower's behavior. The follower will therefore set his price so as to maximize his profits given this behavior of the leader. The assumptions of the follower are correct, and so are those of the leader who sets his price so as to maximize his profits given this behavior of the follower. But while in this respect the leadership solution is superior to the "intersection-point equilibrium," it is not sufficiently superior to make it the true solution of the problem. Here again it is quite arbitrary to assume that one firm desires to be, and succeeds in being, more powerful than its rival *just in that peculiar sense* which is implied in the leadership solution here discussed. Why should the more powerful firm desire to act in the fashion here assumed without ever testing whether alternative types of behavior would not be equally acceptable to the weaker firm, and at the same time more favorable from its own point of view? This criticism also is analogous to the objection expressed in connection with the Cournot leadership equilibria (page 69).

Furthermore, it should be mentioned that in the Bertrand as in the Cournot framework the logical superiority of the leadership equilibria over the intersection-point solution is limited to duopoly. The mutual assumptions cease to be correct in oligopoly because the followers' assumptions about one another are no more well founded that in the intersection-point equilibrium. (For the analogous Cournot-type problem cf. page 70.)

CONJECTURAL VARIATION (PRICE)

It is possible to define price reaction functions which differ from those described in the preceding section in that they do not rest on the assumption that the rival firm keeps its price invariable but, instead, are based on the notion that the price of the rival firm depends in some fashion on one's own price and that therefore the rival firm will change its price by some definite magnitude per unit change of one's own price. This is analogous to conjectural variation in relation to output. The problem of conjectural variation is worth considering for undifferentiated as well as for differentiated products. For undifferentiated products and perfect markets it is obvious that a producer would undercut slightly any price to which he assumed his rival would stick regardless of his policies.[28] But if conjectural variation is introduced, a producer might not believe that his rival is going to stick to the new price and consequently the price reaction functions might

---

[28] Unless the new price forced him out of business.

assume all kinds of shapes for undifferentiated as well as for differentiated oligopoly. If they intersect for positive prices and if the intersection point is "stable" in the usual sense, then the objection to such a determinate solution is the same as has been expressed repeatedly against these intersection-point equilibria. It should be added that in undifferentiated oligopoly any intersection point must be at the *same* price for the competing producers. It is possible to define reaction functions which yield intersection points for different prices, but these reaction functions must shift [29] before the intersection-point equilibrium can stabilize itself. To say that the oligopoly is undifferentiated (and the market perfect) is another way of saying just this.

Even with reaction functions intersecting for identical prices, the objection expressed on pages 73–4 continues to apply. The model loses its validity as soon as the producers discover that their reaction functions are based on incorrect assumptions. They are bound to discover this.

Let us now turn to the leadership problem. If the follower knows that he faces a leader, the leadership solution reverts to the Bertrand assumption proper (that is, to zero conjectural variation), just as in the case of output reaction functions it reverts to the Cournot problem proper (zero conjectural variation). Leadership equilibrium is characterized by the fact that the leader selects a point along the reaction function of the follower. If the follower knows that this is happening, he will set up a reaction function indicating his output or price, as the case may be, for alternative given (constant) outputs and prices of his rival. But this means the Cournot or Bertrand assump-

---

[29] I.e., anticipations with respect to rival behavior (and therefore the conjectural variation) must change.

tions proper, with zero conjectural variation.[30] At this point the difference between homogeneous and differentiated products acquires significance. In the Bertrand model proper (for homogeneous products) there is no significant leadership problem (cf. pages 85–6); in the analogous model for differentiated products there may very well be such a problem (for example, the leadership points on any of the reaction functions of footnote 27, p. 89, possess logical validity).[31]

GENERALIZATION OF CONCLUSIONS: FURTHER VARIABLES

For the two variables "price" and "quantity of output" the conclusions so far reached may be thus summarized. Reaction functions can be defined for a duopolist or an oligopolist on the assumption that, for given values of the competitors' variables, the firm in question chooses a value for its own variable such as maximizes its profits. The relevant range of these functions is that in which the firm establishing the function makes profits or—at least —avoids losses. In the straight Cournot and Bertrand cases the firm acts in this fashion on the specific assumption that the value of the competitors' variables will remain unchanged, while in the cases in which the conjectural variation is other than zero the value of the competitors' variables is assumed to adjust in a definite

---

[30] As was pointed out before (p. 76) the leader may be said to operate with correct conjectural variation in any leadership model. But he cannot be said to establish a reaction function with (or without) conjectural variation.

[31] In the Cournot-type model there is the problem of leadership (p. 64), and also in the analogous model with product differentiation.

way. Furthermore, in the straight Cournot and Bertrand cases all firms produce the identical product, while in alternative models they may be assumed to produce close substitutes of each other's products. Consequently, we may derive a family of models containing the straight Cournot and Bertrand cases as well as such variants as allow for conjectural variation, for product differentiation, or for both. The shape and the characteristics of the reaction functions depend on which member of the family we consider and on what specific assumptions we make about cost functions and consumer preferences. The most "favorable" cases for determinate equilibrium are those in which the reaction functions of the competing firms intersect and in which the intersection point is "stable" so that the equilibrium will be restored after small disturbances. However, even in these "favorable" cases, the "stability" in question should not be considered stability in the relevant sense. The equilibrium position will be restored only if the reaction functions remain unchanged. Yet any movement away from the intersection point—and, generally speaking, any movement along the reaction functions—will reveal instantaneously that the assumptions on which these functions are based are incorrect. Therefore, it should not be implied that the reaction functions remain unchanged whenever movements occur along them. This is another way of saying that the assumption of independent reaction functions, which determine the equilibrium by their intersection, is not a fruitful assumption in oligopoly theory. The resulting theory is not "realistic"; and it is not fruitful on the "pure theory" level because it does not isolate a meaningful complex of problems. There is no point in relegating to a theory of disequilibrium all phenomena produced by the fact that people do not act in this arbitrary fashion!

Further variation of these assumptions results in the leadership problem. In the leadership models not all competitors have reaction functions in the usual sense. The leader selects a point along the follower's reaction function, and this behavior is different from setting up a reaction function in the usual sense.

For the straight Cournot problem it is easy to define a "leadership" variant. This is true also of several other members of the family derived from the Cournot and Bertrand cases, although it is not true of all members of this family. Some of the leadership equilibria so obtained are superior in the sense of not resting on mutually incorrect assumptions. For example, the leadership variant of the straight Cournot case in duopoly (but not generally in oligopoly) gives rise to an equilibrium which rests on mutually correct assumptions about rival behavior. But even in cases such as this, to assume that the equilibrium in question will ever be established is highly arbitrary. For such an equilibrium presupposes that one firm is weaker than the other in a sense which has no independent meaning. The strength of the leader and the weakness of the follower *are defined implicitly* by postulating that the leader may select a point along the reaction function of the follower and that the follower lets him do this. But this is not the formal description of a power relationship which is intuitively (or otherwise) meaningful. It is merely the implicit description of a power relationship which yields equilibrium. Why don't the producers try out some other pattern of behavior which might be more profitable for both and might also yield stability?

This brief summary provides justification for *not* extending the foregoing type of analysis to the further variables entering into the problem of market equilibrium. To be sure, one of the reasons why the old-fashioned oligopoly analysis is unrealistic is that it is concerned exclusively with price-quantity relationships while in the actual world other variables must also be taken into account. Firms can vary their products, and this gives us a third dimension. Advertising might perhaps be interpreted as a specific type of "product variation" yet it is sufficiently different from variation *in the usual sense* to justify distinguishing it as a fourth dimension in which firms may operate. Given the production functions and the supply functions which the firms are facing, their profits depend not merely on the quantity they produce and on the price they realize but also on the type of product they produce and the selling costs they incur. But while a useful model should include these variables, to work them into the kind of reaction-function analysis summarized in the preceding pages does not seem promising. Even in a complex model containing all the relevant variables simultaneously, it will have to be true that the reaction functions express arbitrary assumptions about mutual behavior and that these assumptions are incorrect *except* (accidentally!) in the "intersections" of these functions where they are mutually compatible and where they could be termed quasi-correct. Any movement out of these intersections—and any movement along the functions themselves —will reveal their incorrectness. It will also have to remain true of the leadership equilibria corresponding to these more complex models that they express completely arbitrary implicit definitions of the power relationship between the stronger and the weaker firms. It is impossible to attribute any meaning to this relationship other than the purely formal one implied in the definition of the problem and of the equilibrium. There is no reason to assume that leaders will want to behave in this fashion or that followers will allow them to.

CHAPTER THREE

Stackelberg's Indifference Maps: Extension of the Analysis to Related Market Structures

THIS chapter contains a discussion of Heinrich von Stackelberg's oligopoly analysis, as developed in his *Marktform und Gleichgewicht*. Stackelberg was particularly successful in linking the oligopoly problem to that of a family of related market structures. Any oligopoly theory should be capable of developing these links because the type of analysis applying to oligopoly is suitable for examining a whole family of market structures. Stackelberg's theory brought this out very clearly. However, the specific oligopoly theory he developed is not the kind of qualified joint-maximization theory we outlined in Chapter I. It is a sophisticated version of the kind of theory we attempted to appraise in Chapter II and *from which* we shall subsequently develop a transition toward qualified joint maximization. In connection with a discussion of Stackelberg's theory we may therefore show what emerges for the family of related market structures (not merely for oligopoly itself) from the classical type of theory considered in Chapter II; and we may construct the bridge toward joint maximization for these structures, too.

GENERAL CHARACTERISTICS

Stackelberg operates with reaction functions which—just like the F functions of Figure 1—express each producer's individual profit maximization for given values of the rival's variables. These reaction functions are derived from the profit-indifference maps of the individual participants as drawn against axes along which the value of the producer's own variable and that of his rival's variable are measured. In other words, the profit-indifference map of a producer shows those combinations of the value of his own variable and of that of his rival's which give the producer in question identical aggregate profits. From these indifference maps it is possible to indicate how a producer maximizes his profits, given the value of his rival's variable. The model includes as possibilities the Cournot type of intersection-point equilibria, the corresponding leadership equilibria,[1] and the disequilibrium developing if both parties strive for leadership. Moreover, since the reaction functions are derived from the underlying indifference map, it is possible to indicate which of these possibilities is likely to materialize. We can find out at what point of his profit-indifference map a producer arrives if he adjusts the value of his own variable to given values of his rivals

---

[1] I.e., the equilibria characterized by the fact that one firm selects the (from its point of view) optimal point along the reaction function of the other.

variable, and where he arrives if he is successful in inducing his rival to adjust. The intersection-point equilibrium *à la* Cournot tends to be established if, in view of the individual indifference maps, both firms find followership (that is, the leadership of the rival) preferable to leadership. This is the case if the leadership point of the rival lies at a higher profit-indifference level for both firms than does the "own" leadership point. In this case both firms will adjust to the given value of the leader's variable and by so doing they will gradually move into the intersection point of the reaction functions. This is because each firm takes the value of his rival's variable as given. Leadership equilibrium materializes if leadership is more favorable than followership to the firm in question, while followership is more favorable to the other firm. However, if the indifference maps are such that leadership would be preferable to both firms, then both will be striving for leadership equilibrium, but the two firms will, of course, be striving for different equilibria. Each will select the (from its point of view) optimal point along the reaction function of the other; yet "the other" will not in reality be moving along its own reaction function but will also be trying to select the (from its own point of view) optimal point along the reaction function of its rival. This struggle may last any length of time, or it may end by the submission of one party into followership. Stackelberg discussed the outcome on many alternative assumptions and he found that mutual striving for leadership is likely to develop in a disconcertingly large number of possible cases.[2] We shall call such an outcome "Stackelberg dis-

---

[2] For an analogous problem, described by Professor Bowley in a framework where reaction functions are defined with conjectural variation, cf. footnote 14, p. 73.

equilibrium." At the time when he published his book (1934) he seems to have felt that the likelihood of such disequilibrium on a great many markets provided justification for the corporate state. This idea is expressed in a separate brief section at the end of the book.

THE SCOPE OF THE THEORY

(1) *With respect to the variables included*: The theory is based on reaction functions expressing individual profit maximization for given values of the rival's variable. In the initial definition of the concepts, no limitation is introduced on *what* the variables are. In the detailed analysis of the problem, the technique is handled in such a way that quantity of output *or* price may be "the" variable. Undifferentiated duopoly and undifferentiated duopsony are exceptions. In these cases "the" variable is *unequivocally* the quantity of output. Interpreting the variable as the price would here lead into the straight (unmodified) Bertrand problem which Stackelberg does not consider a legitimate problem. For undifferentiated duopoly and duopsony, he rejects the assumption that the firms may believe that their rival's price is given regardless of what price *they* set because it must be obvious to both firms that the two prices must be the same if both firms are to be on the market simultaneously. Under all other market structures, where the products are not identical, it is conceivable that one firm should set its price on the assumption that the price of the other firm is given. This is, in fact, the follower's attitude, with price as the relevant variable, and it is analogous to the attitude of output followers in the framework of the Cournot-type model (where

output is the relevant variable). Thus, follower's policies
on the part of both firms result in an equilibrium corresponding to the intersection point of the two reaction
functions, while leadership policies of one firm coupled
with follower's policies of the other result in leadership
equilibrium,[3] and leadership policies on the part of both
firms result in Stackelberg disequilibrium. In the cases examined by Stackelberg, the profit-indifference maps are
analyzed for output as the relevant variable, for price as
the relevant variable, and for the possibility that "the"
variable means output for the one firm and price for the
other.[4] The attempt is made to read from the indifference
maps whether the two firms, respectively, are likely to
strive for (price or output) leadership or for (price or
output) followership. The conclusion is that, in most cases
examined, both firms are likely to strive for leadership.
Sales expenditures and the product itself are not treated
as further variables.

(2) *With respect to the number of firms*:   The
graphic method, which is supplemented by mathematics
in the appendix of *Marktform und Gleichgewicht*, lends
itself to the analysis of duopoly and duopsony but not to
that of oligopoly and oligopsony. Consequently, the
theory is developed for two-firm markets, with occasional
hints at the extension of the conclusions to markets with
more firms. There is a presumption that the addition of
more firms increases the likelihood of Stackelberg disequi-

---

[3] That is to say, in an equilibrium marked by that point along the
follower's reaction function which is optimal from the leader's point
of view.

[4] Except that undifferentiated duopoly and undifferentiated duopsony are analyzed only for output as the relevant variable.

librium. For, whenever duopoly or duopsony result in
Stackelberg disequilibrium, the addition of further firms
cannot produce equilibrium: the striving of two firms for
leadership is sufficient to exclude equilibrium, and there is
no reason to assume that the addition of other firms will
typically induce either of the two original firms (which
were striving for leadership) now to strive for followership. And when duopoly or duopsony result in intersection-point equilibrium, or in leadership equilibrium, the
addition of further firms may very easily produce Stackelberg disequilibrium. Given the general premises of his
theory, Stackelberg's conclusions would seem to hold *a
fortiori* under oligopoly and oligopsony. But technically
the theory is developed only for two-firm markets.

(3) *With respect to market structures*: From our
standpoint, the most significant feature of the theory is
its broad scope with respect to market structures. It includes several market relationships which in one form or
another give rise to the *kind* of difficulty with which we are
faced in duopoly theory. In addition to undifferentiated
duopoly and duopsony, the following market structures
are included: two firms producing substitutes (differentiated duopoly), two firms producing complementary
goods, two firms buying substitutes (differentiated duopsony), two firms buying complementary goods, and two
firms, one of which sells to the same competitive industry
from which the other firm buys. Some relationship of this
general character is very much more common than duopoly or duopsony in the narrower sense, but a significant
problem of the kind here considered arises only if the relationship between the products in question is sufficiently
close to be taken into account in policy formation.

STACKELBERG'S TYPES

If along the abscissa we measure the value assumed by the variable of firm A (for example, A's output), and along the ordinate we measure the value assumed by the variable of firm B, then we can draw a profit-indifference map for firm A, letting the indifference levels rise or fall as we move upward from the abscissa; and we can draw a profit-indifference map for firm B, letting the indifference levels rise or fall as we move to the right from the ordinate. The indifference curves of which these maps consist connect pairs of values (of the two variables, respectively) such that along an indifference curve the aggregate profit of a firm remains the same.

The indifference curves may be *concave* viewed from the axis to which they are drawn; [5] and the maximum point of the successive curves may lie increasingly *toward the other axis* as we move upward from the axis to which they are drawn (cf. Figure 3, page 106). If both these conditions are met, the map is said to be "Type α." Secondly, the curves may be *concave* but the maximum point may lie increasingly *away from the other axis*, as we move upward. This characterizes Type β (cf. Figure 4, page 107). We have Type γ if the curves are *convex* and the minimum points lie successively *toward the other axis* as we move upward from the axis to which the curves are drawn (cf. Figure 5, page 108). Type δ is characterized by *convexity* plus the condition that the minimum points lie increasingly *away from the other* axis, as we move up (cf. Figure 6, page 109).

---

[5] I.e., viewed from the abscissa for firm A, and from the ordinate for firm B.

The meaning of concavity (viewed from the axis to which the curves are drawn [6]) is that the firm in question suffers if the rival raises the value of *his* variable. The meaning of convexity is that the firm in question benefits from this circumstance. This can be seen by the following consideration. Draw a straight line parallel to the axis to which the indifference map is drawn,[7] that is, perpendicular to the axis along which the variable of the rival is measured. The straight line expresses a given value of the rival's variable, and it becomes tangent to an indifference curve at some point. It is well known that such a point of tangency expresses maximum profitability for a given value of the rival's variable only if the indifference curves are concave and the indifference levels *fall* as we move away from the axis *to which* they are concave; or if the indifference curves are convex and the indifference levels *rise*. Otherwise these tangencies are minima and no maximum is discernible. If these points of tangency express minimum (rather than maximum) profitability,[8] the economically insignificant cases develop in which for a given value of the rival's variable profits rise monotonically and indefinitely as the firm in question moves from the point of tangency toward infinite output (or prices) on the one hand, and toward zero output (or prices) [9] on the other. Barring this assumption, that is, for the economically significant cases, *concavity (α or β) means that "own" profits fall, and convexity (γ or δ) means that they rise, as the*

---

[6] I.e., viewed from the abscissa for firm *A*, and from the ordinate for firm *B*.

[7] I.e., parallel to the abscissa for *A*, or to the ordinate for *B*.

[8] And if, therefore, the area lying outside an indifference curve marks higher profits than the area encompassed by the same indifference curve.

[9] Generally speaking, toward infinite and zero value of the variable which is measured along the axis of the firm in question.

rival *increases the value of his variable.*[10] This is required
for the establishment of maximum profit values for given
values of the rival's variable.

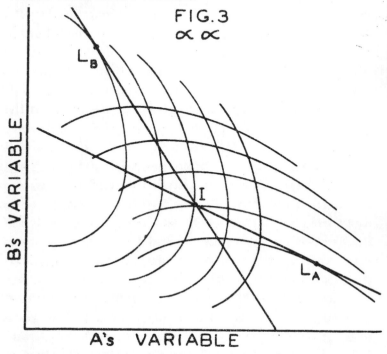

FIG. 3
∝ ∝

We have seen that for Types α and γ the points of tangency (with lines perpendicular to the axis of the rival)
lie increasingly close to the axis of the rival as we move
upward from the axis to which the indifference map is
drawn. The contrary is true of Types β and δ. This means
that *in Types α and γ an increase in the value of the rival's*

---

[10] The argument implies that an indifference curve is concave or
convex throughout its course. Conditions are conceivable in which the
indifference curves turn from convex or concave and *vice versa* as we
move along them. In this case some points of tangency might mark
minimum profits and others maximum profits. But even in this case,
economic analysis must be focussed on the areas in which maximization
takes place, and for these areas the argument of the text is valid.

variable induces the firm in question to select a smaller value for its own variable, while the contrary is true in Types β *and* δ*. The points of tangency with lines perpendicular to the axis of the rival are, of course, the maximum*

FIG. 4
ββ

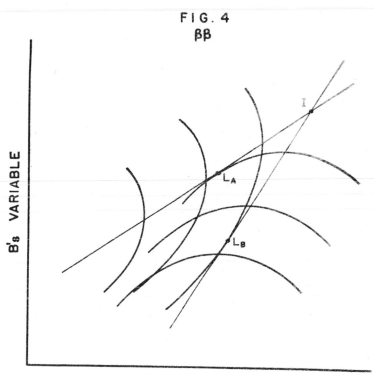

A's VARIABLE

points of concave indifference curves and the minimum points of convex indifference curves. In both cases they are maximum-profit points for given values of the rival's variable. The reaction function of a firm is the locus of these points. The leadership point of a firm is found by identifying that point of the *rival's* (follower's) reaction function where it becomes tangent to an indifference curve *of the firm in question* (the leader). The followership point is the same as the rival's leadership point, and it is found by the analogous procedure. If both indifference maps are known, it is possible to say whether both firms will be striving for leadership (Stackelberg disequilibrium) or for fol-

FIG. 5
YY

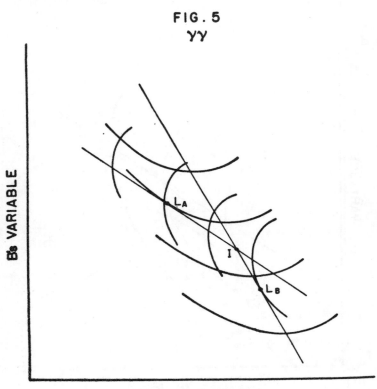

B's VARIABLE

A's VARIABLE

lowership (which leads to the intersection-point equilibrium), or whether the one will be striving for leadership and the other for followership (leadership equilibrium).

Stackelberg distinguishes four types (α, β, γ, and δ), and consequently he is faced with sixteen combinations. Using his symbols, the type to which firm A belongs is

written first and the type to which firm *B* belongs second.
For example, αα means that both belong to Type α, while
αγ means that *A* belongs to Type α and *B* to Type γ. For
discussion of the economically significant cases it is not
necessary to examine all sixteen combinations in detail. We

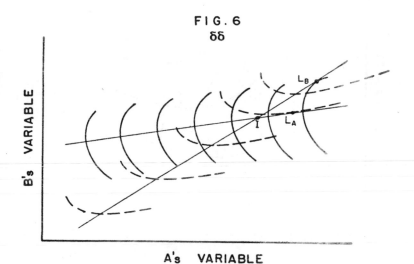

FIG. 6
δδ

B's VARIABLE

A's VARIABLE

*In this graph A's indifference curves are drawn with broken lines because
it is difficult to distinguish them visually from B's indifference curves*

shall limit ourselves here to representing graphically the
combinations αα, ββ, γγ, δδ, δα, and δβ. These play the most
important role in Stackelberg's analysis, although complete reproduction of the analysis would require examining more than these six combinations.

In the following diagrams the intersection point of the
reaction functions is marked *I*, the leadership point of
firm *A* (which lies on the reaction function of *B*) is marked
L_A, and the leadership point of firm *B* (which lies on the
reaction function of *A*) is marked *L_B*.

FIG. 7
δα

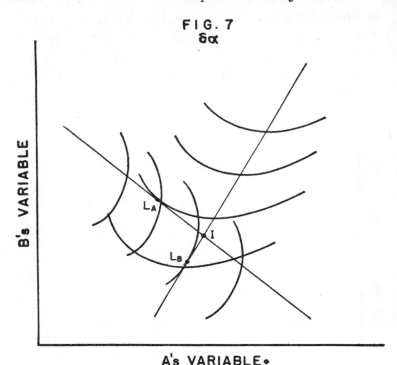

A's VARIABLE•

THE SPECIFIC MARKET STRUCTURES

Cases 1 and 2. Undifferentiated duopoly and undiffer-
entiated duopsony: On normal assumptions about demand and cost functions these are αα cases. As was pointed
out, the variable of both firms is interpreted here unequivocally as output. Each firm suffers by a rise in the output
of its rival (hence *either α or β*), and the profit-maximizing output *falls* for each firm if the rival's output, which
is taken for given, *rises* (hence α). This follows from the
italicized passages on pages 68–70. Stackelberg mentions
β as an exceptional possibility, without discussing the nature of the exceptional assumptions which would have to

be made. These assumptions would certainly have to be very peculiar, and we are not quite satisfied that they are consistent with the usual definition of these market structures. It seems obvious, by inspection of Figure 1, that under $\alpha\alpha$ each firm will be striving for leadership. Hence, Stackelberg disequilibrium.

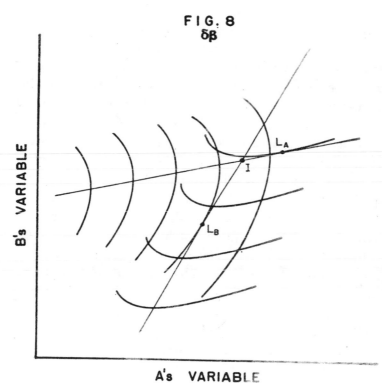

FIG. 8
δβ

A's VARIABLE

Case 3. Two firms producing rival goods, (duopoly with product differentiation):[11] If "the" variable is interpreted as quantity of output, the relevant combination

---

[11] Duopoly with product differentiation is really a special subcase of Case 3 characterized by very high cross-elasticities. Case 3 merely requires positive cross-elasticities. Cf. footnote 13 p. 113, and also the Appendix to Chapter 1.

is $\alpha\alpha$. For each firm suffers from a rise in the value of the rival's variable, and normally each firm will reduce its output if the rival's output (to which it is "adjusting") rises. If the variable is interpreted as price, the relevant combination is $\delta\delta$. For each duopolist will gain by a rise in the value of the rival's variable, and each firm will raise its price if the rival's price (which is taken for granted) increases. Stackelberg disequilibrium arises from $\alpha\alpha$, while $\delta\delta$ produces *either* intersection-point equilibrium *or* leadership equilibrium.[12] Are the conclusions derived from $\alpha\alpha$ or those derived from $\delta\delta$ relevant? In cases of this kind Stackelberg applies the following technique to find out whether the ultimate outcome is likely to be such as in combination $\alpha\alpha$ or such as in combination $\delta\delta$. For the sake of an "experiment" he interprets A's variable as quantity of output and B's variable as price, and he examines the combination $\delta\alpha$, from A's point of view (cf. Figure 7, p. 110). In the combination $\delta\alpha$ the leadership point of B means *price* followership for A because this point is B's optimal point along the *price* reaction function (δ-type reaction function) of A. The leadership point of A is a *quantity* leadership point because it is A's optimal point along the quantity reaction function (α-type reaction function) of B. Examination of $\delta\alpha$ establishes that quantity leadership is superior to price followership, from A's point of view (because L_B must lie southwest of the intersection point of the reaction functions, while L_A must lie northwest of the same point and consequently north of L_B).

---

[12] It produces intersection-point equilibrium if L_B lies higher than L_A in A's indifference map and also L_A lies higher than L_B in B's map (so that both strive for followership); it produces leadership equilibrium if either L_A or L_B lies higher in both maps. But inspection of the combination shows that if L_A lies above L_B in A's map, L_B cannot lie above L_A in B's map. This excludes Stackelberg disequilibrium.

The same statement may be made for B, after exchanging their roles in the foregoing analysis. Hence, $\alpha\alpha$ is the relevant combination, and Stackelberg disequilibrium may be expected. Intersection-point equilibrium of the $\delta\delta$ variety assumes that each firm strives for price followership, with the other firm operating along a δ map, while $\delta\delta$ leadership equilibrium assumes that one firm strives for price followership with the other firm operating along a δ map. Analysis of the $\delta\alpha$ combination excludes these equilibria because it establishes the proposition that firms strive for quantity leadership rather than for price followership if their rivals operate along δ maps. Furthermore, the $\delta\alpha$ leadership equilibrium is excluded because both firms strive for leadership in the $\delta\alpha$ combination just as in the $\alpha\alpha$ combination.

Case 4. Two firms producing complementary goods:[13] If the variable is interpreted as quantity of output, the combination $\delta\delta$ is established. The argument is analogous to those by which the relevant combinations were established for Cases 1, 2, and 3. Again by analogous reasoning,

---

[13] Complementarity may here be interpreted to mean that two goods are in such a relation that the demand for one rises if the supply of the other rises. If the demand for a good falls with a rise in the supply of the other then they are rival goods, as in Cases 3 and 5. These rival goods are sometimes called "substitute goods." To call them rival goods is preferable because the contrary relationship (complementarity) does not imply that the elasticity of substitution between the goods is zero. In other words, complementarity does not imply fixed proportions, or *perfect* complementarity. Cournot discussed conditions under perfect complementarity, and he showed that if one firm produces the one and the other produces the other good, and if A believes that the price charged by B remains unaffected by what A is doing, and B believes that the price charged by A remains unaffected by what B is doing, then a determinate equilibrium will be established (cf. *Mathematical Researches*, ch. ix.) This, of course, is the same kind of intersection-point equilibrium which Cournot had established in his Chapter VII for undifferentiated duopoly, except that it applies to two producers supplying perfectly complementary goods (rather than

αα is established for price as "the" variable; and examination of the combination δα establishes the likelihood that both firms will seek price leadership. In other words, the outcome is likely to be the same as in the combination αα— Stackelberg disequilibrium.

Case 5. Two firms buying rival goods [14] *(duopsony with product differentiation)* : If the variable is interpreted as quantity of output, the familiar kind of reasoning establishes the combination αα (with possible but unlikely exceptions). If the variable is price, ββ is established. Examination of the combination αβ leads to the conclusion that the outcome will be the same as in αα—Stackelberg disequilibrium.[15]

Case 6. Two firms buying complementary goods : If quantity is "the" variable, the combination δδ is established; if price is "the" variable, γγ. Examination of δγ leads to the conclusion that the outcome is likely to be the same as in γγ, where for each firm its own leadership point is superior (resulting here in an attempt, by both, to establish *price* leadership).[16]

Case 7. One firm selling to a competitive industry from

---

perfect substitutes) and except that price rather than output is treated as the relevant variable. In other words, while Cournot did not extend his analysis from undifferentiated duopoly to the whole family of related market structures, he did extend it to one, rather narrowly defined, member of that family. In comparing the results he also showed that while on his assumptions the undifferentiated duopoly price was always lower than the monopoly price, the prices charged by the two producers of perfectly complementary goods were higher than those which would be established if the two producers formed a monopoly.

[14] Cf. footnotes 11 and 13, pp. 111 and 113.

[15] We have not drawn αβ.

[16] We have not drawn δγ.

which the other buys (indirect bilateral monopoly): If quantity is "the" variable δδ is established, while interpretation of the variable as price leads to δβ. In the combination δδ both firms strive for followership (intersection-point equilibrium), or one firm for leadership and the other for followership,[17] while in δβ both strive for leadership. Examination of the relevant hybrid combinations leads to a presumption that the ultimate outcome is likely to be the same as in δβ, not as in δδ.

In summary, it may be repeated that Stackelberg disequilibrium is the most typical outcome. And, given the framework in which the reasoning is carried out, disequilibrium is even more likely than would appear at first sight. For, while Stackelberg does establish a presumption for his kind of disequilibrium in many cases, he does not prove the existence of a *stable* intersection point (in the first quadrant) in the cases where the tendency might be toward intersection-point equilibrium.[18] This, however, is of no great significance because the outcome almost always is Stackelberg disequilibrium. In fact, in the brief summary here given this was consistently the outcome. In one or two cases, exceptional possibilities were mentioned even in this brief summary. It is not easy to interpret these. Some of the exceptional possibilities of Stackelberg's schemes were not pointed out explicitly in our account. In some of these cases one is led to expect intersection-point equilibrium.[19]

---

[17] Cf. footnote 12, p. 112.

[18] The first quadrant is of course the only economically meaningful quadrant.

[19] As Stackelberg points out, his kind of disequilibrium becomes even more likely for oligopoly than for duopoly because equilibrium requires that *all* oligopolists (or *all* oligopolists *except one*) be striving for followership.

CRITICISM OF CLASSICAL OLIGOPOLY
THEORY EXTENDED

The type of oligopoly analysis in which Stackelberg's system belongs is technically characterized by the use of reaction functions expressing individual profit maximization for given values of the rival's variable. Limiting the approach to reaction functions of this sort stems from the desire to exclude collusion and spontaneous co-ordination and thereby to separate the problem at hand from the monopoly problem. It seems more promising to look elsewhere for the distinctive features of the oligopoly problem and of the problem of related market structures. Co-ordination under oligopoly is typically limited or incomplete and the distinctive features of oligopolistic markets reflect themselves in these limitations.

The attempt to exclude the problem of collusion by the quasi-mechanistic use of reaction functions has not only led to unrealistic results but has proved rather unsuccessful even on its own grounds. Leadership equilibria can scarcely be said to exclude quasi-agreement. Under leadership, the policies of any one firm are based on the *correct* assumption that the other firm is acting in a specific way, and the other firm would have no reason to act in this fashion if *it* did not *correctly* assume that the first firm acts in a specific way. Yet, while leadership equilibria may be said to contain an element of collusion or of spontaneous co-ordination, they represent an arbitrary and unintelligent form of co-ordination if leadership expresses itself in selecting a point along a reaction function of the traditional kind (which expresses follower's individual profit maximization for given values of the leader's variable).

Such leadership equilibria stand in no meaningful relationship to joint-profit maximization. The value of the market variables at which industry profits are maximized is quite different from the values established if one firm maximizes its profits on the assumption that the values of the rival's variables are given and the other firm sets the (from its point of view) optimal values on the understanding that the first firm behaves as just described. Yet, given the relative strength of the rival firms, each firm earns higher profits if joint profits *are* maximized. It is true that, on realistic assumptions, unlimited (or complete) oligopolistic co-ordination should not typically be expected. The reasons are connected with the fact that, in the passage of time, the relative strength of the rival firms changes in an unpredictable way, and with the fact that sometimes the relative strength of the firms is insufficiently known even "as of now." Consequently, the prevailing forms of co-ordination are incomplete forms; they contain "outlets." This gives rise to the most important specific problems in oligopoly theory. But it is impossible to interpret the leadership equilibria (along the traditional reaction functions) as resulting from co-operative arrangements with *meaningful* outlets. These equilibria, while "collusive" in a sense, deviate from the maximization of the industry profit *blindly*, that is to say, not in a meaningful manner.

It might be objected that the intersection-point equilibria are not collusive in the foregoing sense, and that therefore they are at least consistent with the postulate that collusion should be excluded from the analysis of the problem. This is true but the objection does not establish the usefulness of the equilibrium concept in question. For these "equilibria" rest on arbitrary and incorrect notions regarding rival behavior.[20] It is quite arbitrary to assume that just these notions will be formed, or that, if formed, they will never be tested for validity. Along Stackelberg's line of reasoning this becomes particularly apparent. Intersection-point equilibria are said to result from a mutual attempt at followership, that is, at the rival's leadership. However, what is accomplished is not the rival's leadership but something different. Each firm assumes that the other firm will select a point along a reaction function which in reality plays no part whatsoever in shaping the policies of the other firm. Therefore, the function has no *raison d'être* for the analysis of the problem under consideration, unless it is maintained that a very special kind of incorrect assumption is made about what the rival is trying to do and that the individual firms are incapable of interpreting their experience which shows clearly enough that their assumptions are incorrect.

The foregoing criticism applies to an entire stage of development of oligopoly theory from which Stackelberg's system emerged as its most mature product. The concept of the Stackelberg disequilibrium (stemming from a mutual attempt at leadership) does not call for qualifying this appraisal. Stackelberg disequilibrium may either be interpreted as resulting from the arbitrary and incorrect assumption, mutually held, that the rival moves along a reaction function which in reality is non-existent for the rival; or it may be interpreted as resulting from an attempt to force the rival into reacting along such a function and thereby to force him into accepting the role of the follower. But if one firm has the power to force the other

---

[20] The arbitrary and incorrect notions derive from the assumption that the value of the rival's variable is given regardless of one's own moves.

firm into anything, why would it not prefer to force its rival into something more favorable for the powerful firm, and possibly also for the weaker firm? These objections uniformly point to the likelihood of attempts at joint-profit maximization, with qualifications (or deviations) which must be subject to reasonable interpretation.[21] This is true of oligopoly as well as of the family of related market structures. For all these market structures it seems reasonable to assume ability to agree on relative strength on the basis of factors (a) through (d) of Chapter I (pages 24–9); and to assume a tendency toward joint maximization. It then becomes necessary, however, to examine separately the specific circumstances which produce deviations from the maximization of the joint profit. In other words, the effective limits of oligopolistic co-ordination must be examined.

---

[21] When considering Stackelberg's system the most mature product growing out of the preceding stages of development, we imply that reaction functions with conjectural variation have proved a blind alley. Stackelberg takes no cognizance of them and in fact none of the difficulties here discussed could be solved by introducing them. Reaction functions with conjectural variation are necessarily based on arbitrary and incorrect notions regarding rival behavior. At the intersection point these assumptions happen to be quasi-correct in the sense that each firm lends its variable the value which the other firm expects. This cannot be true at any other point because wherever it is true the functions must coincide. But if this is true only in the intersection point, then even in the intersection point each firm "maximizes its profits" in a nonsensical way. They maximize their profits on the assumption that the reaction functions, which intersect at that point, are valid; and that, therefore, if either firm moved out of the intersection point, the other would react in a definite fashion. But the functions are not valid, and each firm can convince itself easily enough that, if it moved out of the intersection point, the other firm would not react along its alleged reaction function.

CHAPTER FOUR

The Pure Theory: Maximization
of Joint Profits

THE ANALYTICAL TRANSITION TO
QUASI-AGREEMENTS

THE leader may be unwilling to select any point along a reaction function that expresses the follower's individual profit maximization for alternative values of the leader's variables. Instead, the leader may try to force the follower into setting up reaction functions of a different kind. Reaction functions expressing the follower's individual profit maximization for alternative values of the leader's variables have no significance if the leader refuses to select values for his variables within the range for which the function is established. Refusal to select values within the relevant range means that the leader assumes a "cutthroat" attitude; he selects values that make losses inevitable for the follower so that the follower would have to go out of business if the leader persisted in his attitude long enough. To such a range of values the follower's reaction function does not apply. If his rival sets such values he can choose only between retaliating with cutthroat policies of his own, or quitting. The follower may therefore be in no position to establish an individual profit-maximizing reaction function on the assumption of given values of the leader's variables because if he should tentatively set up such a function he may be made to realize that it is unacceptable to his rival and hence lacks validity. However, the follower may still set up reaction functions if they are of such a kind that the leader *is* willing to select values along them. The leader may exclude certain reaction functions but another family of reaction functions may retain their potential significance. In this case the follower should be expected to establish the (for him) most favorable function of this family—or, as we shall presently see, some range of this function.

Followers may be unwilling to establish reaction functions for the entire range of values in which they could make profits or avoid losses. Instead, they may establish functions for smaller ranges of distinctly satisfactory profitability from their own point of view, and they may assume a cutthroat attitude if leaders do not select a point within this narrower range. In this case too, a cutthroat attitude is one of forcing losses on the rival so that he would have to go out of business should the policy persist long enough. As long as a finite range of a reaction function is established and the leader selects a point in this range, the leader-follower relationship still exists. The limiting case in which this relationship ceases to exist is that in which the "range" of the reaction function is reduced to a reaction point, that is, to definite values of the variables. In this case both select a point, and equilibrium assumes that they agree on the point selected.

Firms frequently agree on reaction functions rather than directly on points because it is often left to one firm—the leader—to make a judgment on the position of the market functions (demand and supply functions facing the industry). The leader then sets the values of his own variables—for example, price and output—and the reaction functions of the followers show the values of their variables for alternative values of the leader's variables. Reaction functions will be acceptable to the leader if, for the alternative choices he can make in view of the market functions, they give the followers no greater profit share than corresponds to their relative bargaining strength. Therefore, in such cases, the quasi-agreement relates to reaction functions indicating the prices, outputs and other market-variables of the followers for given values of the leader's variable. But aside from the problem of evaluating the market functions, we have to expect that reaction *points* are reached directly because we have now assumed that any function which may be established results from quasi-agreement (must be acceptable to *all* participants) and there is no reason to assume that the quasi-agreement would leave a firm the choice of getting more or less along some reaction function at the expense of its rival. The agreement would have to relate to a point, that is, to definite prices, outputs, and so on. Leadership assumes that the leader is given a choice between values included in the reaction functions of followers. Under quasi-agreement this can be justified only in view of necessary adjustments to changing market functions.

The transition from the "reaction-function" approach

discussed in the preceding chapters to the more realistic problem of quasi-agreements may therefore be said to consist of two steps. In the first place, starting from the leadership model, we should include in our arsenal of tools reaction functions other than those defined to express followers' individual profit maximization for given values of leaders' variables. Followers' reaction functions are significant only if the leader is willing to make a selection along them. Any meaningful solution assumes that the behavior pattern of the rivals is mutually acceptable. For the same reason, the second step of the transition consists of allowing for the possibility that the reaction function of the follower may be limited to one range of potential values of the leader's variables, to that range within which the outcome is more favorable for the follower than in other ranges. The limiting case is that of a reaction point, rather than function, and in this case the transition from the original leadership model to quasi-agreement is so complete that all features of the leadership model have disappeared. For, in this case, the "leadership" has become mutual, and mutual leadership is indistinguishable from mutual followership. It seems, however, that in the real world the transition is in many cases less "complete" so that certain firms may make a selection within certain ranges of reaction functions, although there is no reason to assume that the selection expresses follower's individual profit maximization for given values of leader's variables. The reaction functions typically express such follower's behavior *as is acceptable to the leader;* and, presumably, from among these behavior patterns they express the one most favorable from the follower's point of view. Thus, instead of expressing individual profit maximization for alternative leader's values, reaction functions become the objects of quasi-agreement containing significant constraints. *In a sense*, they may still be said to express followers' individual profit maximization but *not* simply "for alternative values of the leader's variable." *They express profit maximization, given not merely the leader's values but given also his (assumed) willingness and power to accept certain reaction functions and to refuse others.* Furthermore, the leader can only be said to maximize his position given the follower's willingness and power to establish certain reaction functions and not to establish others. For the individual participants, this is not a maximization problem *in the usual sense*. It is maximization for the follower individually, and also for the leader individually, only in view of the assumed behavior of the rival which in turn is known to be influenced by one's own behavior.

Moreover, the reaction functions of these models of quasi-agreement cannot be derived from the individual profit-maximizing reaction functions by introducing the concept of conjectural variation. In relation to the behavior pattern actually established, the conjectural variation is zero. Choices which express quasi-agreement are choices in which the participants are believed (correctly) to acquiesce. Something in the nature of conjectural variation enters merely into the decision to set up or to accept certain reaction functions and not others due to the assumed unwillingness of the rival to accept other functions. But this again is very different from conjectural variation in the usual sense. The functions themselves do not include conjectural variation; they are established by followers on the correct assumption of zero variation in the sense that the leader will go on doing what he does if the follower adjusts along the function. However, it may be said that conjectural variation plays a role in deciding to establish a function, that is, in the comparison of alternative functions but not in the comparison of points along the function actually established. Furthermore, the leader in any leadership model operates with conjectural variation in the sense of knowing that followers will adjust along their reaction functions (page 76). But since leaders establish no reaction function we are not faced here with reaction functions which would include conjectural variation.

The "transition" from the leadership model discussed in the preceding chapter to models of quasi-agreement can be made for reaction functions defined in relation to a single variable, as, for example, output (Cournot model). The same transition may also be made for multi-dimensional reaction functions, defined in relation to several "simultaneous" variables and expressing the values of all these variables for "followers," given the values of the same variables for "leaders." In the real world the relevant reaction functions are multi-dimensional. However, they frequently are hybrids in the sense of expressing quasi-agreement for certain variables and competition for others. We shall return to this problem in the next chapter. Incompleteness of co-ordination will be considered an "imperfection" which will be discussed subsequently at some length.

We have now described an analytical transition from models earlier discussed to quasi-agreements. We must realize, however, that in this analytical transition it is impossible to select a stage at which the model has just assumed the characteristics of quasi-agreement. Elements of "agreement" are contained in all stages of the transition. The original Cournot and Bertrand models, if extended multi-dimensionally to all significant variables, may be said to imply no element of agreement because the functions which determine the equilibrium are assumed to be established and to be consistently maintained regardless of the behavior of the competitors.[1] We have seen that these models lead into insuperable difficulties. The leadership models derived from the Cournot and Bertrand type of reaction functions do contain an element of agreement, and these models served as the starting point for the analytical transition with which we are concerned in this section. Consequently, elements of agreement are implied in all stages of the transition, but of course they become increasingly predominant in the course of the transition.

Any leadership model implies an element of agreement about the manner in which economic strength is distributed. It not only implies that agreements have been reached by which certain firms are made leaders and others followers; it also assumes that the leadership function is exercised in a definite way (along certain reaction functions) and that followers behave in a definite way (by keeping to these reaction functions). In the earlier sections it was pointed out that the agreement which was *implied* with respect to the manner in which leadership is exercised is a highly arbitrary "agreement." Indeed it is a meaningless agreement in terms of the basic, underlying forces. There is no reason to assume that leaders will in general select points along functions expressing followers' individual profit maximization for given values

---

[1] However, if these models are not extended multi-dimensionally but are defined in relation to a single variable, then the corresponding equilibria may be said to imply "agreement" on the variable in terms of which the adjustment is supposed to take place.

of leaders' variables. Other implicit agreements may be more profitable to all firms concerned.

The analytical transition described in this section renders the element of agreement, which is implicit in all leadership models, less arbitrary. The model at which we now arrive assumes that the selection of the leader is made along functions sufficiently favorable to him and at the same time to his rivals to be acceptable to both. After this analytical transition we no longer assume that the competing firms limit themselves to functions expressing followers' individual profit-maximization for given values of leaders' variables. As long as we operate with this limiting assumption, "implicit agreement" (or quasi-agreement) is meaningless in any terms other than the mechanistic terms defined in the model. The analytical transition here considered leads us to models in which quasi-agreement becomes meaningful. Once this analytical transition is completed, quasi-agreements, and the distribution of power on which they are based, may acquire meaning in terms of underlying forces such as were distinguished in Chapter I (under (a) through (d), pages 24–9).

The greater the emphasis placed on the element of quasi-agreement, the more do the functional relationships which determine the industry profits come to the foreground. The models discussed in the preceding chapters imply that no attention is paid to maximizing industry profits. This is another reason why the "rules of the game" underlying these models are arbitrary and unrealistic. Why should the competing firms adopt such rules if quasi-agreements establishing different rules could secure higher profits for all rivals? Whether it is possible to move from a potential equilibrium point to another so as to improve the position of all rivals depends on whether aggregate industry profits are higher in the second point than in the first. If we do not restrict the permissible quasi-agreements to those implied in the original leadership models [2] but include more flexible patterns of behavior on which the rivals may "agree" in their own interest, then we are turning our attention increasingly to the bearing of alternative patterns of behavior on aggregate industry profits. Whether a quasi-agreement could or could not be "improved" in the interest of all participants depends on the relation between alternative patterns of behavior and aggregate industry profits. If co-ordination were complete, it would always be true that all firms have an interest in the maximization of the joint profit. With incomplete co-ordination this is literally true only on certain simplifying assumptions. Market-sharing is a form of incomplete co-ordination because it does not imply the pooling of resources. On what simplifying assumptions does market-sharing result in joint maximization for the resources of an industry?

If we assume that the average total cost functions of all firms are identical and horizontal in the relevant range, then, in the absence of product (and spatial) differentiation, a simple market-sharing agreement will result in a condition where each participant is interested in the maximization of the joint profit. For, in these circumstances, each firm earns a given percentage of the industry profits and the industry profits do not depend on how the shares are distributed. There is no difference between maximizing an aggregate or a fixed percentage

---

[2] That is, to the models based on reaction functions which express followers' individual profit maximization for given values of leaders' variables.

of the same aggregate. Consequently, on these simplifying assumptions, there will exist a strong incentive
to reach a quasi-agreement which maximizes the joint
profit. This incentive will be strong even if co-operation
does not go beyond the establishment of market shares by
quasi-agreement.

In undifferentiated oligopoly, with identical and horizontal cost functions, reaction functions may be pre-
sumed to express for given leaders' values such followers'
values as are consistent with the "maximization of industry profits" in the sense of maximization for the pool
of available resources. The obstacles standing in the way
of such maximization would not be significant because,
as we have seen, mere market-sharing according to relative
strength accomplishes this objective. Whether reaction
functions will be established—so that certain elements of
the leadership construction are retained—or implicit
agreement will be reached directly with respect to reaction
points (definite quantities and prices) depends on a
variety of circumstances. Establishment of reaction *functions* (in certain ranges of "validity") may serve a useful
purpose. The leader may possess better judgment of the
market function or a more complete organization, in which
case the choice of the price and of his own output may be
left to him, and the reaction functions may express the
followers' willingness so to set the values of their variables
that for each value of the leader's variable similar distributions of shares would result. Given such functions,
the leader will maximize the gains of all participants by
maximizing industry profits. It is also conceivable, however, that leadership is required for technical-administra-
tive reasons—someone must set the pace in the event of
changes—and that such leadership rotates. In the absence

of leadership, the participants must feel out each other's reactions to changing market conditions by tentative price-setting. Leadership eliminates periods of tentative price-setting and price instability which may occur with changing market conditions even if no disagreements concerning relative strength exist. Direct contacts may sometimes also eliminate this kind of instability but in a less dependable way because the question of who is right has to be settled each time anew.[3] It seems therefore appropriate to consider the mere establishment of reaction points a special case and not to dispense with the concepts of reaction functions and leadership.[4] Reaction functions or, if the quasi-agreement relates directly to points, reaction points should be expected to reflect a tendency toward joint-profit maximization. If the aggregate industry profit is not maximized and the less-than-maximum profit is divided in some fashion, it always is possible to give *every single participant* more than he actually gets, by changing the quasi-agreement to a basis on which the aggregate industry profit *is* maximized.

Even on these simplifying assumptions—that is, even if we set aside product differentiation and cost differences —there exists merely a *tendency* toward the maximization of industry profits. Hence, the proposition that quasi-

---

[3] There is no good reason for excluding this kind of leadership problem from the "pure" theory. Pure theory usually is interpreted to exclude discussions of the consequences of errors and of uncertainty but it need not exclude a discussion of the methods by which correct judgments are made.

[4] TNEC Monograph 21, *Competition and Monopoly in American Industry*, prepared by Clair Wilcox (Washington, D. C., 1940), gives the following examples of industries in which effective price leadership exists: steel, non-ferrous alloys, copper and lead, petroleum, glass containers, biscuits and crackers, cigarettes, agricultural implements, cement, newsprint.

agreements maximize aggregate industry profits must be qualified in several respects. These qualifications are partly in the nature of general qualifications to the profit-maximization axiom. Partly they are additional qualifications applying to oligopolistic markets even if we do not consider product differentiation and cost differences. However, if product differentiation and cost differences are taken into account, then a qualification acquires significance which should be mentioned even in the present introductory discussion of the theory.

Cost differences (in the sense of sloping average total cost curves *and* of differences between the cost curves of various firms) and product differentiation (also spatial differentiation) raise the question whether it is always in the interest of all firms to maximize industry profits. If, as is likely, the method of sharing and distributing the profits consists of co-ordinated setting of the values of the market variables—price, product, and advertising expenditures—then the answer is in the negative. In other words, the answer is in the negative if collusion is incomplete. With sloping cost curves, and (or) different cost functions for the various firms, and (or) product differentiation, the maximization of industry profits would require the firms of the industry to pool resources and markets. Such arrangements could be made profitable to the individual firms only if they were accompanied by *inter-firm compensations*. In the absence of pooling—that is, if the income of each firm is what it earns on the market—the attainable joint profit will depend on what the shares of the individual firms are, that is, on their relative strength. If "rationalization" from the standpoint of maximizing industry profits requires a definite allocation of activities among the various firms, then, in the absence of pooling, the actual market shares of the individual firms exert an important influence on how close it is possible to get to the maximization of earnings for the total available resources. The market shares decide *how* "irrational" the no-pooling clause is, that is, by how much the attainable maximum joint profit is lowered through failure to pool. Moreover, granted the absence of pooling, there is no assurance that the firms will get even as near to the point of joint maximization as the given market shares will let them get. Within certain ranges of the relevant variables (for example, price) one firm may gain by a move toward joint maximization, while another may lose, depending on its cost function, its market share, and the popularity of its brand. If the losing firm possesses sufficient relative strength it will not give its consent to the move even though aggregate profits could be increased.

In these cases it remains true that it would be possible to describe a quasi-agreement which would maximize the profits of the industry; and that *if such an agreement were concluded* and the industry profits were divided in the same proportion as that in which they actually are divided, then each firm would increase its profits. Yet the point is that, with cost differences and product differentiation, dividing the maximized industry profits in the same proportion may require the direct transfer of assets from one firm to the other (inter-firm compensation). In undifferentiated oligopoly and with identical, horizontal cost functions the maximized industry profits [5] can always be divided in the same proportion as lower industry profits,[6]

---

[5] I.e., the aggregate industry profits accruing at the price at which the industry profits are maximized.

[6] I.e., the aggregate industry profits accruing at any other price.

without direct inter-firm compensation, by mere regulation of the market variables.[7] This ceases to be true if cost differences and product differentiation (or even merely spatial differentiation) are taken into account. In this event more complete co-operation would be required to maximize the joint profit and thereby to maximize all individual profits, *given* the shares of the individual firms in the total profit. Co-ordination would have to be complete enough to result in the pooling of resources and of their earnings and in direct inter-firm payments.

Direct inter-firm compensations—the transfer of assets from one firm to the other—is frequently not feasible. Agreement including provisions for direct compensation thereby becomes a *true* agreement, that is, it expresses collusion in the narrower sense of the word. Interfirm compensation requires direct contact and it must result from negotiations rather than from merely inplicit bargaining and from quasi-agreement (cf p. 16). In countries with anti-trust legislation this gives rise to difficulties. These should not be over-emphasized because compensations may assume different forms and in many cases it may be possible to conceal the fact that the payment (or, more generally, the transfer of assets) is undertaken in the framework of what essentially is a restrictive agreement. What, however, seems essential to us is that a firm which at the actually established values of the market variables maintains its profitability by receiving compensations from its rivals is at a substantial disadvantage if the agreement is terminated and aggressive competition is resumed. The conditions then ruling are highly unfavorable for the firm because in receiving compensations

---

[7] I.e., price, output, selling effort.

it substituted contacts with its rivals for contacts with the market and with production experts.

In this connection it should be pointed out that joint and organized handling of freight problems cannot be properly interpreted as output-pooling in the face of spatial differentiation. Arrangements with respect to freight absorption and phantom freight are means of market-sharing by the appropriate setting of delivered prices. They imply price discrimination on an "f.o.b. mill" basis because the appropriate setting of delivered prices clearly does not require a firm to set lower prices in the neighborhood of its plant than at points more accessible to its rivals. Joint maximization would require more than this. In the event of non-horizontal cost curves, *or* differences between the cost curves of different firms, *or* of product differentiation, *or* of spatial differentiation, it would require such reallocation of output between the participating firms as disregards the size of the individual profits which can be earned on the market and aims exclusively at maximizing the difference between joint revenue and cost.

We may conclude that the tendency toward maximization of aggregate industry profits is counteracted by several factors. It seems methodologically convenient to place the emphasis on the tendency toward the maximization of industry profits, when the "first approximation" to a realistic theory of oligopoly is developed. But such a first approximation will have to be supplemented by an analysis of the counteracting forces. Alternatively, we may express this by saying that on the level of "pure theory" the conclusion is that aggregate industry profits will be maximized. In the event of cost differences and (or) product differentiation (also spatial differentiation) *this would require the pooling of resources and inter-firm compensation.* As will be seen later, such pooling does not necessarily imply that conditions will be identical with those under monopoly. The pool contains more than one unit of control—more than one firm—and it may very well find it profitable to use more than one unit. What complete pooling does imply is that no attention is paid to how much profit each participant earns directly on the market but only to how much the aggregate of the participants earns. Each participant is compensated from the pool of earnings according to his share. In contrast, the "no-pooling" clause implies that no participant receives profits beyond what he earns directly on the market. Only on wholly unrealistic simplifying assumptions [8] would looser forms of collusion (for example, simple market-sharing) with the "no-pooling" clause accomplish joint maximization in the same sense as that in which profit on available resources can be maximized under pooling. If we start from a theory of unqualified joint-profit maximization, which implies complete pooling, then it will be necessary to modify our first approximation, or pure theory, to a considerable extent, because the looser forms of co-operation with no pooling are much more prevalent and, on realistic assumptions, these cannot be expected to result in joint maximization.

The methodological justification for this distinction between a pure theory of complete oligopolistic co-ordination and a theory of imperfections is that in this fashion we separate a meaningful complex of problems and place it into a separate category. Why is oligopolistic co-ordination incomplete in spite of the fact that one might expect complete pooling to be more profitable? Why are the

---

[8] On assumptions such as those described on p. 126.

available profits not really maximized in oligopoly? This is an articulate complex of problems which is separated out *in toto* for further analysis if in the first approximation we assume joint-profit maximization. In a sense these questions constitute the core of the oligopoly problem. They will be discussed in Chapters V–VII.

THE COEXISTENCE OF OLIGOPOLY WITH A COMPETITIVE SECTOR IN SPECIFIC INDUSTRIES: PARTIAL OLIGOPOLY POWER

Before proceeding further, it is necessary to point out that oligopolistic conditions may and frequently do exist in a section of an industry even if the industry includes a great many small producers who are unaware of their mutual influence on one another, and who therefore are incapable of concerted action. Such an industry may include an oligopolistic section, that is, a few firms big enough not to disregard their influence. It is *conceivable* that such an industry should operate under *fully* oligopolistic conditions because the dominant firms might police a comprehensive quasi-agreement which extends to the small firms. Each individual small firm would know that price-cutting or overstepping market shares results in retaliation by the big firms. However, fully oligopolistic organization by such policing is unlikely because voluntary agreement on the relative strength of each member of a very large group is difficult. Discontented small firms are very likely to take a chance on the unwillingness of the big firms to upset the entire market merely to punish a violator of negligible size. The big firms are more likely

to possess only *partial oligopoly power*; or the outcome
may sometimes fall between the fully oligopolistic conditions just described and the kind of partial oligopoly to
which we now turn. Oscillations may occur between those
values of the market variables corresponding to the unstable full oligopoly achieved by big-firm policing and the
values corresponding to the partial oligopoly into which
the full oligopoly tends to disintegrate.

Partial oligopoly of the big firms is characterized by
the co-ordination of policies among these which, however,
takes the atomistically competitive behavior of the small
firms for granted. If the small firms alone tend to compete
down the price to the zero-profit level of the big firms then
partial-oligopoly power cannot develop because the price
is determined by the automatic market mechanism. If they
compete it down to the zero level of *all* small firms but not
to that of the big firms, then the problem loses its specific
features as a *partial* oligopoly problem because the best
the big firms can do is to drive out the small ones.[9] The
characteristic feature of the "partial oligopoly" situation
here envisaged is that the big firms can sell gradually rising quantities by increasingly undercutting the price
which would prevail in their absence, but that they cannot
drive out all small firms by slightly undercutting. This in
turn assumes that one or more of the following three conditions are satisfied: there must either be obstacles to the
entry of small firms beyond certain limits with the result
that the existing number of small firms is insufficient to
bring the price down to the cost level of any firm; *or* the

---

[9] The threat of entry will set limits to the exploitation of such
oligopoly but we still call it "full" oligopoly because any oligopoly
group, and even a monopolist, may be exposed to this threat. They
usually are.

cost functions of the entering small firms must become increasingly unfavorable, so that the big firms eliminate
some (marginal) small firms but not all small firms as they
undercut the price which would prevail in their absence;
or there must be product differentiation, and the product
of the marginal firm (zero-profit firm) must be markedly
inferior to the product of the big firms. In these cases, the
big firms *may* find it more profitable to live together with
a group of small ones rather than to drive them out *in toto*
by a very low price. The situation will be that of partial
oligopoly because price, output, profits, and so forth, will
depend on the deliberate behavior of the big firms, which
are aware of their individual influence, as well as on the
competitive forces emanating from the area of small firms.
The profit-maximizing price for the aggregate of the big
firms is determinate because the number and the total output of the small firms depend on the price set by the big
ones. The atomistic firms consider the ruling price "given"
(a parameter). Conditions are essentially those described
in Karl Forchheimer's theoretical model, where the
"leader" knows that at any price he might set the followers
will sell the quantity that equates their marginal costs to
that price, leaving the remainder of the market to the
leader. Given this "rule of the game" the leader selects the
price which is most profitable to him.[10] In our case "the
leader" is made up of the oligopolistic group within the
industry.

Further, it should be pointed out that big firms may
coexist with many small firms which, however, produce
merely a semi-finished product. The big firms may be in

---

[10] Karl Forchheimer, "Theretisches zum unvollstaendigen Monopol,"
Schmollers Jahrbuch, 1908 Erstes Heft. Cf. also A. J. Nichol, *Partial
Monopoly and Price Leadership* (Philadelphia, 1930).

a purely (not partially) oligopolistic position on the market for the finished product, but they may not be in full control of the output of the semi-finished product. They finish their own semi-finished output and also that of the small firms. In this event, they should be regarded as oligopolists *for the process of finishing*, as oligopsonists in the purchase of the semi-finished product, and as competitive producers of the semi-finished product. It is true that the analysis of the preceding section has shown that (potentially) they may possess partial oligopoly *power* even as producers of the semi-finished product. As we have seen, partial oligopoly power in the production of the semi-finished product assumes that the semi-finished price which would be established in the absence of the big firms would not be so low as to eliminate the profits of the big firms nor those of *all* small firms. But even if they possess such partial oligopoly power, they will not make use of it. They will buy the semi-finished product at the lowest price at which it is available in view of the competition among small firms; and they will tend to maximize their profits on the process of finishing. The joint-profit maximizing values of the market variables are determinate, just as a monopolist-monopsonist can calculate his marginal cost from the supply function of the monopsonized raw material and then proceed to equate these marginal costs to his marginal revenue.

Finally, big firms may be full oligopolists in the production of a semi-finished product, but they may coexist with many small firms in the process of finishing. The small firms buy the semi-finished product from the big ones, but the big firms finish part of their own semi-finished output. This is essentially the case whenever there is oligopoly on the level of manufacturing and when the

marketing is undertaken partly by the manufacturers
themselves, or their subsidiaries, and partly by small independent firms. (In this event read "marketing," for "finishing.") The big firms may or may not possess partial
oligopoly power in finishing. This depends on the circumstances on which the existence of partial oligopoly power
generally depends when big and small firms coexist, that
is, on whether the zero-profit price of the marginal entrants does or does not leave the big firms and other small
firms with excess profits. If the big firms possess partial
oligopoly power, they will use it in finishing, just as they
use their full oligopoly power in the production of the
semi-finished good. The partial oligopoly power will not
remain latent as in the previous case.

Such partial oligopoly power of big firms which share
the finishing or marketing business with small ones (and
which are full oligopolists in the production of the semi-
finished good) does not necessarily require the big firms
to make use of the power of discriminatory treatment
which they possess over the small ones as sole producers of
their materials. But it is profitable for the big firms to
use this power. For, by this method, they can impose upon
the small firms a pattern of behavior which is more profitable for the big ones than the pattern just considered.
They can force the small firms to behave *as if* they were
comparatively weak partners in a *full* (not partial) finishing oligopoly. The small firms must buy their materials
from the big ones; hence the big firms may determine the
conditions on which the individual small firms obtain
goods. They may set the price at which the small firms
resell, and they may punish violators not only by aggressive price tactics (which is the only means available
when they coexist on the same stage of the structure of

production),[11] but also by failure to supply materials. This power may stabilize conditions approximating full oligopoly. The big firms may have an interest in accomplishing this even if technically they are not themselves in the finishing business. By determining the conditions on which the small firms are allowed to buy and to resell they can indirectly exploit much of the oligopoly profit of the small ones. They can change the small firms into a finishing (marketing) department or agency of the big ones. This again is as if the small firms were weak partners in a *full* "finishing" oligopoly. In all cases considered in this paragraph we are faced with a combination of big-firm oligopoly with Case 3 restriction among the small firms (pages 47–9). The results are similar to those of full oligopoly.

---

[11] Cf. p. 136.

CHAPTER FIVE

Limitations of Profit Maximization: The Monopoly-Oligopoly Problem (Safety Margins; Long-run Objectives; Controlling Groups)

IN OLIGOPOLY, there is a tendency toward the maximization of aggregate industry profits and toward their distribution in accordance with certain underlying forces which were discussed in Chapter I. But it was pointed out that this tendency is counteracted by other forces. In the present chapter these qualifications will be considered in somewhat greater detail, in so far as they apply to monopoly as well as to oligopoly. Subsequently we shall return to specific oligopoly problems.

ECONOMIC AND OTHER OBJECTIVES

One of the qualifications became commonplace early in the history of economic thought. Individuals are not interested exclusively in maximizing their profits; and economic institutions are composed of individuals. All people, without exception, try to live up to certain standards prevailing in their environments. Even in an industrial society, efficient handling of one's own economic problems is merely one of the many "standards" which people try to live up to. But in the contemporary setting it is a highly important standard. Furthermore, in contemporary Western society, "income" (the reward for contributions to current output) accrues to individuals and institutions mainly in the form of a fund in accounting units which can be exchanged for material goods or for services. The income motive—and more generally the *economic motive* of acquiring goods and services by exchanging or technically transforming one's resources—appears mainly in the form of the *profit motive*, so far as business units are concerned.

Articulate discussion of the relative importance of the profit motive would be easier if the other standards could be divided into a group which is complementary to the profit motive and into a group which is competitive. But in general this cannot be done. Most other motives—including some of the typically unselfish ones and including the prestige motive—partly complement the profit motive and partly compete with it. This undoubtedly is true of the power motive which sometimes is considered the other Great Evil. Certain means of exercising power over other people are greatly increased by the accumulation of wealth. Wealth brings direct economic power and frequently implies indirect political power over others. But the routes to direct political power are made substantially more difficult, and they may be blocked, by great wealth. Power, in turn, partly complements, partly competes with

other objectives, some of which are regarded as typically
unselfish.

Labeling certain standards and motives as "selfish" and
others as "unselfish" is not particularly fruitful. Every
significant ethical system has placed considerable emphasis
on the fact that, by attempting to comply with its standards, the individual acts not only righteously but also in
his *true* self-interest. Ethical systems and civilizations
have existed and still exist with standards among which
income-earning efficiency occupies a much lower place
than it does in contemporary western societies. In some
instances this has gone hand-in-hand with significantly
greater prominence of the direct power motive than is
typical of our environment, and emphasis equal to ours
on the importance of material goods. In other instances,
the smaller weight of the profit motive has been associated
with a much greater emphasis on values that do not depend
for attainment on material goods. In the standards of our
present civilization, profit-making efficiency rates high.
This type of society has provided unprecedented opportunities for the development of personality along lines
other than those predetermined by "tradition," and it has
eliminated some of the worst sources of human suffering.
It also has produced a great deal of imbalance and inner
restlessness, and it has consistently produced very prompt
adjustment of "minimum needs" to the maximum that is
available, in spite of the fact that the available has been
growing rapidly. Intelligent appraisal of the profit-motive
requires interpreting it as an element in the system of
motives propelling certain types of society.

Whatever one's appraisal of these different aspects may
be, no one denies that the profit motive plays an important
part in free-enterprise (or in "mixed") economies. Eco-

nomics is concerned with the processes by which the population earns its livelihood. In the type of economy with which this volume is concerned, these processes are conducted very largely under the influence of the profit motive. But it is possible to exaggerate the significance of the profit motive.

It seems appropriate to draw a distinction between two kinds of "qualification to the profit-maximization principle." The first group consists of qualifications which should be made because economic activities are influenced not only by the objective of realizing economic advantage but also by other incentives, and because these other incentives—or other "standards"—may become partly "competitive" with the economic. We shall be concerned here not with these qualifications but with the second group, consisting of qualifications which should be introduced because *profit maximization in the usual sense is not always the most effective way of acting under the economic incentive*. In this chapter *these* qualifications will be discussed in relation to the "monopoly-oligopoly" problem, that is, in so far as they apply to profit maximization under monopoly as well as under oligopoly. The next chapter will be concerned with analogous considerations applying to the oligopoly problem specifically.

The formal validity of statements relating to qualified profit maximization depends on the definition of "profits." The statements relating to profits were here made on the understanding that we mean by profits the magnitudes which enterprise normally interprets as its profits, that is to say, accounting profits, possibly corrected for certain peculiarities of accounting procedures [1] for which internal

---

[1] We say "possibly corrected" for these peculiarities because for certain purposes official balance sheets may be more important than

correction frequently is made when management attempts
to find out what the true earnings of an enterprise are. We
are here using the term "profits" in its customary "business" sense. It is possible to define profits in such a way
as to make profit maximization an unqualified axiom.
This, of course, can be done by considering everything
that has "disutility" a cost, and everything possessing
"utility" a gross revenue. In this event qualifications need
be made *neither* for extra-economic objectives *nor* for differences between "acting under economic incentives" and
"maximizing profits in the technical sense." But in this
case the qualifications assume the form of elaborations on
the definition of profits, and the difficulties tend to be
hidden rather than to be made explicit. We shall not resort to this procedure. We shall use the term "profits" in
what substantially is the ordinary business sense of the
word. Consequently, we speak of "qualifications" whenever
the objective of economic activity is not that of maximizing profits (net income) in the ordinary sense. The objective may still be "economic." Those directing the activities
in question may still be aiming exclusively at the acquisition of goods and services through the exchange or technical transformation of their resources.

SAFETY MARGINS AND THEIR BEARING
ON AVERAGE-COST PRICING

A firm attempting to maximize its profits tries to equate
its expected marginal revenue to its expected marginal
cost. However, at this point a difficulty enters which is the

---

internal results. Whenever this difference plays a role in the reasoning,
explicit reference will be made to the problem.

central theme of the theory of uncertainty but which has received insufficient attention in general economic theory. "Expected" presumably means that which appears most likely in advance—in other words, the best guess of these functions. Alternatively, one might imply that "expected" means "mathematical expectation of these functions" but we prefer to interpret the term as relating to "best guesses" (a vague form of the most probable) because the other terminology suggests a spurious degree of precision. The difficulty is essentially the same, regardless of the terminology used. Managements have to allow for the possibility that their guesses may be wrong. Moreover, the nature of these guesses is such that it is impossible to protect oneself against the possibility of different outcomes by insurance in the ordinary sense or by "discounting for risk" in the technical sense. This is because the frequency distributions themselves from which any measure or property of the expectations (mode, mean, and so forth) must be derived are not objectively established. These frequency distributions—or whatever corresponds to them in the minds of businessmen—are derived from past experience by correcting in some vague fashion for those peculiarities of the past instances in which they differ from the instances "now" faced. Such corrections are carried out by what is called "feel" or individual judgment, and they would not be carried out identically if some other person made the judgment. The "frequency distribution" from which the best guess is derived (or from which any other property of the expectations could be derived) is different for different individuals. Hence no person has complete confidence in this kind of frequency distribution. At the same time it is impossible to attach definite probabilities to the correctness of the judgment itself. Individual allowances must be made for the possibility of surprise, that is, for deviations from best guesses. Not only business problems but a great many problems of everyday life have these characteristics.

The kind of allowance made for the possibility of outcomes other than those corresponding to "best guesses" greatly influences business policy. Firms do not usually maximize their expected profits if by profit maximization we mean equating "best-guess" marginal revenue to "best-guess" marginal cost.[2] The paradoxical character of this statement merely expresses the fact that the probability calculus *is* applied in some vague form but is not *properly* applicable to the maximization of *expected* profits. Whatever we choose to mean by expected profits we have to recognize that allowances are made for the possibility that expectations may be wrong and that these allowances are made although it is impossible to tell *how* probable the correctness of the assumed frequency distribution is.

The effect of these allowances on business policy depends on whether the possibility of favorable or of unfavorable surprise is weighted more heavily; and on whether the allowance is made mainly for the possibility of lump-sum differences as compared with best-guess results, or for differences that are roughly proportionate to the scale of output.

There exists a presumption that the possibility of unfavorable surprise is typically weighted more heavily than that of favorable surprise (which of course does not exclude the possibility that the original "best guess" may frequently be too optimistic). The adverse consequences

---

[2] We shall see presently that maximizing policies would have to be defined in a very peculiar way to include this "qualification" in the concept itself.

of business losses tend to become cumulative at a rate which usually has no equivalent counterpart on the favorable side. The "rating" of a firm which suffers losses may deteriorate in so many respects that the indirect losses caused by this far exceed the original loss. This does have *some* counterpart on the favorable side because profitability raises the rating of a firm; but it does not usually have an *equivalent* counterpart because gains do not tend to become cumulative at the rate at which forced liquidation of an enterprise renders losses cumulative. The psychological weight attaching to these contingencies probably also is higher than that attaching to higher-than-normal gains. To be sure, this is not true of all environments in which firms have operated in history, and even in the contemporary setting it is not true of all firms. Obviously, there always are persons who attach a higher "psychological" weight to the possibility of favorable than to that of unfavorable surprise. In addition, there always are firms for which the more or less "objective" likelihood of favorable deviations from the "most probable" is greater than the likelihood of unfavorable deviations. In certain historical environments both the "objective" [3] and the "psychological" skewness toward favorable surprise may even have been typical for enterprise in general. For example, in the frontier type of setting there very likely existed such a

---

[3] "Objective" is placed in quotation marks because in this kind of vague probability calculus psychological elements enter also into the appraisal of what is *likely*, not merely into the *choice* which is made between alternatives of given likelihood. This is the reason why an approach starting from probability concepts must qualify these with the result that the apparatus turns out to be different from a probability apparatus in the usual sense. Mr. G. L. S. Shackle is opposed to using the probability apparatus even as a point of departure. In his recent *Expectation in Economics* (Cambridge, England, 1949) he elaborates an alternative method of approach.

psychological skewness; and while it is not obvious whether the quasi-objective likelihood of favorable deviations from the "most probable" [4] also was greater than that of unfavorable deviations, it seems reasonable to state that gains exceeding the "most probable" by a very high margin were *not extremely unlikely*.

However, in environments in which extraordinary gains of this sort are very unlikely, and in which the quasi-objective likelihood of moderate favorable deviations [5] is no greater than that of moderate unfavorable deviations, *the quasi-objective factors justify a greater emphasis on the possibility of unfavorable surprise*. This is true because originally moderate losses show a more pronounced tendency to become cumulative than do originally moderate extra gains. On the credit market, the rating of a firm which suffers losses is certain to deteriorate. This results in higher costs of production and possibly even in being cut off from the sources of credit supply. Furthermore, the rating of such a firm on the commodity markets may also deteriorate considerably, and *especially its bargaining power on oligopolistic markets is very likely to be reduced*. Therefore, in the contemporary setting the objective factors point to emphasizing the possibility of unfavorable surprise more than that of favorable surprise. It would be *conceivable* that this should be offset by an opposite skewness of the purely psychological element involved in the problem, that is to say, the pleasure caused by the possibility of moderate extra gains might be felt more intensely than the fear of more significant losses. But

---

[4] "Most probable" in the same partly objective and partly psychological sense as was circumscribed on p. 147.

[5] From the "most probable," that is, from the "best guess."

this is not typical of the economic environment of advanced industrial societies.

We may therefore expect that allowances will be made for the possibility that actual outcome will deviate from best-guess results, that is, for the possibility of "surprise;" [6] and that "on balance" these will assume the form of allowances for unfavorable rather than for favorable deviations (or surprise). This, of course, does not contradict the possibility that the subjective best guesses may frequently be unduly favorable guesses. A person may be congenitally optimistic but he or his accountants may still be trained to make downward allowances before decisions are reached. What is the nature of the surprise for which allowances are made?

If allowances were to be made for the possibility of lump-sum deductions from best-guess profits—deductions unrelated to the rate of output—then the price and output policies of the firm actually operating would not be affected, except that they would presumably develop an increased demand for liquidity.[7] This demand for liquidity —for idle balances, associated with a preference for short-term as compared with long-term securities—would be a consequence of the fact that the possibility of unfavorable surprise makes it desirable to make provisions for self-financing. By this means the cumulative tendency of originally moderate losses can be diminished considerably. In addition to increased hoarding, that is, to lower velocity, these *ex ante* allowances for the possibility of lump-sum

---

[6] "Surprise" as compared with the best guess. Not *much* surprise need be involved in this because the best guess need not always be considered a *much* better guess than *any* of a great number of other guesses.

[7] As compared to a policy of equating best-guess marginal revenue to best-guess marginal cost, *with no allowance for unfavorable surprise*.

deductions would result in reduced aggregate output because certain firms would be unwilling to operate even
though their best-guess aggregate revenue might exceed
their best-guess aggregate costs. Yet the firms actually
operating would continue to equate their best-guess marginal revenue to their best-guess marginal cost. The possibility of lump-sum deductions from "best-guess" profits
does not affect the policy of profit maximization because
there is no difference between maximizing a magnitude, on
the one hand, and maximizing the same magnitude *minus*
a constant, on the other. The identical conclusions hold
mutatis mutandis for favorable surprise, as long as it is in
the nature of lump-sum additions to best-guess profits. If
the possibility of lump-sum addition were weighted more
heavily than that of lump-sum deductions from best-guess
profits, the velocity of money would tend to rise,[8] and the
number of firms operating would become greater.[9] But
the firms actually operating would still tend to equate
best-guess marginal revenue to best-guess marginal cost.

The same may be expressed also by using the concept
of safety margins. Let us define safety margins as the
*margins by which the outcome of a venture may fall short
of the "best guess" without causing losses.* The safety
margin of a firm against lump-sum deductions from best-
guess profits—that is against deductions unrelated to the
rate of output—is maximized under precisely the same
conditions as the best-guess (or "most probable") profits
themselves. Diagrammatically, this safety margin is meas-

---

[8] Because contingency provisions would tend to become unusually
small.

[9] Because a firm might operate even if its most probable aggregate
revenue were but slightly in excess of its most probable aggregate cost
(possibly even if its most probable aggregate cost exceeded its most
probable aggregate revenue).

ured, in terms of dollars, by the total "profit area" of the text-book graphs of price-output determination, if the revenue and cost functions represented in these graphs are interpreted "best-guess" (or "most probable") functions. A firm can afford to forego the greatest lump sum, without suffering losses, if its aggregate profit is maximized.

However, the safety margins against downward-shifting demand functions and upward-shifting cost functions are usually *not* maximized at the rate of output which maximizes "best-guess" profits. For example, the safety margins against *parallel* downward shifts of demand functions and upward shifts of cost functions are maximized at the rate of output for which the gap between the best-guess *average* revenue and the best-guess *average* variable cost is at a maximum. They are maximized by the P_2 prices, rather than the P_1 prices of Figure 13, page 223. This in general, corresponds to a smaller output than does the point of profit maximization, if by "profit maximization" we mean the maximization of best-guess ("most probable") profits.[10] It is reasonable to assume that the unfavorable possibilities against which safety provisions are made are very largely *these* shifts in demand and cost functions. While these potential unfavorable shifts need not always be conceived of as precisely parallel shifts— and while, therefore, the point of maximum safety need not be precisely that of the greatest gap between average revenue and average variable cost—the notion of parallel shifts probably provides a good first approximation. After all, unexpectedly low product prices (for any potential output within the relevant range) belong among the com-

---

[10] Best-guess profits are maximized at the intersection of best-guess *marginal* revenue and best-guess *marginal* cost.

monest causes of entrepreneurial disappointment. Furthermore, while unexpectedly high factor prices and unexpectedly low technological yields do not necessarily express themselves in precisely parallel upward shifts of cost functions, they frequently assume approximately this form. Therefore, we may conclude that safety margin considerations *alone* favor a rate of output which may frequently come close to the point of the maximum excess of average revenue over average variable cost.

Obviously, the rate of output would also be affected by the possibility of deviations from best-guess results if favorable deviations were weighted more heavily than unfavorable. Assuming that these deviations typically express themselves in approximately parallel shifts of the relevant functions the rate of output would then exceed that of most probable profit maximization. Moreover, while the possibility of unfavorable deviations—whatever form these might assume—makes for lower velocity (contingency hoarding) and for greater interest-rate differentials in favor of short-term rates, an asymmetrical [11] weighing of favorable deviations tends to produce the opposite results. It seems to us that unfavorable deviations are usually weighed more heavily than favorable, and this favors placing the emphasis on the fact that safety considerations tend to produce a lower rate of output as well as contingency hoarding. However, it should be repeated that the apparatus here discussed could also be used for developing and examining the contrary hypothesis.

This analysis does not suggest that the maximization of safety margins is the sole objective of firms. It seems much more likely that a compromise is usually sought be-

---

[11] I.e., giving more weight to the possibility of favorable deviations.

tween the maximization of best-guess profits and the maximization of safety margins. Only factual research could answer the question concerning the representativeness of alternative assumptions in this respect. It should be pointed out, however, that problems here discussed may bear importantly on the practice of "average-cost pricing" and on that of charging "mark-ups." A firm maximizing its safety margin against parallel shifts of the revenue and cost functions and *therefore* maximizing the excess of average revenue over average variable cost would be charging its buyers average variable cost plus the maximum mark-up (or differential) the market will bear. It would, of course, be selling whatever the market is willing to take, given the price policy adopted. The output would be selected in view of the objective of obtaining the maximum available mark-up. A firm seeking a compromise between maximizing its safety margins (in the foregoing sense) *and* maximizing best-guess aggregate profits would be charging average variable cost plus a mark-up (or differential) which is less than the maximum obtainable on the market.[12] Again, such a firm will sell whatever the market will take, given the price policy adopted. Logically, all charges arising from past commitments should be excluded in interpreting average costs for the purpose of safety-margin calculations. But if the safety margin is believed to be positive, it is arbitrary whether part (or all) of it is or is not regarded as planned

---

[12] Whenever positive safety margins against parallel shifts are available for certain outputs (i.e., unless the best-guess profit, if maximized, is zero or negative), the safety margin against parallel shifts (i.e. the mark-up over variable costs) is maximized at a lower output than that corresponding to the intersection of the *marginal* curves. Therefore, mazimizing safety margins results in a higher mark-up than does maximizing best-guess aggregate profits, and also in a higher mark-up than does a compromise policy between the two objectives.

amortization of sunk costs. If it is so regarded, the resulting policy may be characterized as an average full-cost
policy. The propositions derivable from this kind of
analysis may sound more familiar to persons acquainted
with business practices than do the propositions based on
the best-guess marginal functions alone.[13]

It is true, however, that the percentage mark-up explainable by this type of theory should vary with shifts in
the market-functions, while some mark-ups seem to show
a high degree of rigidity. Reference should therefore also
be made to a proposition developed by Professor Tibor
Scitovszky. The proposition is based on the notion that
many producers work on the assumption that their average variable and marginal cost curves are approximately
horizontal in the relevant range and also that the shifts
in their demand functions do not change the demand-
elasticity appreciably for the relevant points (so that
demand elasticity is the only property of the demand
function which need be estimated for the purpose of rational price policy). To such producers a *constant* percentage mark-up over variable cost would seem justified
even in the short run, regardless of shifts in the cost and

---

[13] To have focused attention on the difficulties of interpreting actual
price decisions in terms of the usual framework of value theory was
perhaps mainly the merit of Messrs. R. L. Hall and C. J. Hitch (cf.
their "Price Theory and Business Behavior," *Oxford Economic Papers*,
No. 2, March 1939). Of the extended literature pertaining to these
difficulties, cf. Clive Saxton, *The Economics of Price Determination*
(Oxford, 1942); Committee on Price Determination of the National
Bureau of Economic Research, *Cost Behavior and Price Policy* (New
York, 1943); the controversy between Fritz Machlup and R. A. Lester
in the March 1946, September 1946, and March 1947 issues of the
American Economic Review; K. W. Rothschild, "Price Theory and
Oligopoly," *Economic Journal*, September 1947; R. A. Gordon, "Short-
Period Price Determination," *American Economic Review*, June 1948;
also the present writer's "Average Cost Pricing and the Theory of Un-
certainty," *Journal of Political Economy*, June 1948.

revenue functions (cf. pages 224–5). This would be true quite aside from safety-margin considerations (i.e., also for the marginal intersection) and the proposition was in fact developed independently of safety-margin considerations. But the magnitude of the mark-up may be affected by these considerations because maximizing safety margins against parallel shifts would call for moving back to the point where the average variable cost-function turns from downward sloping to horizontal. A compromise solution would call for moving back some way *toward* that point.

By doctoring the concept of profit maximization it would be possible to arrive at a theoretical construction in the framework of which a policy of maximum safety margins could be *called* a variant of the policy of profit maximization. We should merely have to define the expected profits (which are maximized) [14] *not* as best-guess profits but as the profits which are expected in the event that certain comparatively unlikely [15] possibilities materialize. On such a definition of "expected profits," the maximization of safety margins may be made a variant of "profit maximization." Furthermore, each compromise between the maximization of safety margins on the one hand and best-guess profit maximization on the other could then become a further variant of "profit maximization." If we use our concepts in this sense, then profit maximization becomes an unqualified axiom. But if this is done, some of the most essential problems of value theory are hidden so skillfully that it becomes difficult indeed to find them.

---

[14] There can be no doubt that profit maximization should be interpreted to mean the maximization of *expected profits*. The question is, what should be meant by expected profits.

[15] Unlikely as compared with best guesses.

THE SHORT RUN AND THE LONG RUN

There is no reason to assume that firms try to maximize their profits in the short run, unless the policies accomplishing this end happen to be those which *also* maximize long-run profits. Whatever the other qualifications to profit maximization may be, we should realize that the profit incentive is not typically a short-run incentive.

It is not fruitful to "get rid" of this difficulty by simply postulating that profit maximization means *long-run* maximization and that therefore the marginal-revenue and the marginal-cost functions must be interpreted in the long-run sense. In the first place, in the present context the "long run" is not a clear-cut notion. In terms of what periods are managements thinking? Secondly, the pricing problem is in a sense a short-run problem: We are interested in the prices prevailing over limited periods of time and also in price changes from one short period to the other. The same is true to a considerable extent of output, although the average rate of output over a longer period may be a "directly" significant concept for more problems than is the average price over a longer period. Consequently, "long-run" revenue and cost curves, which could be conceived of as determining the point of "long-run" profit maximization, would leave a great number of questions unanswered. These curves would not determine prices and output for periods in which these magnitudes frequently interest us.

The relationship between short-run and average long-run magnitudes is complicated because it consists partly of relationships between *ex post magnitudes* of a period and the *ex ante market functions* which will determine these magnitudes in future periods. The actual price and output of today exert an influence on the price-and-output determining *functions* of tomorrow. This relationship does not move from definite magnitudes which are determined by certain functions to other definite magnitudes, nor from the determining functions to other determining functions; it moves from definite magnitudes which are determined by certain functions to the determining functions of another period. In other words, the problem is similar to that of complementarity and the rival relationship between goods. Complementarity and the rival relationship depend on the effect of changes in the *price* of a commodity on shifts in the position of the demand *function* for another commodity (or on the effect of price changes for a commodity on changes in the shapes of the indifference *curves* between other commodities). The problem here discussed is reminiscent of the problem of complementarity and the rival-goods relationship, except that the comparison is concerned with different time periods and one and the same commodity, rather than with different commodities for the same time period.

It would be difficult to say whether the relationship *over time*, for one and the same commodity, tends to be predominantly that of complimentarity or of the contrary relationship. Do present price reductions predominantly raise or lower [16] the future demand for the same commodity? Do price increases predominantly lower or raise the future demand?

Some of the factors that come to mind would make for complementarity in this sense, others for the contrary. A buyer who is induced to buy *more* today may do so *instead*

---

[16] "Raise" reflects here complementarity, "lower" reflects the rival relationship. In the second question, the other way around!

of buying tomorrow, and *vice versa*. This pattern would clearly be one of "rivalry" over time. This type of rival relationship is quite relevant to the analysis of durable-goods markets. The same assumption may sometimes be realistic for services (one may make a trip now instead of in the future) and also for non-durable materials. On the other hand, certain factors tend to produce the opposite type of relationship between successive time periods. Technological circumstances frequently make it necessary to use quantities of goods in successive periods, if they are used at all. Building materials are an example. Increased use now makes for increased demand for some period to come (complementarity), although it may well make for smaller demand in the more distant future (rival relationship). The "complementarity" pattern may also be produced when the public gradually becomes acquainted with a commodity and gets to like it, as a consequence of lower prices and of increased purchases "now."

Also, within limits, present price reductions may act as deterrents, and present price increases as stimulants, with respect to the present as well as the future, because inexpert consumers sometimes "appraise quality by price."[17] The less expensive commodity may be considered cheap in both senses of the word. Furthermore, within limits, any present price change (reduction *or* raise) may act as a deterrent, for the present as well as the future, because a steady habit is disrupted and the buyer, having been made uncertain of future developments on the market, may start experimenting with substitutes. The last two phenomena—appraisal of quality by price, and the deterrent effect of price changes *per se*—are phenomena of "irra-

---

[17] Tibor Scitovszky, "Some Consequences of The Habit of Appraising Quality by Price," *Review of Economic Studies*, 1944–45.

tionality" in the sense of precluding the application of the theory of rational buyer's choice. Yet they may be quite important in certain cases, and they have to be taken into account in a discussion of the effects of present price changes on future demand. In the discussion of these phenomena of "irrationality" it might, however, be preferable not to use the concepts of complementarity and the rival relationship because these concepts suggest that buyers' preferences can be derived from underlying indifference maps; and an indifference map implies buyer's "rationality" in the sense that preference must be definable without knowing the price which is established for the commodities in question in the same period. In the cases considered in this paragraph, preferences are influenced by the simultaneous price. The cases considered in the preceding paragraph are more nearly comparable to complementarity and the rival relationship in the sense proper. However, the cases discussed in both paragraphs bear on the problem of the relationship between "present" prices and "future" demand functions.

So far we have been concerned with direct economic relationships moving from present price-and-output to market functions which will determine the future market magnitudes. But present prices and outputs (and in particular present *profits*) may affect future market conditions also in another way. Reckless exploitation of monopolistic, monopsonistic, oligopolistic, or oligopsonistic positions may result in regulation by public policy. Even aside from the possibility of legal regulation, it may lead to the formation of blocks of buyers and sellers with aggressive tendencies. These considerations may influence business policy significantly. Furthermore, high profits may induce outsiders to take up competition. Not only

oligopolists but also "pure" monopolists may be exposed
to the menace of competition by newcomers, and to the
same extent. A "pure" monopolistic position need not be
the result of its being literally impossible to take up competition by producing the identical product or its substitutes.[18] Constantly foregoing some of the potential
profits need not be the cheapest nor the most effective
method of keeping out possible newcomers. The alternative
is to acquire the reputation of adopting an aggressive attitude whenever attempts are made at entering the industry. Nevertheless, it is likely that the menace of
newcomers and fear of government interference and of
aggressive block formation frequently do set limits to the
exploitation of short-run profit opportunities. Here are
cases in which "too high" present profits may result in
more than correspondingly lower future profits.

One step toward including long-run considerations can
be made by substituting for the profit-maximization principle the principle of maximizing the present value of the
enterprise. The present value expresses long-run profit
prospects. In Figure 9 the function N expresses the present net worth of the enterprise as a function of the output
of the immediately following short period, given the demand function AR for that period. The enterprise may
be viewed as selecting that point on AR which lies precisely below the maximum point of N. This is point P.
Where complementary relationships are dominant between
subsequent periods, the intersection of the marginal-
revenue function corresponding to AR *with* the marginal-

---

[18] A monopoly may be a "latent duopoly" just as an oligopoly of n
producers may be a latent oligopoly of $n + 1$ (or more) producers.
Cf. Paul Braess, "Kritisches zur Monopol und Duopoltheorie," *Archiv
fuer Sozialwissenschaft und Sozialpolitik*, Vol. 25 (1931), Heft 3.

cost function occurs to the left of P. In other words, if under purely short-period influences the price corresponding to the marginal intersection were selected, the price would be too high for long-run maximization because the beneficial influence of a lower price on future demand

FIG. 9

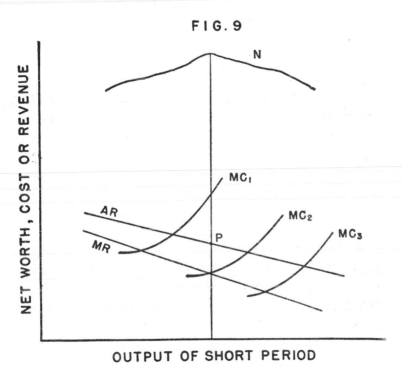

would be disregarded. If on balance we are faced with the inter-temporal rival relationship, the marginal intersection is to the right of P. Only if there is no inter-temporal effect does the marginal intersection lie below P and therefore below the maximum point of N. The intersection points of MR with MC_1, MC_2, and MC_3, respectively, express these possibilities. The MC_2 intersection expresses the absence or neutrality of inter-temporal effects.

In reality the N function need not have the simple shape expressed in Figure 9. The N value corresponding to any selection along AR depends, of course, on what policies are planned for the future, and the shape of the function should always be interpreted as implying optimal future policies for each present selection. But alternative present selections may exist which, in conjunction with alternative future policies, yield identical N values. This introduces indeterminateness only in the event that no combination gives a higher N value than one or several others.

Taking into account the safety-margin qualification discussed in the preceding section, we should have to argue that the absence of inter-temporal effects ought *not* be represented by having the marginal intersection point lie below P (as in the graph for MC_2); they should be represented by having a *point expressing a compromise between safety-margin maximization and short-run profit maximization* lie precisely below P. Later we shall try to bring these two considerations—and others—together. But at present we are concerned with the inter-temporal problem, and we wish to simplify our terminology by leaving the safety-margin problem aside for the moment. A long step toward including long-run considerations can be made by stressing present net worth instead of marginal revenue and marginal cost, as in Figure 9.

If this were all, it might be somewhat too pedantic to speak of a qualification of the profit-maximization principle. All we should have to do is to read: "maximization of the present net worth of the enterprise" when we say: profit maximization. Profits are flows and the present value is a stock concept, but it might be argued that not much fundamental modification is involved in substituting the corresponding stock concept for a flow. Yet even if this

were all, it would have to be pointed out that the present
value is not strictly speaking the stock concept corresponding to expected profits but the stock concept corresponding to expected profits plus expected capital gains.
In many respects, to draw a distinction between income
and capital gains is reasonable. Generally speaking, these
two concepts should not be confused. But a firm acting
under economic incentives in the relevant sense tries to
maximize the sum of the two. This is automatically taken
into account if we postulate that it tries to maximize the
present value of the enterprise. But it is not automatically
taken into account if we express ourselves in terms of
profits.

Moreover, even this is not all. The main reason why it is
advisable to speak of a qualification in this context is that
the "present value of the enterprise" *in the foregoing
sense* is not its potential sales values. This is a consequence
partly of the subjective character of market expectations,
that is, of differences between persons in evaluating probable future market events, and partly of the fact that the
worth of an enterprise may depend on who controls it. The
first of these two factors can never be disregarded; and the
second frequently cannot, especially if an influential (or
"controlling") group among the owners can be discerned.
Maximizing the present value should here be interpreted
to mean the maximization of what to the management appears to be the most probable value, on the basis of a
given evaluation of what is likely to happen on the market,
and on the basis of given assumptions about ownership and
control within the enterprise. The assumptions about
ownership will rarely be such as to imply that the *status
quo* will be maintained indefinitely and under any circumstances. Consequently, the potential sales value will

usually be taken into account among other things. But an estimate of what the market would pay for the whole enterprise implies by logical necessity changes in ownership relations, while the present value *in the sense in which it is maximized* may be largely the result of estimates based on the notion that no such change will occur. To repeat, the value of the enterprise in this sense is not the same thing as its sales value, partly because of differences in the appraisal of uncertainty, and partly because of the dependence of net worth on who is behind the enterprise. Therefore, instead of profit maximization we should say: "the maximization of the stock concept (present-value concept) corresponding to the relevant profit-flow expectations, corrected for expectations of capital gains and losses, and interpreted not in terms of market valuation but on the basis of the management's attitude to probable future market developments and on the basis of its assumption about future ownership and control of the enterprise itself." It is submitted that to call this a qualification of profit maximization in the usual sense is more reasonable than to incorporate all this into the concept of profits. However, it would be possible to choose the latter course. Even if the former course is chosen, the policies of present-value maximization should still be interpreted as being framed under economic motives. But in this case a distinction seems appropriate between policies framed under the economic motives on the one hand and profit-maximization policies, in the technical sense, on the other.

The framing of monopolistic and oligopolistic business policies from the long-run (rather than short-period) point of view is probably largely responsible for so-called price rigidities. It seems very likely that a high proportion of the shifts in the market functions is expected to cancel out in the long run. The adjustments of the price to these fluctuations would give rise to certain direct costs of administrative character, and they might also generate speculative expectations with respect to further price changes.[19] Such speculative magnification of the fluctuations is not in the interest of the industry because it makes the adjustment of production plans more difficult. There is much to be said for not adjusting the price to those fluctuations in the market functions that are expected to cancel out within reasonable periods of time. In other words, there is much to be said for making price adjustments only when (and to the extent that) the shifts are believed to reflect "long-run" changes. Rigid price policies may require somewhat more flexible output policies. Something has to adjust if, in the short run, prices do not. But the advantages are not fully offset by the increased burden of output flexibility since, within limits, a strong firm can act as its own buffer-stock agency. To this extent price flexibility is replaced by inventory flexibility, not by output flexibility. A highly competitive industry cannot behave in this fashion because the weak firms cannot adopt such a buffer-stock policy. They have to reduce their prices. If this happens, the others must follow suit.

An analogy seems convincing. In international-trade theory, no adherent of flexible exchange rates is in favor of adjusting the rate to all fluctuations in demand and supply. There is complete consensus on the desirability of establishing stabilization funds by which short-run fluctuations may be ironed out. In international-trade theory "flexibility" usually means adjustments of exchange rates

---

[19] However, speculation may also have a stabilizing effect.

to such changes as are expected to prevail in the long run. The degree of price flexibility which is analogous to that on a competitive commodity market is not called "flexibility of exchange rates" but is commonly considered a pathological condition calling for intervention. There is good reason *not* to conclude that in general the same degree of flexibility is pathological also on commodity markets because the speculative repercussions of short-run adjustments usually are much less far-reaching on a single commodity market than on markets for entire currencies. The political repercussions also are much less far-reaching. However, this extraordinarily high degree of price flexibility is not a desirable phenomenon *per se*. It is merely an indicator of something that has significant advantages on commodity markets, namely competition. It might prove possible to eliminate "unnecessary" price fluidity on competitive markets—that is, responses to short-run changes which tend to cancel out—*without* interfering with the basic competitive structure of the industry. The main difficulty here is that the stabilization agencies lend themselves somewhat too readily as objects of pressure politics. With respect to the foreign exchange market this disadvantage may be disregarded because the fact that the management is "political" cannot be avoided and in any event the political pressures must be squarely faced. What matters from our present point of view is that any institution—private or public—which is capable of setting prices on a market, and is able to take a long-range attitude, is likely to limit its price adjustments to those changes in the underlying conditions that do not tend to cancel out within reasonable periods. The resulting price behavior is apt to be very much more rigid than that which is observed on the highly competitive commodity markets.

CONTROLLING GROUPS

The profit maximization principle needs to be interpreted with some degree of subtlety also for the further reason that the *owners*, to whose profits the principle relates, are mostly not in direct control of "their" enterprise. Furthermore, whatever control is exercised by owners frequently comes from specific groups rather than from the rank and file in general. In many corporations ownership is so thinly diffused that no ownership control can be exercised. In the United States, of the two hundred largest non-financial corporations, which owned more than one-half of the total assets of non-financial corporations and received about 30% of their total gross revenue, about one-third was found to lack any "visible center of ownership control." The percentage lacking ownership control rises to more than 40 per cent if we exclude from the sample those corporations which were subsidiaries of others. In the great majority of the remaining corporations in which a group of significant stockholders does exist, this group is a minority group. In many of these corporations such minority control is quite effective, in others it may be loose and at best very general.[20] The ownership interest of per-

[20] Cf. Raymond W. Goldsmith, *The Distribution of Ownership in the 200 Largest Nonfinancial Corporations*, TNEC monograph No. 29 (Washington, D. C., 1940); and R. A. Gordon, *Business Leadership in the Large Corporation* (Washington, D. C., 1945).

Some of the most significant enterprises of the country belong in the category of corporations with no "visible center of ownership control." The American Telephone and Telegraph Co., General Electric Co., U. S. Steel Corporation, Bethlehem Steel Corporation, Paramount Pictures Inc., two of the four big rubber companies (Goodyear and Goodrich), Montgomery Ward & Co., and the Radio Corporation of America are examples. The existence of a majority group of shareholders is exceptional (disregarding subsidiaries where the owner is an-

sons actively involved in management is small not merely
"on the average" but also in the great majority of the
individual cases. The average management holdings of

other *corporation*). Among these exceptional cases there are a few in
which the enterprise is wholly owned by a family, such as, for example,
the Ford Motor Co., or the Great Atlantic & Pacific Tea Co. (Hartford
family); and there are several in which a family, or sometimes two or
more traditionally co-operating family groups, own the majority of
stock or, at least, of voting stock. For example, the Mellon family possesses such *majority* in The Koppers Co. (coal, coke, and chemicals)
and in Gulf Oil Corporation, the Pew family in Sun Oil Co., the Kress
family in S. H. Kress and Co., the Duke family in Duke Power Co.,
the Anderson and Clayton families in Anderson, Clayton & Co. (cot-
ton assemblers), and so on. Outstanding examples for the existence of
"*predominant minorities*" (30–50 per cent) are E. I. du Pont de
Nemours & Co. and the General Motors Corporation (in both cases the
Du Pont family), the Aluminum Corporation of America (Mellon family), Cudahy Packing Co. (Cudahy family), Deere & Co. (Deere family),
R. H. Macy & Co. (Straus family), Marshall Field & Co. (Field,
Simpson and Shedd families). Examples for the existence of a "sub-
stantial minority" (10–30 per cent) are the Standard Oil Co. (Rocke-
feller family), the International Harvester Co. (McCormick family),
Colgate-Palmolive-Peet Co. (Colgate family), the Procter & Gamble
Co. (Procter and Gamble families), Firestone Tire and Rubber Co.
(Firestone family), Owens-Illinois Glass Co. (Levis family), U. S.
Rubber Co. (Du Pont family), Pullman Inc. (Mellon family), Climax
Molybdenum Co. (Loeb, Hochschild, and Sussman families), Gimbel
Bros. (Gimbel family), Sears, Roebuck & Co. (Rosenwald family),
Safeway Stores, Inc. (Merrill and Lynch families). *Smaller minorities*
(less than 10 per cent) which nevertheless are strategically significant
exist for example in the paper-manufacturing firm Crown Zellerbach
Corporation (Zellerbach family), in Swift & Co. (Swift family),
Warner Bros. Pictures Inc. (Warner family), and American Can Co.
(Moore family).

In some cases "small" minority owners exert a more active influence
on management than "predominant" minorities or even majorities.
The influence of owner groups is not always exerted actively. Whether
it is does not always depend on whether the minority is big or small.
Case studies show that the influence of owner groups varies—from one
enterprise to the other and also in the passage of time—with the per-
sonalities of which the groups consist and in some cases also with the
phase of development through which the firms are going. For example,
the Zellerbach influence in Crown Zellerbach or the Swift influence in
Swift & Co. seems to be considerably more active than the Duke influence in the Duke Power Co. or the Rockefeller influence in the

voting stock fall short of 5 per cent of the stock outstanding.

In the smaller corporations the link between ownership
interests and management may well be much closer on the
average. In non-corporate forms of enterprise the link, of
course, is even closer. Non-corporate enterprise still pre-
dominates in agriculture and in the service industries and
it does about 40 per cent of all business in trade and in
contract construction (but considerably less elsewhere).

Even where ownership and control are divorced, the interests of honest management are not opposed to ownership interests in any crude sense of the word. To be sure
the management is interested in earning high salaries
which are a deduction from gross revenue in calculating
profits. But this does not make the management less keen

Standard Oil Companies. The Du Pont influence in E. I. du Pont de
Nemours has been decisive all along. The influence of the family in
General Motors was decisive in a significant phase of General Motor's
history when the corporation moved from the extraordinarily rapid rate
of expansion towards more stability (in the early nineteen-twenties).
The influence still exists but it is less direct and less active. The influence
of the McCormick family in International Harvester seems to have been
less active from 1922 to 1941 than before, but it has become more active since 1941.

The absence of ownership influence usually means that the influence
of non-owner managerial groups is correspondingly greater. However in
some cases financial groups which have played an important role in the
expansion of an enterprise exert influence on management. For example, the Morgan influence in the U. S. Steel Corporation seems to
have been decisive in past phases of development. Later it seems to
have diminished considerably in relation to the executive group in
charge but has stayed potentially present owing to the substantial
representation of the Morgan group on the finance committee of the
corporation. The Morgan influence in American Telephone also was
great in the past but it is questionable whether at present the group
has much influence in the company.

Not all corporations mentioned in this footnote operate in oligopolistic or monopolistic conditions. The footnote merely illustrates the
propositions of the text with respect to corporate ownership.

to maximize profits. Managerial money income usually moves up and down along with profitability. A conflict of interests in a less direct sense may develop, however, in connection with several factors.

In the first place, it should be realized that owners (stockholders) do not constitute a homogeneous group in weighing safety-margin considerations against profit maximization. Even if owners were in complete control, the resulting policy would be some kind of policy of average preferences. In reality, the preferences of the management are likely to be of decisive importance in many cases. Whether these express more or less conservatism than do those of the average stockholder is a question to which no general answer is suggested here. The answer depends on the special circumstances in which the enterprise is operating.

On the whole, it may be suggested that *if* owners and managers were precisely the same sort of people *except* for their different roles, then managements would be more conservative than owners. This seems plausible because if owners have good reasons to feel that the risk of loss is too high in relation to the promise of gain, managers have good reasons to feel the same way, while *vice versa* this is not necessarily so. If the enterprise goes bankrupt, managers are full-fledged losers, along with the owners, although in a different sense; yet managers as such are not really full-fledged winners when profits rise. This would point to the conclusion that, for the economy as a whole, managements tend to be more conservative than owners. But the conclusion rests on the assumption that managers and owners are the same sort of people, with the same evaluation of probabilities and with the same preferences, except in so far as their preferences are influenced by the different roles they have assumed. The conclusions based on such an assumption are insufficiently well founded to suggested themselves as *general* conclusions. What matters from the present point of view is that only accidentally could the management's safety preferences be identical with those of the "average" stockholder.

Several other subtle relationships exist in regard to which the interests of managers and those of owners need not coincide. Mergers, for example, increase the prestige as well as the money earnings of certain managerial groups, namely, of the influential groups which survive the merger in leading positions. They frequently also bring considerable gains to financial groups carrying out the transactions resulting in the merger. Whether they enhance the earnings of owners depends on specific circumstances which are partly unrelated to the managerial and financial interests in these matters.

In addition, cost saving and revenue raising may sometimes require not only extraordinary effort but also willingness to sacrifice popularity and prestige. The marginal weighing of these elements results in certain managerial decisions. These need not always be the same as those which would have been reached under direct ownership control.

Conflicts of interest between different groups of stockholders, and between stockholders and those who might *become* stockholders in the event of expansion, may also bear on the appropriate interpretation of the profit incentive. The influential group among the stockholders may not be interested in a project which would bring additional gains to the aggregate of the existing stockholders because some of the other stocks may carry preferential claims. What seems more important, the aggregate of the *existing* stockholders—including the influential groups—

may lose on an expansion project which would increase the net profits of the enterprise because profits per unit of stock may fall. Yet it is not always true that the profits on the existing stock are the relevant magnitude because the old stockholders may participate in new issues, and sometimes under more favorable conditions than the market in general. The participation of the existing stockholders in new issues depends ultimately on the alternative investment opportunities of old stockholders as compared to those of outsiders.

Summarizing this chapter we may repeat that the profit-maximization principle should be interpreted in view of, or with the qualifications imposed by, (a) safety-margin considerations, (b) long-run objectives, (c) the controlling influence of managements and of specific groups of stockholders whose interests do not always coincide with average ownership interests.

CHAPTER SIX

Further Limitations:

The Specific Oligopoly Problem
(Cutthroat Competition and the Desire
to Avoid It; Improvement by
Non-price Competition;
Cost and Product Differences)

THE MONOPOLY-OLIGOPOLY PROBLEM
VERSUS THE SPECIFIC OLIGOPOLY PROBLEM
AND VERSUS ATOMISTIC COMPETITION

THE factors discussed in the preceding chapter apply to the monopoly-oligopoly problem in the sense that they must be taken into account in the interpretation of the profit incentive for monopolistic and oligopolistic firms alike. We do not mean to imply that they necessarily have the same intensity in monopoly as in oligopoly. Yet, a discussion of the question whether they have greater intensity in the one than in the other case would be laborious and inconclusive. It is impossible to arrive at a valid generalization on *a priori* grounds. Consequently, we do not propose to take up a detailed discussion of this question.

A presumption exists that the same proposition applies in an attenuated form to "pure" and to atomistic-monopolistic competition. Safety-margin considerations cannot be afforded if, in the same industry, a considerable number of small firms disregards them. Furthermore, for weak firms, long-run objectives can frequently not be distinguished from short-run objectives because these firms find it difficult to bridge time periods by drawing on their assets or by borrowing. In an atomistic industry, even comparatively strong firms must adjust to the policies of weak competitors. As for the problem of controlling groups among owners, this has less significance in the atomistic industries where non-corporate forms of organization play a more important role.

In perfect (as opposed to merely pure) competition the propositions of the preceding chapter have no validity whatsoever. This follows from the definition of perfect competition. It was stated earlier that the analysis of the preceding chapter relates to problems which were not taken into account in the "first approximation" of the theory, as developed in Chapter IV. This first approximation was said to be on the level of pure theory. Perfect competition also is on that level and consequently the qualifying propositions of the preceding chapter do not apply. To oligopoly they do apply and further qualifications also do.

We shall now turn to the further qualifications applying to oligopoly specifically. *All these are consequences of the fact that the strength of the participating firms in relation to one another changes, and is known to change, in an unpredictable way.* Consequently, it proves impossible to agree on discounting the future in a way that would be required for the true maximization of the joint gain. The potentiality of renewed warfare always exists. This requires the avoidance of certain measures which imply the danger of actual warfare. At the same time it prevents the participants from disarming in relation to one another, even if this should be profitable for the aggregate.

These statements concerning the specific oligopoly qualifications of joint maximization disregard the effects of anti-trust legislation. Later this problem will also be considered.

ADOPTION OF CUTTHROAT POLICIES AND THE DESIRE TO AVOID THEM

Needless to say, aggregate industry profits are not maximized while the oligopolistic firms are "fighting it out" by means of cutthroat competition. The characteristic feature of so-called cutthroat competition is that it is carried on in view of the possibility of co-ordinating business policies. Therefore, it aims either at forcing rivals into some pattern of behavior or at forcing them out. In contrast to this, competition in large groups is carried on in view of the impossibility of colluding. Therefore, it does not aim at influencing the rivals. It takes them for granted. The kind of competition aimed at eliminating rivals or at reducing their bargaining strength is a con-

sequence of imperfect foresight. The relative strength of
the participants needs be tested because it is not known
from the outset. Cutthroat competition performs the function of testing. Any quasi-agreement expresses relative
strength in given circumstances; new testing may become
necessary if conditions change in a significant degree. This
is a very important qualification to the "first approximation" postulating the maximization of industry profits.
However, it is an obvious qualification, and there is little
danger of its being overlooked.

The potentiality of cutthroat competition influences the
behavior of oligopolistic firms even if this kind of bel-
ligerent attitude never becomes actual. No firm knows for
sure what the point of industry-profit maximization is.
This, of course, is true of all market structures, not only
of oligopoly. For firms in general this gives rise to safety-
margin considerations which were discussed in the preceding chapter. But under oligopolistic conditions further
considerations enter. The participating firms usually have
different notions of what policy is appropriate to the
maximization of industry profits, as corrected for the
qualifications discussed in the preceding chapter. Such
differences in the appraisal of the underlying factors
might lead one to believe that some average appraisal will
serve as the basis of the quasi-agreement.[1] This would not
have to be considered a further qualification because there
is no reason to believe that profit maximization on the basis
of the average appraisal, rather than on the basis of some
individual judgment, is less *truly* profit maximization.
On the contrary there may be some reason to assume that
the average appraisal is superior to any individual judg-

---

[1] Cf. Duncan Black, "On the Rationale of Group Decision-making,"
Journal of Political Economy, February 1948.

ment. The reason why an additional qualification enters here is that each firm knows that the others have different appraisals and that they are *mutually* ignorant about what precisely the rival's appraisal is. Consequently, no firm can be *sure* whether the move of a rival is toward a profit-maximizing quasi-agreement or towards aggressive competition; and no firm can be sure how its own move will be interpreted. This is where the desire to avoid aggressive competition enters as a qualifying factor. Even where leadership exists, the leader's moves may be misinterpreted as aiming at a change in relative positions rather than as being undertaken in accordance with the quasi-agreement.

The result is likely to be not profit maximization on the basis of the *average appraisal* but something lying between this on the one hand and the average guess, on the other, *as to what the appraisal of the rival is of the policies appropriate to profit maximization.* This *is* a qualification which is specifically applicable to oligopolistic markets and is not included in the more general propositions of the preceding chapter. How serious is the qualification?

The views expressed in this volume are based on the notion that the foregoing qualification may be serious in some cases but that, generally speaking, it stays a qualification and does not become the central proposition of oligopoly theory. Sometimes however, it *is* represented as the essence or the central thesis of the theory of oligopoly. If this is done, the main conclusion is that oligopoly equilibrium is indeterminate. Everything depends on what I believe the others think, which in turn depends on what they believe I think, and so on. Admittedly it is impossible to refute this kind of "theory" on purely *a priori* grounds. But economic behavior is not typically of this sort. Such a view is analogous to opinions that could be—and occasionally have been—expressed in many other areas of economic thought. In fact we do not live in a world of permanent hysteria which threatens to explode all the time. Very much depends on people's thoughts about other people's thoughts concerning their own ideas, but, aside from certain margins of error, people usually have a reasonably accurate appraisal of what other people want and they usually also assume that the other people have a reasonably accurate appraisal of what they want.

The qualification just discussed *may* produce a higher degree of price rigidity than would exist under monopoly. Downward price adjustments which would be required for the maximization of industry profits may not materialize for fear that they might be misinterpreted by rivals. On the other hand, if the adjustment is undertaken and is misinterpreted, a very high degree of flexibility (warfare) may ensue. Moreover, fears of starting warfare by an attitude which is misinterpreted by rivals *need* not always produce rigidity. Considerations of the same sort may also induce oligopolists to change prices in periods of expansion for fear that failure to raise them might be misinterpreted as an aggressive attitude to rivals; while a monopolist might keep his price unchanged on the assumption that he is faced with a phase of oscillations which cancel out in the long run. It is not at all clear on *a priori* grounds whether oligopolistic price rigidity, that is, oligopolistic failure to adjust price to shifting revenue and cost functions, is greater or smaller than monopolistic price rigidity.[2] This gives rise to some misgivings concerning the so-called "kinked oligopoly demand curve"

---

[2] Cf. George J. Stigler, "The Kinky Oligopoly Demand Curve and Rigid Prices," *Journal of Political Economy*, October 1947.

hypothesis, which has received much attention recently.[3]

Formally, the kinked oligopoly demand curve hypothesis merely maintains that oligopolistic firms are apt to believe correctly that their rivals will follow suit in the event of price reduction but not in the event of price increase. This makes the individual demand curve similar to Chamberlin's *DD'* curve *downward from the ruling price*, and similar to Chamberlin's *dd'* curve *upward* (unless the oligopoly is completely undifferentiated, in which case the producer runs into perfectly elastic demand if he tries to *raise* the price but still operates on *DD'* if he lowers it). The discontinuity (or hole) in the marginal-revenue function, which corresponds to the kink in the demand function, makes it appear likely that, within certain limits, a shift in the price-determining functions will fail to affect the optimum price for the firm. The hole in the marginal-revenue function always appears just below the price actually prevailing [4] (that is at the output to which the prevailing price corresponds), and hence no shift in the marginal functions affects the price as long as the intersection of the marginal functions still falls in the same hole.

The disadvantage of expressing an oligopoly hypothesis in this fashion is intimately connected with the technical circumstances that individual demand functions are inconvenient tools of oligopoly analysis, unless the functions themselves as well as the movements along them are inter-

---

[3] Paul Sweezy, "Demand under Conditions of Oligopoly," *Journal of Political Economy*," June 1939; also Oscar Lange, "Note on Innovations," reprinted from the February 1943 issue of the *Review of Economic Statistics*, in *Readings in the Theory of Income Distribution*. Cf. further Bernard F. Haley, "Value and Distribution," chap. I in *A Survey of Contemporary Economics*, edited by Howard S. Ellis.

[4] Because at this price there exists no well-defined elasticity. The elasticity jumps; it is different upward from what it is downward.

preted as expressions of quasi-agreement. The kinked demand curve implies no quasi-agreement because it is intended to show the consequences of rival response to autonomous price changes undertaken by a firm. The kinked function does not show these satisfactorily because it is not realistic to assume that the rivals will generally "follow suit" in the event of price reductions and that they will generally remain inactive in the event of price increases. If a firm reduces its price, the rivals may follow suit or they may undercut (or conceivably they may stay inactive) depending on the impact (cost-change) under which the firm moves; and if under certain impacts the firm does not raise the price *sufficiently*, the rivals may undercut. It would not be legitimate to argue that these impacts shift the demand curve rather than affect its shape because any movement along a function is a consequence of some impact (or change) and hence the shape of a function must show what happens under certain impacts. The difficulty here is that the shape of a non-collusive individual oligopoly demand function should be different for a practically infinite number of possible impacts and reactions. This of course means that such a function is a highly inconvenient tool of analysis. The general suggestion of the kink hypothesis that, for fear of retaliation, oligopoly price is likely to be particularly rigid, is subject to the significant qualification that the fear of retaliation may induce firms to raise prices under impacts which may not induce a monopolist to move.

Returning to the main thread of the argument, we may conclude that cutthroat competition, as well as the desire to avoid it, makes for deviations from the condition of industry-profit maximization. Aggressive competition, while it lasts, produces a high degree of fluidity. Awareness of the potentiality of aggressive competition may frequently produce downward price rigidity. But the fear of aggressive competition may also produce upward price flexibility. It is likely, therefore, that, while actual price warfare makes for lower prices, the *potentiality* of warfare raises prices beyond the monopoly level, provided warfare is avoided.

INCOMPLETE COVERAGE OF DYNAMIC SHIFTS BY QUASI-AGREEMENTS: COST AND PRODUCT VARIATION

While oligopolistic firms typically live in a state of quasi-agreement, quasi-agreements do not typically cover the entire range of the market variables. The main reason for this appears to be that the relative strength of the participating firms is apt to change, and, if quasi-agreements included no outlets, the pressure exerted by the firms whose relative strength has increased would, in most cases, soon destroy the existing arrangements.

The most significant reason for changes in relative strength derives from inventiveness. Quasi-agreements frequently allow the participating firms to handle certain variables on an individual-competitive basis; and these variables are apt to be more nearly associated with inventiveness than are the variables regulated by the quasi-agreement. The lowering of costs of production, product variation, and gains from advertising are more nearly related to inventiveness than pricing. Inventiveness is the faculty of improving the conditions under which one is operating, by adopting methods which are unpredictable. [5]

---

[5] That is to say, which are "new."

Technological improvement, product variation, and changes in advertising stem more nearly from this faculty than does price policy.

These statements imply that, aside from the desirability of creating outlets for inventiveness, quasi-agreements would have to be expected to include restrictions on product variation, advertising, and on technological improvement other than product variation. This is clearly true of product variation and of advertising; true maximization of joint profits becomes impossible without concerted action concerning these two. It is perhaps less clearly true that firms have an interest in preventing their rivals from unilaterally adopting improved methods, as long as the quality of the product, the sales effort, and the price are covered by quasi-agreement. Consequently, one might argue that while incompleteness of oligopolistic co-ordination concerning product variation and advertising *is* an imperfection requiring discussion and explanation in this section, incompleteness of co-ordination concerning cost-saving innovations (or even the absence of such co-ordination) should be taken for granted. But this is not so. In the first place unilateral cost-saving improvement may create such radical shifts in relative strength that adjustments on the product market are practically unavoidable. Secondly, and perhaps more importantly, a very high share of cost-saving innovations is linked to improvements of the product, and these, of course, are of direct concern to the rivals. Therefore, the question *should* be posed in the form in which it was: What makes for incompleteness of spontaneous co-ordination in relation to technology, product variation, and changes in advertising?

In all these cases the essence of the matter is that it is

impossible to discount the future changes in relative strength which will be brought about by these manifestations of inventiveness. Or, alternatively expressed, the present value of this future flow of inventiveness cannot be calculated with sufficient accuracy to include it in the present appraisal of relative strength. Therefore, in many cases competition remains less restricted, or possibly even unhampered with respect to these variables, especially if the oligopolistic group is not quite small.

For the very same reason, competitive handling of these variables is less dangerous than price competition would be for the individual firms and for the industry. In the event of non-price competition the extent to which it is possible to "retaliate" effectively within a given period of time is also dependent on inventiveness which is in the nature of a scarce resource. Consequently, there is much less danger of the kind of cumulative retaliation which results in cutthroat competition. Price is the foremost variable to be regulated by quasi-agreements because there is no special skill (no unpredictable faculty) involved in undercutting. There are no limits to effective retaliation, even in the very short run. If price competition were the only available weapon, and if inventions of all sorts could be disregarded, presumably only two alternatives would exist. Either it would be possible to make a mutually acceptable estimate of present relative strength and to reach a quasi-agreement, or price policy would be handled competitively with mutual unlimited retaliation. The latter alternative would gradually result in an estimate of "present" relative strength, and, therefore, would lead back to the former. The other variables, however, introduce the difficulties connected with inventiveness and at the same time they open a third avenue. They can be handled com-

petitively, thereby avoiding the problem of discounting
the future changes in relative strength; and competitive
handling of these variables need not degenerate into cumulative, cutthroat retaliation.

However, competitive handling of the non-price variables is not an ideal solution from the standpoint of the
industry. If an estimate of the future changes in relative
strength could be made beforehand, this would be much
superior for all individual firms because in this event they
could limit themselves to that amount of cost-saving investment, product variation, and new advertising which
raises the level of aggregate industry profits. In other
words, inventiveness would not become a bar to the practice of maximizing industry profits and of sharing in the
maximized profits according to relative strength. In reality, non-price competition and investments in cost-saving innovations express themselves in policies intended to
benefit the individual firm *at least partly* at the expense of
the other firms in the industry. The same policies may also
benefit the industry as a whole but even if they do the adverse effect on the rivals makes the beneficial effect on
total industry profits smaller than they would be under
collusive handling of the same variables. Furthermore, the
effect on total industry profits may be neutral or adverse,
because the adverse effect on the rival firms may be equal
to, or greater than, the favorable effect on the firm making
the outlays. If repercussions are taken into account, *all*
may firms lose on the competitive handling of these variables—in an absolute sense, that is, not merely as compared with the results of collusive handling of the same
variables—because the rival firms may copy the measures
of the initiating firm, and, therefore, the intended benefit
at the expense of the rivals may not materialize.

We may take for granted that competitive handling of cost-saving innovations, of product variation, and of gains from advertising always result in a *relative* loss, that is, in a loss as compared with the results of the collusive handling of the same variables. *Absolute* loss for the industry as a whole—that is, reduction of industry earnings in consequence of these activities—is least likely to develop in connection with investment in cost-saving innovations, and it is most unlikely to develop in connection with advertising. Product variation probably assumes an intermediate position because, while it shares some of the essential characteristics of technological innovations, part of the product variation actually occurring is superficial enough to be likened to dynamic advertising. It is impossible to draw a sharp line between product differentiation and advertising because the advertised product is different from the unadvertised in the sense that the elasticity of substitution between the two is not infinite. But advertising is sufficiently different from other methods of product differentiation and variation to warrant distinguishing it. Cost-saving innovation, viewed in isolation, may be assumed to result typically in a net favorable balance from the standpoint of aggregate industry profits,[6] while certain kinds of product variation, including advertising, may frequently not yield such a balance because they are too largely directed against rival firms. However, as was pointed out before, cost-saving innovation and product variation are frequently linked very closely and may in many instances be inseparable. Whenever any of these activities results in absolute loss for the industry, the in-

---

[6] The cases in which this is not true are those in which the only justification for the individual outlay is that it increases indirectly the relative position of the firm at the expense of the others.

centive to undertake them derives wholly (not merely partly) from the desire of individual firms to gain at the expense of the others. But, if retaliation follows, all firms may suffer reductions of the earnings. Absolute reduction of earnings in the industry as a whole is a necessary but insufficient condition of the case in which the competitive handling of these variables results in reduced earnings for all firms individually (with the complete elimination of excess profits as the limit).

The certainty of relative loss and the possibility of absolute reduction of earnings provide an inducement for extending quasi-agreements to cost-saving innovations, product variation, and advertising. The obstacle is uncertainty concerning the inventiveness of the individual firms and concerning the changing relative strength brought about by the unpredictable manifestations of inventiveness. But to some extent even this unpredictable factor is tested in the passage of time. Therefore, the presumption exists that quasi-agreements tend to become extended to these variables, as an oligopolistic constellation matures in time. The least mature oligopoly may be involved in testing by aggressive price competition the relative standing power of the individual firms. In the intermediate stage of maturity the present relative strength may be known well enough to exclude price competition—but *only* price competition—by quasi-agreement. Completely mature oligopoly may be willing to exclude competition with respect to cost-saving innovation, product variation, and new advertising because the guesses as to "relative inventiveness" may have become good enough. This probably assumes that the firms should be thoroughly familiar with each others' characteristics and that the market demand should not change violently.

However, it is likely that the "completely" mature oligopoly is more a theoretical abstraction than a realistic concept, especially if the oligopolistic group is not quite small. A more realistic assumption is that the highest degree of "maturity" actually attained is characterized by the placing of limitations on all varieties of competition rather than by the complete elimination of competition with respect to cost-saving innovation, product variation, and advertising. In the passage of time all factors bearing on relative strength tend to change. This is true not only of the factors connected with inventiveness in the foregoing interpretation of the word but also of the financial strength, quality of management, extraneous factors influencing the demand, [7] and so on. Moreover, in the long run, new entries and sometimes the liquidation of individual firms may play an important part. It seems, therefore, realistic to conceive of oligopolistic constellations as moving *towards* a high degree of maturity for certain periods and then being occasionally thrown back to a lower stage of maturity from where a next move *toward* higher maturity starts, and so on. In the life history of an oligopolistic industry even price competition will not be excluded all the time. The other varieties of competition certainly are observable in most cases, although it also is well known that, in varying degrees and in certain periods of development of oligopolistic industries, limitations have been placed on these varieties of competition. These circumstances also explain why firms are usually more reluctant to enter long-term commitment than to accept common patterns of behavior which can be abandoned whenever they see fit.

---

[7] I.e., of changes other than those induced by the sales effort of the firms themselves.

A word should be added concerning the meaning of the competitive handling of certain variables in the framework of collusive arrangements. The extreme case of unhampered competition for non-price variables is characterized by (a) the selection of a "collusive" price structure for the industry with mutually acceptable product qualities, sales efforts, and actual sales of the individual firms at some base date (where the combination of these variables tends to maximize industry profits, given the techniques of production, except for the qualifications of Chapter V and this chapter); (b) the adoption, in the passage of time, by the individual firms of new production and sales techniques, coupled with product variation, by which their individual profits are increased beyond the original level, on the assumption that the techniques, sales effort, and product quality of their rivals is uninfluenced. Assumption (b) is known to be unrealistic but rivals may be assumed to react with such a long lag or with such inferiority of skill that their reactions are ineffective. However, they cannot all be ineffective relative to one another, and non-price competition will become subject to restrictions as soon as there is sufficient mutual willingness to lower one's estimate of one's own abilities in relation to those of the rivals, or as soon as there is sufficient unilateral willingness on the part of one group of firms. Restricted non-price competition (or partial non-price collusion) differs from the foregoing in that certain methods of sales promotion and of technological improvement, plus product variation, will not be applied on the mutually correct assumption that the rival will also refrain from these unless someone violates the agreement. Complete co-ordination with respect to change and improvement would limit the scope of changes to only those changes by which relative positions would remain unchanged or would change in a mutually accepted way. Choice between mutually exclusive changes which benefit the participants in different proportions would have to remain a matter of relative bargaining strength. However, the participants would still be earning their profits on the market, individually. Pooling of profits would require not merely collusion concerning change and improvement but also complete collusion on the static level.

INCOMPLETE COVERAGE ON THE STATIC LEVEL: COST DIFFERENCES AND PRODUCT DIFFERENTIATION

Differences between the cost functions of the individual firm as well as differences between costs for alternative outputs of the same firm [8] lead to deviations from the principle of industry-profit maximization. This is because direct inter-firm compensations and the rational reallocation of quantity of output and of brands between the plants of different firms (pooling arrangements) are not typical features of quasi-agreements. The existing cost differences and product differentiation to be discussed in this section are the static counterparts of the dynamic concepts of cost changes and product variation which were discussed in the previous section. In view of sloping cost functions, differences between cost functions and product differentiation, the failure to pool resources (on the static level) makes for deviations from joint maximization, just as failure to co-ordinate new moves does.

---

[8] I.e., non-horizontal average total cost curves and (or) different cost curves for different firms. Cf. pp. 128–36.

If each firm operates a vary large number of plants the deviations, due to non-horizontal cost curves, tend to lose their significance, unless important inter-plant economies remain unexhausted even by these multi-plant firms. Each multi-plant firm tends to carry out all measures of rationalization within its own limits. In the *absence* of inter-plant economies and diseconomies (which relate to changes in unit cost specifically attributable to the operation of an increasing number of plants by one and the same management, given the unit cost in each plant when separately operated) [9] the following short-run proposition applies to firms operating a very large number of identical plants: If not all plants can be utilized up to the minimum points of their average variable cost functions, then some plants will be so utilized, and the others will be kept idle; while if the output of the firm equals or exceeds the quantity required to utilize all plants to the minimum point of their average variable cost curve, then each plant will produce the identical output. In the long run—that is, after adjustment of the number of plants—each plant will be producing at the minimum point of its average cost curve. [10] This assumes that the firm output is very large in relation to the optimum output of a single plant so that the firm operates a very large number of plants. If this is so, and all plants of the industry operate along identical cost curves, then in the long run, aside from unexhausted inter-plant economies, the pooling of firms would ac-

---

[9] Intra-plant economies and diseconomies are those developing along the cost curve applying to a plant when separately operated. Cf. fn 4 page 202.

[10] Cf. Don Patinkin, "Multiple-plant Firms, Cartels and Imperfect Competition," *Quarterly Journal of Economics*, February 1947. Cf. also comments by W. Leontief and rejoinder by Don Patinkin in *Quarterly Journal of Economics*, August 1947.

complish nothing. In the short run, it is not necessarily true that no gains could be obtained from pooling because some firms (those with small market shares) may operate part of their plants at minimum cost, and they may keep some plants idle, while other firms may operate all their plants beyond minimum cost, producing the identical output in each. Yet the qualification that industry profits cannot be maximized without pooling tends to lose its importance as the number of plants per firm rises, because in the long run all would tend to produce at least cost (firm minimum cost). On the other hand, if the firm output is not very large in relation to the optimum output of the single plant, the industry may be far removed from the cheapest possible industry cost curve. Therefore, the maximization of industry profit may require pooling of the plants and the earnings of different firms, which, in turn, requires inter-firm compensations. In the absence of such compensations, the quasi-agreement deviates from the maximization of the joint profit. As for differences between the cost curves of the various firms, these would obviously require inter-firm rearrangements of output for joint maximization. In the absence of compensations, such arrangements will also not take place.

In American manufacturing multi-plant firms are more typical than single-plant units.[11] Before the last war more than 60 per cent of the value product of the manufacturing industries was produced in plants operated by "central offices" that also operated other plants; almost 60 per cent of the total value added accrued in such plants; and more than one-half of the manufacturing workers was employed in such plants. Not in all cases, but in the great majority of them, the central offices operated

---

[11] Cf. TNEC monograph No. 27.

more than one plant in one and the same industry (horizontal intergration), although in the great majority of the cases they also operated plants belonging to different "industries." The average number of plants per central office was 4.6. While to view the American manufacturing industries as typically consisting of single-plant units would be unrealistic, it would be an exaggeration to assume complete rationalization within the limits of the individual firms. Firms do not usually operate a "practically infinite number" of plants. Therefore pooling would increase the joint profit. Furthermore, if inter-plant economies remain unexhausted by the single multi-plant firms, then pooling would of course further reduce costs, regardless of the number of plants operated by each firm, and even if cost conditions were identical in each plant, taken separately.

Product differentiation (also spatial differentiation) increases the likelihood of deviations from joint maximization, and it increases the gains which could be obtained from inter-firm pooling. This is because the actual degree of differentiation is partly determined by the gains which —really or supposedly—can be realized at the expense of competitors. In the preceding sections this was pointed out in connection with product *variation*, that is, in connection with changes in product differentiation which belong in the same category of concepts as technological *change* and dynamic advertising. Here it should be emphasized that the same considerations apply also to given degrees of product differentiation and advertising which belong in the same category of concepts as of existing costs of production (rather than technological change). Not only progress but also cost differences and product differentiation (also spatial differentiation) on any given level of development preclude joint maximization in the absence of pooling.

Non-horizontal cost curves, differences between the cost curves of the various firms, and product differentiation make maximization of joint profits impossible in the absence of pooling partly because the available joint profit is smaller if high-cost production and excessive differentiation are not eliminated by pooling. But this is not the only reason. The failure to pool makes it appear unlikely that even that "highest" joint profit *which is compatible* with given individual costs, given market shares, and given brands will be earned. For, within significant ranges of the relevant variables, certain firms will fare better with values of the variables (price, output, and so forth) which do not maximize the joint profit. Only by accident could relative strength be so distributed as to maximize the joint profit *even in this qualified sense;* that is, *even with the constraint* that individual costs, brands, market shares, and the absence of profit pooling should be taken for granted. If the quasi-agreement provided for different market shares at different prices in such a way that the relative profit shares would be the same at all prices, then there would be a common interest in maximizing the joint profit *in the qualified sense* of maximizing it when the shares in question and the absence of pooling are taken for granted.[12] But even this qualified maximization is unlikely to occur because quasi-agreements are likely to come nearer to distributing fixed market shares than to

---

[12] Maximization still would be qualified by the circumstance that the actual profit shares decide by how much the available maximum profit is smaller than that available under complete pooling. In other words, these shares decide *how* "irrational" the failure to pool is in the given circumstances.

distributing variable market shares such as correspond to
fixed profit shares at alternative prices (cf. p. 217).

If the quasi-agreements provided for direct inter-firm
compensation, each firm could derive higher profits from
a greater total. But direct inter-firm compensations are
associated with considerable difficulties, among which the
following should be repeated from our earlier discussion:
(a) a firm maintaining its profitability by the receipt of
compensations is at a substantial disadvantage on the market if the agreement is discontinued and warfare is renewed; (b) this difficulty can be somewhat reduced (but
not eliminated) by long-term commitments which, however, give rise to difficulties of another kind because they
imply abandoning unforeseen future opportunities; (c)
direct compensations make it more difficult to conceal the
co-operation. In view of (a) and (b) it must be stressed
that the incompleteness of co-operation *on a static level*
(that is, for existing cost differences and product differences) is also largely a consequence of the fact that the
potentiality of changes in relative strength and therefore
the threat of warfare is ever present. Hence the incompleteness of co-operation on the static level (for existing
cost and product differences) has basically the same roots
as the incompleteness of co-operation for dynamic change
(product variation and technological progress).

Does it follow from the foregoing that the complete
pooling of resources would always result in the monopoly
output for an enlarged firm (which of course would be a
multi-plant firm if the output is produced more economically in several plants)? This does not follow with general
validity. The proposition is valid only with what we will
call the "inter-plant diseconomies qualification." If the
inclusion of the plants of several firms under a single man-

agement is subject to *inter-plant* diseconomies,[13] the oligopolistic pool may find it profitable to have groups of plants operated ("governed") separately, while a monopolist, by definition, operates all plants. Joint operation results in the fullest exploitation of intra-plant economies and in minimizing intra-plant diseconomies, and it also results in the fullest exploitation of inter-plant economies. But to the extent to which inter-plant diseconomies may offset these gains, the completely pooled oligopoly would establish more independence between various plants or groups of plants than a monopoly, and hence a completely pooled oligopoly *might* operate along a cheaper industry cost curve (cf. page 202). The reason is that the pool contains more than one unit of entrepreneurship (or of firm-control or "government") and it may find it profitable to use more than one unit.[14]

---

[13] Cf. p. 192.

[14] To this argument the objection has been raised in discussion that even a monopolist (one firm) may always give its various managers enough independence to avoid inter-plant diseconomies. According to this view "inter-plant diseconomies" could only be attributed to inertia and they should have no place in the pure theory of the firm. This would call for omitting the statement contained in the last paragraph of this chapter because the output of the completely pooled oligopoly would be identical with the comparable monopoly output. The writer disagrees because he believes that the concept of the firm implies a single "government" which, at least in certain matters, has jurisdiction over the entire firm. Pooling of resources under oligopoly does not imply this. The analogy with government is taken from Professor Robertson's *The Control of Industry.*

CHAPTER SEVEN

Concise Statement of Limited
Joint Maximization

QUASI-AGREEMENTS

THE theory resulting from the preceding three chapters is one of qualified joint-profit maximization. At this point it seems convenient to list the reasons for the various qualifications:

a. Unwillingness to pool resources and their earnings and to agree on inter-firm compensations, in order to maximize profits in the presence of non-horizontal cost curves (pages 191–7ff.)

b. Same unwillingness in the presence of differences between cost curves of the various firms (pages 191–7ff.).

c. Same unwillingness in the presence of product differentiation, implying unwillingness to pool brands, or in the presence of spatial differentiation, implying unwillingness to reallocate output between points with different locations, pages 191–7ff.).

d.   Incompleteness of co-ordination concerning future changes in advertising, product quality, and technological methods (pages 183–91ff.).

e.   Safety-margin considerations (pages 146–57ff.).

f.   Long-run considerations which relate to the maximization of the present value of the enterprise, in a particular sense, more than to "profits" technically (pages 158–68ff.).

g.   The adoption of cutthroat policies or the desire to avoid them (pages 177–83ff.).

h.   The existence of controlling groups among owners (pages 169–74ff.).

Of these (e), (f), and (h) apply to monopoly as well as to oligopoly. The others are the specific oligopoly qualifications. All qualifications belonging in the latter group may be interpreted as consequences of the fact that, while the relative strength is known to change, the changes are unpredictable. They cannot be discounted in advance. It is not advisable to disarm in relation to one's rivals. The potentiality of struggle is always present. This accounts for the incompleteness of oligopolistic co-ordination on the static level as well as with respect to changes in the market variables. The monopoly-oligopoly qualifications, on the other hand,[1] reflect the circumstance that profit maximization in the technical sense (that is, the marginal-functions proposition) cannot be conveniently formulated in such a way as to express everything pertaining to the pursuit of economic advantage; too much would become implicit.

We will now try to integrate these qualifications diagrammatically, as well as seems possible.

If merely qualification (a) is taken into account, and if

---

[1] That is to say, (e), (f), and (h), applying to monopoly as well as to oligopoly.

the firms in undifferentiated oligopoly are assumed to be
of equal strength, the conclusion is that which was suggested by Professor Chamberlin's oligopoly analysis.
Chamberlin too suggests this more as a possibility or as a
limit than as a definitive conclusion.[2] With two firms—and
there is no need to go beyond duopoly in this attempt at
diagrammatic presentation—Figure 10 results. The figure shows that each firm will produce the quantity indicated by the intersection of its marginal-cost curve with
the marginal curve corresponding to its *DD'* demand
curve. The *DD'* curve stands here for a duopolist's portion
of the market demand curve in *undifferentiated* duopoly,
where the share results from dividing the market by quasi-
agreement, or sometimes by more explicit varieties of
agreement, in accordance with relative strength.[3] In Figure 10 it is assumed that the two shares are equal.

The *DD'* curves remain valid even if the industry includes an atomistic sector which stays outside the quasi-
agreement. In this case the big firms possess "partial
oligopoly power" and the *DD'* curves express their individual shares not in the total market demand but in the
market demand minus the sales of the small firms at each
price. The small firms equate their marginal cost to the
price set by the big firms. This determines the quantity

---

[2] An outcome such as that in Figure 10 is explicitly suggested by
Chamberlin for differentiated oligopoly, as a possibility or as a limit.
His assumptions are in the nature of those described on p. 211 for differentiated oligopoly. Hence they are applicable to undifferentiated
oligopoly with identical cost curves and equal market shares. He argues
in general that joint maximization is a possibility also in undifferentiated oligopoly, but he does not discuss market-sharing *explicitly*.

[3] *DD'* implies that the two firms set the same price. The *dd'* demand
curve, implying that the other firm keeps its price at a given level,
is not significant for oligopoly theory. Its significance is limited to the
analysis of the "large group."

of their sales which is taken into account in the *DD'* curves. Consequently, the *DD'* curves are applicable to "partial" as well as to "full" oligopoly. This is true of Figure 10 which represents qualification (a) without the other qualifications of joint maximization. It also will be true of the subsequent graphs which will include the further qualifications.

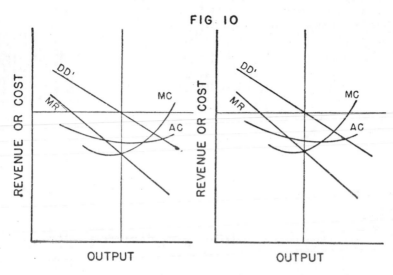

FIG. 10

Qualification (a) expresses itself in the fact that we do *not* derive a single cost curve for the two firms with the aid of the method described by Patinkin (cf. pages 192ff. Assuming that each firm operates only one plant the method described by Patinkin would require that we draw first an average-cost curve such as the curve applying to each plant in Figure 10; secondly, an average-cost curve indicating the lowest possible cost for each potential output if two plants are used; and finally construct a cost curve by using the first or the second of these curves for alternative outputs, depending on whether the first or the second is lower for the output in question.[4] This cost curve would have to be used in the absence of qualification (a)—that is, in our "pure theory" or "first approximation"—and it would have to be set against the market

---

[4] The main characteristics of such a combined cost curve may be illustrated by the following graph. The left-hand U-shaped curve is the first curve described in the text. The right-hand U-shaped curve is the second curve of the text. The fully drawn (unbroken) parts of the two curves make up the relevant curve (combined or synthetic curve) in the absence of qualification (a).

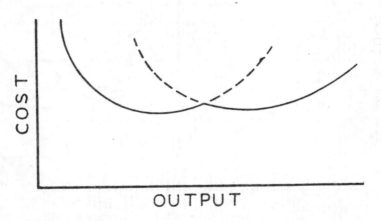

The curve is drawn on the assumption that there are no inter-plant economies or diseconomies (p. 192). In this event an oligopolistic pool *or* a monopolist would be operating along a synthetic cost curve of this kind. In the event of inter-plant economies the second minimum of the synthetic curve would be lower than the first; in the event of inter-plant diseconomies it would be higher for a monopolist but not for an oligopolistic pool. Assume that it is lower (inter-plant economies). On this assumption an oligopolistic pool as well as a monopolist would again operate along the identical synthetic cost curve, which, however, in this case expresses the existence of inter-plant economies. Assume now that the second minimum is higher than the first, i.e., that inter-plant diseconomies are expressed in the curve. A monopolist would be operating along this synthetic cost curve, which expresses the existence of inter-plant diseconomies. An oligopolistic pool would have the choice between such a synthetic curve and two separate curves, both of which have their minima at the level of the first (lower) minimum of the synthetic

demand curve (that is, against the sum of the two DD' curves, horizontally added). If each firm operates two plants, then, in the absence of qualification (a), Figure 10 should contain two separate cost curves each of which is of the variety now described, that is, each of which is such as the curve of footnote 4; and in the absence of qualification (a) two such cost curves would have to be synthesized by the same method, and the resulting cost curve would have to be set against the market demand curve. If each firm operates a very great number of plants, then the propositions of pages 192–3 hold and qualifi-

---

curve.

The pool would make its choice depend on which of the two solutions results in lower unit cost for the output in question. For example, for an output corresponding to the second (higher) minimum, separate operation would obviously be preferable because both plants could be made to operate at the first (lower) minimum. For outputs slightly exceeding that at which the synthetic curve turns down (i.e., slightly exceeding the point where the second branch of the synthetic curve starts), joint operation would clearly be preferable because for such outputs the single-plant cost curve indicates unit costs which can be read by extending the upward range of the first branch of the synthetic curve beyond the point at which the synthetic curve turns down. For such outputs joint operation is preferable, by definition, to producing all output in one plant; otherwise the synthetic curve of the monopolist would not turn down (the second branch of his curve would not start) where it does. The oligopolistic pool must find joint operation also preferable *to* producing in one plant the output at which the synthetic curve of the monopolist turns down *plus* producing in a separately operated plant a *very small* output. The unit cost of producing a very small output in a separately operated plant is very high, as is indicated by the initial range of the first branch of the synthetic curve. Hence, in the event of inter-plant diseconomies, a completely pooled oligopoly does not use the same cost curve as a monopolist, but for some outputs the cost curve of the pool may indicate the same costs as that of the monopolist. This illustrates the "inter-plant diseconomies qualification" applying to the proposition that completely pooled oligopoly operates like monopoly (cf. p. 196). If the second minimum of a synthetic curve of the monopolist is higher than the first (inter-plant diseconomies), then such a curve is *not* at the same time the synthetic cost curve of the completely pooled oligopoly. The second minimum of the synthetic cost curve of the pool can be no higher than the first.

cation (a) tends to lose its significance, except for inter-plant economies. It loses its significance also if we are faced with two identical horizontal cost curves. At present we are considering two single-plant firms with identical but sloping cost curves and we include qualification (a) but none of the other qualifications. We assume definite and equal market shares. This is how Figure 10 is drawn.

The outcome in Figure 10 is "determinate" in a sense in which oligopoly results usually are not, because the firms are assumed to be duplicates of one another in every respect. Relative strength (bargaining power) expresses itself in the market shares and hence in the DD' curves, but given these curves, the equilibrium *point* is determinate with no regard to relative strength.

Relative strength enters also into the determination of the equilibrium point (given the curves) if we assume that one firm is more powerful than the other. The DD' curve of one duopolist would then have to be shifted to the right and that of the other to the left. One firm would prefer one price, while the other firm would prefer a different price, and in the price range between the two limits it would be impossible to indicate the price which is optimal for both firms. *Within* this price range, any change benefits one firm and is harmful to the other. Their interests are diametrically opposed. Outside this price range they have a joint interest in changing the price by moving toward the critical range just described.

The outcome will therefore depend on relative strength which—with unequal shares—decides not only the position of the two DD' curves, subject to the constraint that they must add up to the market demand curve, but also the selection along the price axis and thereby along the quantity axis. It is possible to *describe* the price which will

maximize the sum of the two profits, given the constraint
that no pooling is permitted and that the two DD' curves
are such as to make them accord with relative strength.
However, in selecting the price within the relevant range,
one firm will have an interest in a price lower than that
maximizing the joint profit price, the other in a higher
one. The actual bargain may be the result of two mutually
acceptable reaction points, in the sense that the two firms
feel out their reactions to tentative prices and then agree
directly on price and quantity; or it may be the result of
leadership selection. In the latter case the follower is
known to accept the leader's price and to sell the quantity
indicated by his DD' curve for this price. This defines his
reaction function. The leader may possess better judgment
concerning the industry demand function, or a more complete organization and therefore more information; or
leadership may be required for purely technical reasons
and it may rotate.[5] But in the leadership case the leader
must be assumed to set the price in accordance with
relative strength, on which quasi-agreement was reached,
and to know that price warfare will develop if, with changing demand or cost functions, he is caught at not observing
this limitation. Moreover, from the outset, certain prices
may be acceptable to the followers, while prices lying outside a range may not.

Figure 11 expresses the limits of the price range within
which interests diverge and within which the actual price
will be determined by relative strength. This is the figure
expressing joint maximization *with qualification (a)*,
given definite but unequal market shares. Figure 10 expresses joint maximization with qualification (a) only
on the special assumption of equal market shares. Equal

[5] Cf. pp. 129–30.

but sloping cost curves are assumed in both figures.

On the assumptions of Figure 11 both firms could increase their profits by sharing the market demand curve on a different principle. The *DD'* curves here drawn are of the *iso-market-share* variety: they show an unchanging percentage distribution of sales for alternative prices. and hence the curves of the two producers possess the

FIG. II

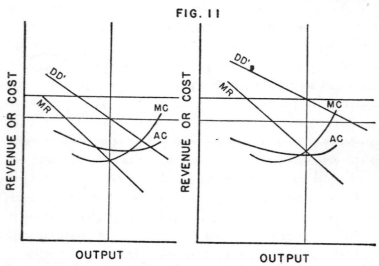

same price-elasticity. These curves correspond to a different distribution of profits for the alternative prices measured along the ordinate. Let us assume that, at the price which is reached by quasi-agreement and which lies between the two limits shown in Figure 11, one firm makes one-third of the sum of the profits, and the other two-thirds. It would be possible to construct *DD'* curves showing those quantities *for alternative prices* which distribute the sum of the profits in the given proportion one-third to two-thirds.[6] These quantities would correspond to chang-

---

[6] If the market demand curve can be written $x = f(y)$, where the quantity sold by the industry is x and the price y; if the proportion in

ing market shares, along the price axis. If such *iso-profit-share DD'* curves were derived from the industry demand curve, then both firms would be interested in establishing one and the same price, namely, that which maximizes the sum of the profits, with the constraints that the sum

---

which the first producer shares in x is called α and the proportion in which the second shares is called $1 - \alpha$; if we wish to construct DD' functions along which the profit shares are identical and are determined by the condition that the profit of the second producer equals K times that of the first; if, finally, the aggregate cost function of each producer is $\varphi(x)$, i.e., that of the first producer is $\varphi[\alpha f(y)]$ and that of the second $\varphi[(1 - \alpha)f(y)]$ then for any given y the value of α is determined by the equation

$$y\alpha f(y) - \varphi[\alpha f(y)] = K[y(1 - \alpha)f(y)] - \varphi[(1 - \alpha)f(y)]$$

At all prices at which—each producer's share in the market demand does not exceed the quantity required to equate the price to marginal cost—i.e., in the relevant range—a diminution of α will reduce the profit of the first producer and raise that of the second continuously. It may be seen from the previous equation that, assuming a constant α, K will not change with changing y if cost curves are identical and horizontal, or if cost curves are identical (but not horizontal) and $\alpha = 1 - \alpha = \frac{1}{2}$ (i.e., the market shares are identical). If one of these two conditions is satisfied, then the iso-profit-share DD' curves are at the same time iso-market-share DD' curves. On realistic assumptions α will have to change along the DD' curves to keep K constant. Furthermore, on realistic assumptions α will rise with rising prices in some ranges and fall with rising prices in others if K is to remain constant. This is because with constant α the profit share of a firm would rise with rising prices in certain price ranges and it would fall with rising prices in others. Take, for example, iso-market-share DD' curves (constant α curves) for two producers with sloping cost curves. Assume different market shares. It is not necessary to assume that the two cost curves are different; it may be assumed that they are identical. In the range between the low price which is optimal for the high-market-share producer, and the high price which is optimal for the low-market-share producer, a price increase must of course raise the profit share of the low-market-share producer. Consequently, the market share of the low-market-share producer would have to be decreased with rising prices, in order to keep the profit shares constant. But moving further up into the region of higher prices the contrary must become true somewhere, since along iso-market-share DD' curves (constant α curves), the profit of the low-market-share producer will become zero (due to intersection of his DD' curve with his average cost curve) *before* the profit of the high-market-share producer

must be distributed in the proportions ⅓ : ⅔, and that there is to be no pooling—qualification (a).[7] A bargain which turns out to establish the ⅓ : ⅔ profit ratio in the iso-market-share framework of Figure 11 gives neither producer the maximum profit compatible with the ⅓ : ⅔ profit ratio and with the no-pooling clause. The bargain puts each firm on that point of its ⅓ : ⅔ iso-profit-share DD' curve which happens to be compatible with the market

---

is reduced to zero. Therefore, in these high-price regions the market share of the low-market-share producer will have to be increased with rising prices, in order to keep the profit shares constant. On realistic assumptions, α will rise with rising prices in certain regions of iso-profit-share DD' curves, and it will fall with rising prices in other regions. Further, it is possible that in certain price ranges one of the two iso-profit-share DD' curves may be upward sloping because a price increase *with constant individual sales* may increase the profit of one producer in a smaller proportion than that in which the profit of the other producer is increased with the same price rise plus such a reduction of his sales as is required to satisfy the market demand curve. In this event the first producer must be permitted to make a greater absolute amount of sales at the higher price if the profit shares are to remain constant. *However, in the neighborhood of the price which maximizes the joint profit and also the two individual profits, the iso-profit-share demand curves must be downward sloping because the corresponding marginal-revenue curves must intersect with the marginal-cost curves precisely below the profit-maximizing price.* Moreover, if the marginal-cost curve is upward sloping at the optimum output of both producers and if the cost curves are identical, then the iso-profit-share DD' curve of the small-profit-share producer must be steeper at the optimum point. This is because its marginal-cost curve lies at a greater distance below the DD' curve and hence the marginal-revenue curve must also lie at a greater distance below DD'.

Using the symbols introduced in this footnote, the iso-market-share DD' curves may be written as $x_1 = \alpha f(y)$ and $x_2 = (1 - \alpha)f(y)$; the iso-profit-share DD' curves as $x_1 = \phi(y)f(y)$ and $x_2 = [1 - \phi(y)]f(y)$ where $\phi(y)$ stands for the α consistent with a given K according to the main equation on p. 207, this footnote.

[7] This, of course, *is* a constraint. The maximum joint profit available in such circumstances is smaller than under pooling, and the difference depends on the proportion in which profits are shared. In the event of constant and equal average total cost (in undifferentiated oligopoly) this would, naturally, not be true.

shares expressed in the iso-market-share DD' curves of the figure. This is not even the highest-profit point on any *iso-market-share* DD' curve because one firm is interested in establishing a lower price and the other a higher price than that corresponding to maximum profits along given iso-market-share curves, and they will have to agree on a compromise solution. With iso-profit-share DD' curves both firms would make higher profits than with iso-market-share DD' curves, assuming the same distribution of the sum of profits (but not of the market) as that which actually emerges with iso-market-share curves. In spite of this, we shall not imply iso-profit-share DD' curves but we shall have Figure 11 represent "joint maximization with qualification (a)." The reasons will be explained presently (page 217).

Inclusion of qualification (b), (page 198) leaves us also with limits *such as* those of Figure 11, except that one cost curve would have to be shifted up or down. This is how we represent joint maximization with qualifications (a) and (b). The proposition still holds that each firm could earn higher profits with iso-profit-share DD' curves, in which case they would be interested in establishing the identical price (so that given the quasi-agreement with respect to profit shares there is no *further* "indeterminacy"). However, after inclusion of qualification (b) it cannot be taken for granted that the firms would be capable of distributing the profits (by iso-profit-share curves) in *any* proportions that may occur to them. The cost inferiority of one firm in relation to the other sets limits to the proportions in which the profits *can* be distributed. But they certainly *could* distribute the profits in the proportions in which these *actually* are distributed when the bargain is reached along iso-market-share curves, be-

tween limits such as those of Figure 11. Both could increase their profits by agreeing on iso-profit-share DD'
curves with the same profit shares as are actually established, because in this event the maximum joint profit
would be earned which—in the absence of pooling—is
compatible with these profit shares. In Figure 11 they do
not earn the highest joint profit compatible with either
the profit shares actually established by the bargain, or
with the market shares expressing themselves in the position of the DD' curves, because within a range surrounding these highest-profit points [8] they have conflicting
interests. This is true regardless of whether we do or do
not shift up or down one of the cost curves of Figure 11
to take into account qualification (b) as well as (a). A
basically new element enters with (b) merely by the circumstance that while—aside from inter-plant economies
—qualification (a) tends to lose its significance gradually
as the number of plants *per firm* increases, qualification
(b) does not. Even qualification (a) need not lose its
validity completely in the short run because one multi-
plant firm may keep some of its plants idle and operate
the others at the minimum AVC point, while another
multi-plant firm (with a higher market share) may operate all its plant beyond the minimum point, in which case
pooling would be clearly profitable. But in the long run,
aside from inter-plant economies, all firms with a great
many plants would accomplish cheapest-possible production within their own limits. This would be achieved by
disinvesting or building new plants, provided all plants
operate along the same cost functions. Yet certain *firms*
(not merely certain plants) may well possess lower cost

---

[8] In the qualified sense of "highest profits compatible with these
definite market shares."

curves than the others, and hence there is no reason to assume that qualification (b) loses its importance with a rising number of plants per firm, even if qualification (a) does tend to. However, the significance of qualification (b) may also become reduced if *each firm* operates high-cost as well as low-cost plants.

At this juncture it should be recalled that if all cost curves were horizontal and identical, then all iso-market-share demand curves would at the same time be iso-profit-share demand curves and they would distribute the market in the same proportion as that in which the profit is distributed. Furthermore, the pooling of output and of profit would be of no advantage, even if all firms operated merely a single plant.[9] If we are faced with sloping cost curves but the cost curves are identical and an undifferentiated market is shared in equal proportions, it still is true that all iso-market-share demand curves are at the same time iso-profit-share demand curves and that the market and the joint profit are distributed in identical proportions (cf. Figure 10). But in this case pooling is required for maximizing the profits that in view of the production function and of consumer behavior are available to the industry. Profits will be maximized only in the restricted sense which takes the no-pooling clause for granted. We have seen that as soon as the conditions are further relaxed, it is true not only that pooling is required for maximization but also that the iso-profit-share *DD'* curves become different from the iso-market-share *DD'* curves. Along the iso-market-share curves the joint profit will not be maximized in the foregoing restricted sense. A further restriction is introduced.

---

[9] Except possibly for inter-plant economies which are not logically excluded even on these assumptions.

We may now integrate qualifications (a) and (b) with (c) (page 198) obtaining Figure 12. We still have the price limits, as in Figure 11, in a framework which is analogous, except that the meaning of the DD' curves is now somewhat different.[10] The implications of these

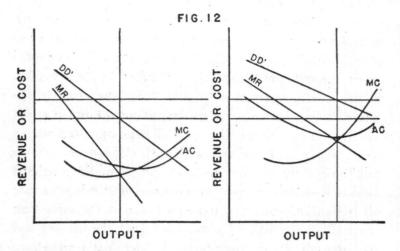

FIG. 12

curves are more complex than those of the curves applying to an undifferentiated market. The DD' curves pertaining to undifferentiated markets assumed identical prices for the producers, and constant market shares along the curves; or, when we described our iso-profit-share curves, without drawing them, they assumed identical prices for the producers, and constant profit shares. They, of course, assumed a given product and "equal"—namely, zero—advertising cost. The shares were determined by relative bargaining strength. These assumptions cannot be carried over into differentiated oligopoly without modifications.

---

[10] Also the difference between the two cost functions is now expressed in the graph, while—when discussing qualification (b)—we merely asked the reader to shift one of the two curves of Figure 11 in his imagination.

The reason is that in differentiated oligopoly the buyer has a say in the matter of market shares and in that of profit shares at equal prices.

We shall distinguish between the following alternative ways of modifying the undifferentiated *DD'* assumptions. For oligopoly with product differentiation it is possible to assume that (1) the functions, throughout their course, imply such price ratios [11] between the products in conjunction with such advertising expenditures by the rivals and with such product qualities as will establish iso-market-share *DD'* curves; (2) the functions, throughout their course, imply such price ratios between the products in conjunction with such advertising expenditures by the rivals and with such product qualities as will establish iso-profit-share *DD'* curves in accordance with relative strength; (3) the functions, throughout their course, imply a constant (absolute or proportionate) price ratio between the products and given advertising and product quality. In all three cases the unwillingness to pool—in the sense of qualification (c)—expresses itself in the fact that brands exist if a producer finds it profitable to produce them, given the brands of other producers, and *not only if the sum of the profits is increased* by the separation of markets which the existence of the brands makes possible. It should be emphasized that the sharing agreement (market- or profit-sharing) *need not relate directly to sharing* in any of the three cases just distinguished, that is, in any of the cases under product differentiation. A quasi-agreement relating to price ratios, advertising policy, and product variation policy *is* implicitly a sharing agreement. This is always true under product differ-

---

[11] In this case and in the subsequent ones the price ratio *may* be 1:1 (price identity).

entiation and also under merely spatial differentiation of an otherwise homogeneous product.

In the presence of *spatial* differentiation, the three cases distinguished on page 213 still apply. In the event of f.o.b. mill pricing (that is, identical mill-net prices to all customers of a firm) the prices measured along the ordinate of Figure 12 should be interpreted as *f.o.b. mill prices*. Quasi-agreement on the price ratios between the firms for the entire course of the curves will determine the market shares, given the sales expenditures, and the quality of the product. The spatial element does not require specific analysis in the event of f.o.b. mill pricing. It does require specific analysis in the event of freight absorption and (or) phantom-freight charges (for example, basing-point pricing),[12] although the analysis may continue in terms of the three cases distinguished on page 213. In this event, the price ratios by which the individual shares of the participants are partly determined are best interpreted as applying to *delivered prices*. The *actual* freight burden of the individual firm must then be deducted from the prices indicated by the *DD'* curve, before the optimum of the firm in question is calculated. The three cases discussed on page 213 apply to spatial differentiation as well as to product differentiation but in the event of spatial differentiation with freight absorption the corrected *DD'* curves resulting after deduction of the freight burden—that is, the curve from which the optimum of the individual firm is calculated—must be interpreted in terms

---

[12] The system of uniform delivered prices is essentially a variety of the basing-point system with each buyer located at a "base." It will be argued in Chapter XI that freight-absorption does not assume the basing point system.

of the theory of discriminating monopoly and not in terms of Figure 12. The net-of-freight ("mill-net") prices realized by any seller at different places of delivery cannot be identical if a definite relationship is to be maintained between the delivered prices of various sellers differently located; and this means price discrimination on a net-of-freight ("mill-net") basis because price advantages given to certain customers do not extend to others. Consequently, in the event of spatial differentiation and freight absorption, the DD' curves of Figure 12 (expressing the price relations between the products for alternative prices) should be interpreted as applying to delivered prices, after which the actual freight burden should be deducted from each price, the resulting net-of-freight ("mill-net") DD' curve should be divided into constituents applying to the different places of delivery, and these curves should be used to calculate the discriminating-monopoly optimum output and optimum prices of the individual firm, by equating each constituent marginal revenue to marginal cost. Finally, a compromise between the various firm optima will be established unless the DD' curves are iso-profit-share curves (in which case the firm optima are identical). In the event of product differentiation or of spatial differentiation with f.o.b. mill pricing there is no price discrimination. Figure 12 applies, in which the firm optima are calculated from the DD' curves in the manner of simple monopoly and then a compromise is reached (unless the DD' curves are iso-profit-share curves in which case the firm optima so calculated are identical).

After these observations on the meaning of the DD' curves of Figure 12 under product differentiation and spatial differentiation, respectively, we now return to the

three cases distinguished on page 213. Regardless of
whether we are faced with product differentiation, with
spatial differentiation, or, as is frequently the case, with
a combination of the two, the meaning of the *DD'* curves
of Figure 12 will depend on whether the *DD'* curves are
established in accordance with the first, the second, or the
third case there distinguished.

In the second of the three cases, the quasi-agreement
should be expected to establish—throughout the course of
the iso-profit-share *DD'* curves—that combination of
price differential, advertising, and product quality which
maximizes the sum of the profits, given the constraint that
there is to be no pooling of output or of earnings and that
profit shares are to be distributed in a definite way. It is
conceivable that several combinations of these variables
would accomplish such qualified maximization (that is,
that several maxima of equal height exist), in which case
the choice is a matter of chance. Yet, aside from this possibility the choice of the combination gives rise to no further indeterminateness, once the question of profit shares
is settled; and the choice of the optimum point along the
iso-profit-share curves so established also precludes further indeterminateness. The interests of the rivals coincide
and the joint profit as well as the individual profits will be
maximized, with the "no-pooling and given-profit-shares"
constraint. Not so in the first and the third cases distinguished on page 213. In the first case (iso-market-share
case), the optimum combination of price difference, advertising, and product quality, compatible with given market
shares, will usually be different from the standpoint of the
different producers because each producer prefers that
combination which gives him the highest profit, given his

market share.[13] Consequently, in this case—as distinct from the iso-profit-share case—the quasi-agreement will have to bridge a conflict of interest with respect to the combination of price difference, advertising, and product quality as well as a conflict of interest with respect to the market shares. Moreover, after settling the matter of the combination of variables, the quasi-agreement also must bridge a conflict of interests with respect to the point to be chosen along the iso-market-share curves so established, since in this respect the same conflict develops as was observed in connection with "undifferentiated" *DD'* curves of the iso-market-share variety. Hence, profits will not be maximized even in the qualified sense which takes the no-pooling clause and the market shares for granted. The same is true of the third case distinguished on page 213 unless the given (constant) price differences, advertising, and product qualities happen to be consistent with the iso-profit-share case. But they are much more likely to be crude approximations to the iso-market-share case or to be quite arbitrary in some respects.

Should we therefore assume that quasi-agreements typically establish iso-profit-share *DD'* curves for differentiated as well as undifferentiated oligopoly? The reason for not suggesting this is that the iso-profit-share construction implies a degree of indifference concerning contacts with the market which *borders on* the indifference which would be required for pooling and therefore for dropping even qualifications (a), (b), and (c) (cf. page 198). A firm which takes the attitude that it prefers

---

[13] For undifferentiated markets the market share decides the profit shares for the alternative prices, but this is not true of differentiated markets.

a considerably smaller share of the market if thereby it
increases its profits places itself at a grave disadvantage
in relation to its rivals if the quasi-agreement should be
discontinued and new testing of relative strength should
become necessary. The most important obstacle standing
in the way of profit-pooling and inter-firm compensation
tends, at the same time, to block iso-profit-share arrangements. We should not go quite to the point of maintaining
that it is logically inconsistent to assume the no-pooling
clause—qualifications (a), (b), and (c)—and then to construct iso-profit-share curves. Some obstacles stand in the
way of pooling which need not interfere with the iso-profit-
share construction. But the most important obstacle does
apply to both and hence we suggest that iso-market-share
curves are more realistic than iso-profit-share curves. For
differentiated oligopoly, the "third case" on page 213 may
possibly be realistic more or less as an approximation to
iso-market-share curves. We therefore suggest that the
joint effect of qualifications (a), (b), and (c) should be
expressed by Figure 12, as interpreted in terms of the first
or the third case on page 213.

However, the main purpose of this analysis is to submit
a conceptual framework which can be used for further
inquiry, and consequently the iso-profit-share construction
should not be excluded. The preceding pages contain what
is required for reinterpreting the functions of our graphs
in terms of the iso-profit-share assumption for cases in which
it appears realistic. In some cases the actual DD' curves
may lie between the two pure varieties here described.

In differentiated as in undifferentiated oligopoly, the
actual bargain may be established by coinciding reaction
points, or, if the better information or more complete or-

ganization of certain firms warrants leadership, by followers' reaction functions along which leaders make their selections.[14] But if leadership exists, the followers' reaction functions must be acceptable in the sense of reflecting conditions of the quasi-agreement concerning shares (or possibly concerning established price differences, sales efforts, and product-qualities).[15] Furthermore, in all cases in which the various firms have different interests concerning the selection of a point along the DD' functions—that is, in all cases *except that of iso-profit-share curves*—the leader must know that retaliation follows unless he observes the conditions of the quasi-agreement with respect to bridging the conflict.

Let us now turn to qualification (d) on page 199. This expresses itself in the fact that the market shares established by the original DD' curves need not remain unchanged in the further course of events. Certain changes will not be considered violations of the quasi-agreement. Let us assume at first that any improvement in the market share of a firm is permissible if it is produced by increased advertising, or product variation, or technological progress.[16] This means that the "sharing" agreement assumes

---

[14] Such reaction functions may show, for example, that the follower will always sell at a price which bears a definite relation to the leader's price and that he will sell a product and incur selling costs which bear definite relations to those of the leader.

[15] The parenthetical clause relates to the "third case," on p. 213.

[16] We may assume that certain changes at the expense of rivals are permissible if the participants can establish "claims" on the basis of newly acquired technological superiority, even if this is not accompanied by improved quality of product. In the event of iso-market-share DD' curves the innovating firm becomes interested in a lower price, and one way of defining an unchanging bargaining power is to assume that the price actually is lowered (because, say, the midpoint of the range in which the two parties have divergent interests is lowered).

the form of a quasi-agreement relating merely to price differentials between the brands, with no provision for the handling of any other market variables (non-price variables). If the firms wrongly assume that their rivals are slow and ineffective, then such conditions may result in the elimination of profits. They *need not* have this result, but joint profits will at any event be reduced below the collusive level, and they *may* be reduced absolutely. They do not have to be reduced absolutely because the moves of each firm may be widening the market of the industry, as well as its own market relative to that of its rivals, *beyond* the extent to which they raise its costs, and consequently the joint profit may be rising, even if the improvements of the firms *in relation to one another* cancel out partly or wholly. In this event the joint profit would be rising absolutely, and, if the improvements in relation to one another cancel out, all individual profits would also be rising absolutely; yet, even in this event they would be rising less than if (by concerted action) *only* those changes were undertaken which would have a favorable effect on the joint profit, and no mutually cancelling intrusions into rival markets were taking place. Furthermore, the effect on the sum of the revenues and on the sum of the costs *may* be unfavorable on balance, absolutely (not merely as compared with those on the collusive level). If in such circumstances the improvements relative to one another cancel out by retaliation, then, of course, all firms suffer reduced

---

In addition, the bargaining power of the innovating firm may also increase because in the event of cutthroat competition it is at an advantage. With iso-market-share *DD'* curves the non-innovating firm suffers a disadvantage. With iso-profit-share *DD'* curves both profit unless the share of the innovating firm is increased sufficiently to eliminate the gain of the other.

earnings *absolutely*, while if some of these intrusions into rival markets do not cancel out a firm *may* obtain an absolutely (not merely relatively) higher profit share out of a smaller total. If the shrinkage of the total proceeds far enough, then all will lose individually.

Conditions of this sort can exist only if there is serious disagreement concerning the evaluation of relative skills. Disagreement is likely to arise because we are dealing here with persons who have chosen a profession primarily suitable for those who believe that they can outdo their rivals. Businessmen do not probably believe that they are more skillful than their rivals in cutting the price; hence price warfare is not a normal feature of oligopolistic markets, except when it is necessary to test relative standing power. But businessmen *are* apt to believe that they are more skillful than their rivals in such things as technological and organizational improvement, product variation, and advertising; hence they may never end testing their skills in these respects. Yet non-price competition on the assumption that the rival is completely uninfluenced or impotent is an extreme case. Limited non-price competition which restricts itself to certain methods of improvement and of new advertising is more likely, especially if it is felt that these methods are tied more closely to certain "skills." The corresponding quasi-agreements would not interpret these methods as violations and they would permit such shifts in the shares (market shares and profit shares) as are attributable to these methods, while other methods would "tacitly" be interpreted as violations, and they would give rise to price warfare and cutthroat competition. Complete oligopolistic co-ordination with respect to the non-price variables, without dropping the *other* qualifications of joint maximization which have so far been considered,[17] would express itself in quasi-agreements which continuously limit technological improvement, product variation, and sales effort to what pays, given the shares originally established or given certain mutually accepted changes in the relative shares.[18]

Qualifications (e) and (f) outlined on page 199 will now be included. Figure 13 results.

The qualifications now discussed express themselves in the circumstance that the price limits of Figure 12 are not truly governed by the intersection points of marginal revenue with marginal costs but by more complex considerations. If they were governed by marginal intersections, then the P_1 points of Figure 13 would mark these limits and Figure 13 would be no different from Figure 12. But now we take into account that the P_2 points would be the points of maximum safety margin against parallel downward shifts of demand functions and upward shifts of average variable cost functions.[19] Therefore, the P_3 points express compromise solutions between the maximization of safety margins *in this sense*, and the maximization of best-guess aggregate profits. If, on balance, favorable surprise were weighted more heavily than unfavorable, then the point actually chosen (P_3) would lie to the right of P_1. In developing a general framework this possibility should

---

[17] I.e., without dropping qualifications (a), (b), and (c) (p. 198).

[18] As was shown above (p. 216), in the event of iso-market-share curves the quasi-agreement must contain provisions concerning the combinations of price difference, sales effort, and product variation which may be chosen, because several combinations may be compatible with the established market shares and the various firms have conflicting interests with respect to the choice between these combinations. Their interests do not conflict in the event of iso-profit-share curves.

[19] Because the gap between average revenue and average variable cost is at a maximum here.

FIG. 13

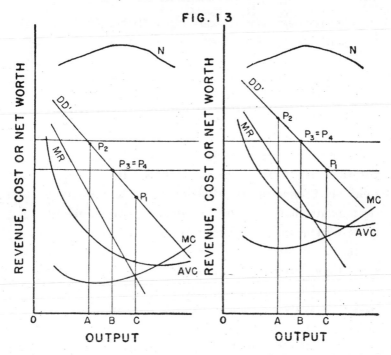

not be left out of account but we will here assume that P_3
lies between P_1 and P_2, thereby implying that the relevant
entrepreneurial decisions are based on an appraisal of the
outlook plus on the notion that some allowance should be
made for unfavorable surprise. The figure assumes that
the compromise expressed by P_3 is the desirable compromise as viewed by each producer. Consequently, the gap
between average revenue and average variable cost *for the
output OB* will be set as the required excess of price over
variable cost; or the gap between average revenue and
average total cost *for the output OB* will be set as the required excess of price over total cost.[20] (In Figure 13 only

---

[20] *OB* is a compromise point between *OA* and *OC*, and *OA* is defined
by the maximum excess of price over average variable cost. But once
OB is established, it is arbitrary whether we express price on a "variable

the average-variable-cost curve was drawn. The average-total-cost curve was omitted.) Such a policy can always be expressed as one of charging "average cost plus necessary profit margin," therefore, essentially as some variety of the "mark-up" policy. Given the required gap between the average functions, there is, of course, a determinate quantity which "the market will take."

To charge a constant percentage "gap" over average variable costs during periods in which the relevant functions shift may imply a belief that most shifts of the revenue and the cost functions do not change the optimum margin by much. In this event the unchanging percentage mark-up may be justified even in terms of short-run considerations. Such a policy may appear to be justified to some producers. It follows from Professor Tibor Scitovszky's analysis [21] that this may frequently be the case because producers may work on the assumption that their average-variable-cost curve is horizontal in the relevant range and that the shifts of their DD' curves do not result in appreciable changes in demand-elasticity from one equilibrium point to the other. To such producers the profit-maximizing price will remain marginal cost divided by the expression 1 minus $\dfrac{1}{\text{elasticity}}$, regardless of any shifts in the cost and revenue functions. Furthermore, on these assumptions we may write average variable cost instead of marginal cost. Consequently, on these assumptions the percentage mark-up which must be added to variable

---

cost plus profit-margin" basis or on a "total cost plus profit margin" basis. The margin may always be interpreted as amortization of sunk costs, and part of it is usually so interpreted.

[21] Professor Scitovszky's analysis is being developed in a book on which he was working at the time of the writing of this volume. The writer had the benefit of several discussions with him.

cost in order to arrive at the P_1 prices of Figure 13 remains the same, regardless of shifts in the revenue and cost function;[22] and if originally the price was not at the P_1 level but corresponded to the kind of compromise expressed by P_3, then, after the shifts of the functions, the unchanging percentage mark-up will deviate from the new profit-maximizing price (P_1) in the same direction as before (that is, in the direction of higher safety margins) and it will deviate in the same proportion. If the average-variable-cost curves are horizontal in the relevant range and if the shifts of the DD' curves are iso-elastic, then a policy of constant percentage mark-up is justified even in the short run. These assumptions may frequently seem realistic to entrepreneurs, and in many cases they may actually be realistic. In cases where they are *not* realistic, a policy of constant percentage mark-up is not justified *in the short run* because the shifts in the revenue and the cost functions would call for a variable percentage mark-up over variable costs in the passage of time. In other words, if these assumptions are not realistic, the policy of constant percentage mark-up is an unduly "rigid" price policy from the short-run viewpoint, although usually less rigid than the policy of keeping prices constant.[23] Rigid price policies

[22] In other words, with horizontal average-variable-(and marginal) cost functions, the elasticity of demand uniquely determines the profit-maximizing mark-up. Cf. also Wassily Leontief, "Elasticity of Demand Computed from Cost Data," *American Economic Review*, December 1940. This follows from the general proposition that marginal revenue divided by the expression appearing in the text equals price. If profits are maximized we can write marginal cost for marginal revenues; and on the assumptions here made we can write average variable cost for marginal cost.

[23] Only on highly unrealistic assumptions could a policy of keeping prices constant be justified in the short run in view of shifting cost and revenue functions. In periods in which prices tend to rise (fall) costs also tend to rise (fall).

may be justified *in the long run* if the shifts of the functions are assumed to cancel out cyclically in the passage of time. This leads us to the next qualification which is concerned with long-run considerations.

"Qualification (f)," (page 199) means that the price limits are ultimately set *not* by the values indicated by the AR functions for outputs such as OB but by the prices corresponding to the maximum points of net-worth functions such as N. These functions are those which were represented also in Figure 9, page 163, except that in Figure 9 we disregarded allowances for the possibility of surprise (such as safety-margin considerations) while here we include them. In other words, the N function of Figure 13 expresses an appraisal of present net worth which is not based exclusively on most probable cost and revenue functions for successive periods but is corrected for safety considerations. In Figure 13 the price and output corresponding to the maximum point of N happens to coincide with the price and output corresponding to the "appropriate" compromise between marginal intersection (P_1) and maximum safety margin (P_2). In other words, P_3 happens to coincide with the ultimately relevant P_4. But this need not be so, and P_3 is not ultimately relevant unless the conditions prevailing during the period to which the graph applies can be assumed to continue in the future. This cannot usually be assumed. Moreover, future conditions depend partly on present decisions. Inter-temporal complementarity tends to make P_4 lie to the right of P_3, while the inter-temporal rival relationship tends to produce the contrary result. *Fear of new entries tends to move P_4 to the right of P_3.* The adverse long-run consequences of "faring too well" may also have this effect. The belief that a great many shifts of the cost and revenue functions cancel out in the longer run tends to make P_4 lie to the left of P_3 in periods of contraction and to the right of P_3 in periods of expansion because adjustments are costly and they may create a great deal of uncertainty. This may result in failure to change the price in the face of short-run fluctuations; or it may result in mere failure to adjust the percentage excess of price over average variable cost (a policy which usually corresponds to a smaller degree of "rigidity" than does the failure to change the price).[24] Any price rigidity implies a correspondingly higher degree of flexibility of sales or of "output for the market." But such flexibility of "output for the market" may be partly or wholly offset by inventory accumulation and diminution.

This is the place to allow for qualification (g) (page 199). The desire to avoid cutthroat competition tends to make for downward price rigidity and for upward flexibility. Hence it tends to move P_4 to the left of P_3, in the long run. Actual cutthroat competition cannot be expressed in terms of such a diagram because the diagram applies to quasi-agreement. Cutthroat competition can also not be conveniently expressed by individual oligopoly demand curves of a different kind because the reaction of the rivals and therefore the price-demand relationship itself depends on how the producer in question "moves along the demand curve."

Qualification (h), (page 199) expresses itself in the circumstance that the N function should be interpreted as the net worth of the effective interests in the enterprise (cf. pages 169ff.). This may sometimes shift P_4 to the left of P_3 because the absolute share of "old owners" may sometimes fall if aggregate profits are increased by the

---

[24] Cf. footnote 23, p. 225.

investments of "new owners." On the other hand, the effective ownership interests may be closely linked with management interests, and these may be favored by "irrationally" high output. This may shift P_4 to the right of P_3.

The foregoing allowances for qualifications (e), (f), (g), and (h) were expressed on the assumption that the more realistic framework is one of iso-market-share DD' curves, or of DD' curves implying fixed price differentials (Cases 1 or 3, page 213). In this event the framework itself need not be changed, and the qualifications relate merely to the price limits which—as was seen—become different from those shown in Figure 12. But if we start from iso-profit-share DD' curves, then qualifications (e), (f), (g), and (h) introduce indeterminateness which, without these qualifications, is not inherent in the iso-profit-share construction. This is because without these qualifications the outcome is determinate: there is no conflict of interests. Yet, due to these qualifications, the producers cease to be interested in profits *alone*, and hence they may wish to realize different points along their iso-profit-share DD' curves. Consequently, at this level we arrive at a model with price limits such as Figure 13 portrays, regardless of whether we start from iso-market-share curves or from iso-profit-share curves.

The discussion of this chapter has assumed that the resources of a firm can be used merely for the production of one product. The problem of the multi-product firm has not been considered. On the level of factual inquiry, the problems arising in connection with the multi-product firm are involved but the general principle by which the foregoing analysis may be extended to the multi-product firm can be indicated briefly. If the resources of the firm can be used for producing different products in variable proportions, then the marginal profits foregone by not producing Product A should be included in the marginal cost of Product B and vice versa. This principle will make it possible to find out at what point it ceases to be profitable to substitute the production of one product for that of the other. Alternatively we may say that the total profit should be calculated for all possible product-proportions *without* including foregone profits for alternative products, and the proportions should be chosen which yield the maximum total profits. However, if the objective is not purely that of expected profit-maximization along given individual DD' and cost functions (that is, if we are concerned with P_4 rather than with P_1 points), then the points of the N function should be compared which can be realized by producing alternative product-combinations, and the maximum should be chosen. All this applies merely to cases where product-proportions are variable. Where they are fixed, we may treat the bundle of products as one commodity. In this case the single-product analysis here developed does not require adjustment.

CARTELS

So-called cartel agreements differ from the quasi-agreements here considered in that they involve explicit agreement.

In the United States concluding cartel agreements is a violation, except where special legal exemption is granted to certain groups (as is the case for workers, agricultural producers, exporters). In some countries cartels are not illegal but the courts usually do not enforce the obligations resulting from them (Great Britain).[25] In other countries the courts enforce these obligations; or they enforce them if the cartel is registered and submits to government supervision. In some cases the governments themselves have organized cartels and they have distributed quotas according to formulae possessing legal force. This is like Case 3 restriction (p. 47), except that the group so organized need not be atomistic. Such a line of policy was followed also in the United States during the short-lived NRA period.

Co-ordination is likely to be tighter under explicit cartel agreements than under quasi-agreements. This may be true even where the courts refuse to enforce the obligations, but it is especially true where the obligations are enforced. The limits of oligopolistic co-ordination depend on the likelihood of warfare developing from inability to agree in the future. Legal agreement excludes or reduces this likelihood for definite periods of time. On the other hand, legal agreement may facilitate public supervision. We shall return to this problem.

The analytical framework suitable for the discussion of cartel problems is not fundamentally different from that developed in the preceding pages. The qualifications of joint-profit maximization are usually weaker for organized cartels than for quasi-agreements and in specific cases some of the qualifications previously discussed may even lose their validity completely. Yet we can arrive at useful generalizations about cartels. In connection with any factual cartel problem—just as in connection with factual oligopoly problems—it is advisable to ask the question

---

[25] In Great Britain the new Monopolies and Restrictive Practices Act (1948) makes it possible to suppress restrictive practices by *ad hoc* ministerial orders which, however, must be approved by resolutions of both Houses of Parliament. Furthermore, certain practices were considered illegal even before this act was passed.

whether the various oligopoly qualifications do or do not apply, and, if so, to what extent. Qualifications (e), (f), and (h) apply in any event because they apply to monopoly as well as to oligopoly. The extreme case of the completely pooled cartel is that in which qualifications (a), (b), (c), (d), and (g) do not apply *at all*.

In this extreme case we may construct a joint cost function for the industry on the principles considered on page 201; we may set this against the industry demand functions; and finally we may correct the result of marginal analysis for qualifications (e), (f), and (h), so that the actual equilibrium will deviate from the marginal-intersection equilibrium in the same way as in which P_4 is different from P_1 in Figure 13. The difference between this result and the outcome of our "pure-theory analysis" for oligopoly is merely that in the pure-theory, qualifications (e), (f), and (h) possess no validity and consequently the marginal intersection, as established from industry cost curves and industry demand curves, marks equilibrium. In pure theory there is no uncertainty but for cartels there is. However, in both cases—in the pure theory of oligopoly as well as in the extreme case of organized full co-ordination —the pooling of earnings is complete. This implies among other things that only the brands and product qualities coexist which increase the joint profit in a sense *similar* to that in which price discrimination is profitable. Creation of separate markets through product variation is, of course, associated with extra production costs and sales costs. But it will be profitable to push differentiation and variation to the point where the marginal extra cost to which it gives rise equals the marginal gross extra revenue.[26]

---

[26] For a formal treatment of this problem, and especially of that optimum advertising expenditures under monopoly, cf. N. S. Buchanan,

The extreme case of the complete pooling of earnings is rare (perhaps even non-existent) because relative strength may change and therefore the firms of an industry do not usually wish to disarm in relation to each other. Completely dropping qualifications (a), (b), (c), (d), and (g) assumes unlimited willingness of the firms to disarm. However, the validity of these qualifications is considerably limited for certain cartels; partial pooling and the exclusion of the possibility of cutthroat competition for extended periods are not uncommon features of cartels. These features are observable also in the framework of quasi-agreements. But it is a reasonable guess that the formalization of obligations tends to reduce fears of adjustments to changing relative strength *via cutthroat policies;* and the co-ordination of business policies tends to be more complete if there is less desire to stay "armed" for a possible period of cutthroat competition.

We shall now turn to the problem of qualified joint maximization in relation not only to oligopoly but to a family of similar market structures. This will be undertaken in terms of indifference-curve analysis.

"Advertising Expenditures: A Suggested Treatment," *Journal of Political Economy*, August 1942.

CHAPTER EIGHT

Limited Joint Maximization for the Family of Market Structures

BY USING Stackelberg's analytical apparatus, it is possible to integrate the results of the analytical transition to quasi-agreement for the entire family of market structures of which oligopoly is a member. The transition leads to the following propositions.

(1) If the agreement concerning distribution, on the basis of factors (a) through (d), pages 24–9, is so tight that it results in complete pooling of resources and earnings, then the Stackelberg indifference maps lose their meaning. Output is determined by a synthetic cost function such as was described on page 201 and by the market demand function. This is the monopoly output, aside from the inter-plant diseconomies qualification (pages 196, 203). This qualification relates only to the cost functions along which the oligopolistic pool, on the one hand, and a

monopoly, on the other, may operate. The agreement provides for appropriate division of the gains by direct compensation.

(2) In the absence of pooling, or with incomplete pooling, Stackelberg indifference maps may be obtained for all market structures here considered. Let us first assume the absence of pooling, in the sense of taking into account qualifications (a), (b), and (c) (page 198). Two subcases should be distinguished.

The *first subcase* is that in which *iso-profit-share DD'* curves are established. The meaning of these was made clear for oligopoly in Chapter VII. The analogous functions can be defined for all market structures in question. For example, in oligopsony the iso-profit-share *SS'* curves (which are analogous to the iso-profit-share *DD'* curves of oligopoly) express the fact that the rival firms buy, at alternative prices, different shares of the aggregate purchase in such a way that the profit shares will be the same.[1] Furthermore, in all these market structures iso-profit-share *DD'* curves or *SS'* curves emerge not only if they are directly established; on certain simplifying assumptions sharing of a different kind (for example, market sharing) coincides with profit sharing. For example, the oligopsony analogues of iso-market-share *DD'* curves are individual market-sharing supply curves which give each firm the same share in the aggregate purchase at different prices. These coincide with iso-profit-share supply curves on the same simplifying assumptions which produce identity of iso-market-share *DD'* curves with iso-profit-share *DD'* curves.[2] In the first subcase now under con-

---

[1] These are the individual supply functions faced by the oligopsonists. They are derived by spontaneous co-ordination from the supply functions faced by the oligopsonistic industry.

[2] Cf. p. 211.

sideration—that is, if iso-profit-share *DD'* curves are established—we have to *connect the points of tangency of the Stackelberg indifference curves with one another* and thus derive a *contract curve* of the Edgeworth type (which, however, was not applied by him to this problem). The actual bargain will come to lie on this curve, and it will be expressed by that point of the curve which corresponds to the accepted distribution of the joint profit. The aggregate joint profit is not constant along these contract curves; the contract curve merely satisfies the condition that the individual profit of both participants can be increased by moving from any point outside the curve to some point on the curve, while the individual profit of both cannot be increased by moving away from the contract curve or by moving along it. This does not imply that by moving along the contract curve the profit of one participant cannot rise more than the profit of the other falls. Indeed, it is obvious from the analysis of Chapter VII that the joint profit is affected by the magnitude of the individual profit shares.[3] This is because the shares decide the extent to which the no-pooling clause reduces the available maximum joint profit. Only if pooling is not required for joint maximization—that is, with constant average total cost in undifferentiated oligopoly—does this joint profit remain unaffected by how it is shared (so that the sum of the two profits remains constant along the contract curve). In realistic analysis this possibility may be disregarded. The sum of the two profits changes along the contract curve. The establishment of iso-profit-share curves means, in all market structures here considered, that a curve should be drawn across the corresponding

---

[3] That is, by the position of the iso-profit-share *DD'* curves, given the individual cost curves.

Stackelberg map (for instance, across the map in Figure 3, page 106), showing the output combinations, or price combinations which distribute profits in given proportions. The information contained in our Figures 3–8 is not sufficient to draw such "profit-share paths" because the profit-indifference curves are not labeled for the magnitude of the profit in question. But they could be so labeled, and then profit-share paths could be drawn. What matters here is that these profit-share paths would become tangent to an indifference curve of one producer precisely at the point at which they become tangent to an indifference curve of the other producer, that is, on the contract curve (cf. Figure 14). Both producers have an interest in moving to the point of the profit-share path which expresses maximum joint profits *for these profit shares*, that is, to the point of intersection of the profit-share path with the contract curve. With more market variables and more firms the problem becomes more involved. The principles remain the same, except that there may be several combinations of price, output, sales expenditures, and product quality which jointly produce identical profits.

In the *second sub-case*, when no iso-profit-share *DD'* curves are established, the line which expresses the quasi-agreement and which cuts across the Stackelberg indifference map becomes tangent to an indifference curve of one producer at one point and to that of another producer at another point. For reasons discussed in Chapter VII, this would seem to be the more realistic assumption for all market structures here considered. For example, in the Stackelberg map with *output* as the variable, the "market-share path," corresponding to *iso-market-share DD'* curves in oligopoly, is a straight line moving northeast from the point of origin of the Stackelberg map. The slope

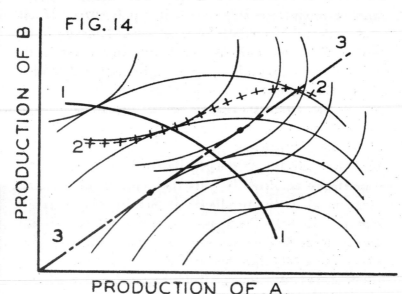

FIG. 14

PRODUCTION OF B

PRODUCTION OF A

1–1 = *The contract curve.* 2–2 = *A profit share path. (Different profit share paths go through the different tangencies of the indifference curves with one another; these distribute the joint profit in different proportions.)* 3–3 = *A market share path. (Different market share paths proceed northeast from the origin at different angles; these divide the market in different proportions.)*

of this line shows the constant market shares. The same is true of the analogous market-share paths in oligopsony and in the other market structures, if output is chosen as the variable. The shape of these market-share paths in the Stackelberg maps becomes different for price as the variable because it depends on what prices are compatible with the output combinations in question. But none of these market-share paths will reach tangency with the two families of indifference curves at one and the same point (the tangencies will not lie on the contract curve) unless the market-share paths happen to be also profit-share paths, that is, unless the market-sharing demand curves or supply curves established by the quasi-agreement coincide with iso-profit-share DD' curves or supply curves. If not, each party will be bidding for the point of tangency of the market-share line with its own indifference curve in the Stackelberg map, and the quasi-agreement will have to bridge this difference as well as the conflict of interests with respect to the shares themselves. The actual bargain will not maximize the joint profit compatible with the profit shares which emerge nor will it maximize the joint profit compatible with the given market shares (unless the compromise accidentally puts the point on the contract curve in which the producers cannot be said to have a mutual interest). These results apply not only if iso-market-share DD' curves—or their analogues for oligopsony—are established but in all cases in which no iso-profit-share curves emerge from the agreement. Figure 14 may help in visualizing the propositions here developed. We used an $\alpha\alpha$ map for illustration.

(3) We have now arrived at translating certain propositions of Chapter VII into indifference-map analysis for the whole family of related market structures. In the terminology used in Chapter VII, we have taken into account qualifications (a), (b), and (c) (page 198) but not the others. Figure 14 is more on the level of Figure 12 than of Figure 13 (Chapter VII). Qualification (d) may be included by stating that, within the framework of existing quasi-agreements, the tangency points of market-share paths with the indifference curves may change in the passage of time, and the compromise points reached between these tangencies may also change. This is because changes in the angle of the market-share-paths produced by the competitive handling of certain variables are frequently "permissible"; and also because new techniques of production and of marketing change the indifference

curves themselves. We will stop here because nothing would be gained by showing how the actual outcome differs from that here established, in consequence of qualifications (e), (f), (g), and (h) (page 199). We would merely be repeating what was said in Chapter VII. It should be added that the validity and significance of some qualifications may not be the same for all market structures. But too little is known about this by general observation alone. This is a matter for detailed factual inquiry.[4]

---

[4] In his interesting paper "Some Observations on Duopoly Theory" (*American Economic Review, Papers and Proceedings*, May 1948), H. Gregg Lewis used a Stackelberg map such as that of Figure 14 to show that certain traditional oligopoly equilibria (Cournot, Bertrand, and others) do not lie on the contract curve. He maintains that a rational solution must place the outcome on the contract curve. In our terminology this means that the outcome would have to be the same as that resulting from the establishment of iso-profit-share DD' curves. The following question may, however, be raised. Why does rationality *not require* the complete pooling of resources and of earnings, in which case the superimposition of two indifference maps would become as illegitimate as it is under simple monopoly? Our answer is: *because* future relative strength is unpredictable, and therefore the potentiality of warfare is always present. No firm wishes to disarm by withdrawing from the market for the sake of direct compensation. But if so, it may be argued that the same circumstance favors the establishment of DD' curves such as do not result in contract-curve solutions (for example, iso-market-share rather than iso-profit-share curves). This argument was developed on page 217.

CHAPTER NINE

Bilateral Monopoly on Product Markets

BILATERAL oligopoly—that is, the oligopoly-oligopsony relationship—is encountered on some product markets.[1] The interpretation of bilateral oligopoly requires a theory of bilateral monopoly, in addition to the previously discussed theory of limited joint maximization for oligopoly and for oligopsony.

The bilateral-monopoly problem is different from the duopoly problem. But in essential respects it is possible to establish *analogies* with the result that the corresponding conclusions follow for bilateral monopoly from a framework which stands in the relationship of *mutatis mutandis* to the duopoly framework.

It is true that in bilateral monopoly explicit negotiations and the conclusion of an agreement are postulated,

---

[1] For illustration, cf. the last paragraph of footnote 1, page 20.

while the relations of duopolists to each other need not be so regulated. But this difference is more superficial than it seems at first sight because bilateral monopoly does not thereby become the counterpart of a tightly organized cartel, based on explicit agreement for an extended period. The bilateral-monopoly relation on product markets does not possess inherent properties which would make co-ordination tighter or would exclude the recurrence of cutthroat policies with more assurance than is the case under oligopoly. Agreements are explicit, but if they relate merely to *ad hoc* purchases and sales, this does not make much difference. A vocabulary can be described with the aid of which the main propositions of duopoly theory can be "translated" into the language of bilateral monopoly. Let us now turn to this vocabulary.

(1) *Intersection-point equilibria*: One approach to the duopoly problem is characterized by the assumption that each duopolist sets up a reaction function expressing his individual profit maximization for given values of the rival's variables, and that equilibrium is established at the intersection of these reaction functions. This is analogous to assuming that, in bilateral monopoly, the monopolistic seller sets up a supply function (which is his marginal-cost function), and the monopsonistic buyer sets up a demand function (which is the marginal value product function of the commodity or service purchased), and that equilibrium is established at the intersection of these functions. In both cases—duopoly and bilateral monopoly—such behavior could be termed "competitive" in *some* sense. In bilateral monopoly, this behavior is competitive in the *usual* sense because supply and demand functions are based on the notion that the price at which the indi-

vidual seller sells, and the price at which the individual
buyer buys, are given to him. On these assumptions the
output is the competitive output in the usual sense (so-
called ideal output). In duopoly, the corresponding behavior is merely "analogous" to competitive behavior. The
reaction functions are also based on the notion that the
value of some variable is given to the individual producer,
but this variable is not the price at which he sells or buys.
Instead, it is the variable at which his rival operates (that
is, the price at which the rival sells, or the output which the
rival produces, and so forth). The equilibrium output is,
of course, not the "ideal" output. The vocabulary we are
developing translates the concepts applying to a vertical
relationship in the structure of production (a buyer-seller
relationship) into the terminology applying to a horizontal relationship (a relationship between rivals).

In both cases the "equilibrium" is based on false ideas
of the producers concerning the behavior of their rivals.
Furthermore, in both cases it is practically inconceivable
that the producers should not discover this. The values of
the variables in question can, of course, not really be
"given" to both producers.

(2) *Leadership equilibria*:   The leadership equilibria
of duopoly theory is characterized by the assumption that
one producer selects the (from his standpoint) optimal
point along the reaction function of the other. The
analogous assumption for bilateral monopoly is that the
buyer selects the (from his standpoint) optimal point
along the supply function (marginal-cost function) of the
seller or that the seller selects the (from his standpoint)
optimal point along the demand function (marginal value
product function) of the buyer. If the buyer makes the

selection along the supply function (marginal-cost function) of the seller—that is to say, if the buyer is the leader —he will buy the quantity which equates the marginal function corresponding to the supply function of the seller *with* his own marginal value product function,[2] and he will pay the price indicated by the supply function (marginal-cost function) of the seller for this quantity. This is monopsony equilibrium. If the seller makes the selection along the demand function (marginal value product function) of the buyer—that is to say, if the seller is the leader—he will sell the quantity which equates the marginal function corresponding to the demand function of the buyer [3] *with* his own marginal-cost function. He will charge the price indicated by the marginal value product function (that is, by his demand function) for this quantity. This is monopoly equilibrium. Here, and in connection with the subsequent paragraph, the reader might find Figure 15 helpful.[4]

---

[2] On these assumptions, the marginal-cost function of the seller is the supply function. Therefore, from the buyer's point of view, it is the *average*-cost function of the commodity or service which he buys. To maximize his profits he will equate the marginal function corresponding to *this* function with the marginal value product function of what he buys.

[3] This is the marginal function corresponding to the marginal value product function. It is the marginal-revenue function of the seller because on these assumptions the marginal-value product function is his demand function (or average-revenue function).

[4] The figure is reproduced from an earlier article of the writer. Cf. "Prices and Wages Under Bilateral Monopoly," *Quarterly Journal of Economics*, August 1947. This article also contains references to the literature on bilateral monopoly, mainly to works of Knut Wicksell (in *Archiv für Sozialwissenschaft und Sozialpolitik*, 1927), Joseph A. Schumpeter (ibid.), A. L. Bowley (in *Economic Journal*, 1928), J. R. Hicks (in *Econometrica*, 1935), Heinrich von Stackelberg (*Marktform und Gleichgewicht*), Gerhard Tintner (in *Journal of Political Economy*, 1939), and Wassily Leontief (in *Journal of Political Economy*, 1946). The two leadership points here discussed and the joint-profit maximiz-

FIG. 15

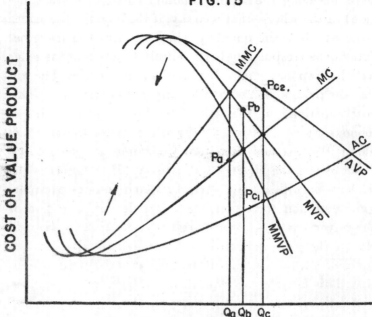

QUANTITY OF COMMODITY

AC = *Average Cost;* MC = *Marginal Cost;* MMC = *Marginal to Marginal Cost;* AVP = *Average Value Product;* MVP = *Marginal Value Product;* MMVP = *Marginal to the Marginal Value Product;* Q_a = *Quantity Produced if Buyer Dominates;* P_a = *Price Paid for Commodity if Buyer Dominates;* Q_b = *Quantity Produced if Seller Dominates;* P_b = *Price Paid for Commodity if Seller Dominates;* Q_o = *Quantity Produced if Joint Profit is Maximized;* P_{c1} = *Lower Limit of Price if Joint Profit is Maximized;* P_{c2} = *Upper Limit of Price if Joint Profit is Maximized*

The arrows indicate the direction in which the functions shift if close substitutes are introduced on both sides of the market.

These cases of the dominance of buyers or sellers are analogous to the leadership equilibria in duopoly theory. The corresponding equilibria—in contrast to the intersection-point equilibria—are *not* based on false notions of the producers about the behavior of their rivals. But to

ing point were first described by A. L. Bowley in his note "On Bilateral Monopoly," *Economic Journal*, December 1928.

say that no collusion is involved in these leadership equilibria is arbitrary. In these cases, the solution is derived from very definite "rules of the game" by which each producer is given a specific role. It is not convincing to assume that producers attempt to secure themselves just these roles. These "rules of the game" do not maximize joint profits. Furthermore, the deviations from joint-profit maximization are "blind." They are not meaningful expressions of effective limits to co-operation.

(3) *Joint-profit maximization*: We may now turn to the counterpart, in bilateral-monopoly theory, of the profit-maximizing quasi-agreements of duopoly theory. This counterpart consists of setting the output of the seller (and the purchase of the buyer) at the level which equates the marginal cost of the seller with the marginal-value product of the buyer. The output measured by the abscissa of this intersection maximizes the joint profit. The price is one of the means—the easiest means—of distributing the joint profit in accordance with relative strength. *Aside from* considerations pertaining to relative strength, the price (in contrast to the output) would have to be regarded as "indeterminate." The range of indeterminancy is limited by the average-cost function from below and the average value product function from above. Within the range lying between these "zero-profit limits," the *price* is determined by relative strength. The profit-maximizing *output* is unequivocally that which equates the marginal cost with the marginal-value product, and it is measured by the abscissa of this intersection point. For all prices *other than that measured by the ordinate of the intersection of the marginal-cost curve with the marginal value product curve* the profit-maximizing contract must

include an all-or-none ("take it or leave it") clause. The
one price for which this is not necessary—namely, the ordinate of the intersection point—is merely one of the
prices lying between the average cost and the average-
value product for the joint-profit maximizing output.
There is no reason to assume that the relative strength of
the parties will be such as to establish just this price. For
all other prices an all-or-none clause is required because, at
any price that may be set, the seller would prefer to deliver
the quantity by which he equates his marginal cost to the
price, while the buyer would prefer to buy the quantity
by which the equality of the marginal-value product with
the price is established. Generally speaking, joint-profit
maximization requires setting the sale of the seller and
the purchase of the buyer, with the aid of an all-or-none
clause, at the level equating marginal cost with marginal-
value product; and agreeing on the price, within the
zero-profit limits, in accordance with the relative strength
of the parties. In bilateral monopoly on product markets
the application of an all-or-none clause merely means that
price offers and quantity offers go hand-in-hand, that is,
that the other party is not free to accept a price offer as
such and then to select the quantity he wants to buy or
sell. There is nothing peculiar in this so far as bilateral
monopoly on product markets is concerned. Sales contracts usually apply to price and quantity alike. They
imply all-or-none clauses whenever price quotations are
not divorced from quantity offers.

If the joint profit is maximized, then the contract lies
along Edgeworth's familiar contract curve. If along the
ordinate we measure the price of the commodity passing
from seller to buyer in bilateral monopoly, and along the
abscissa we measure the quantity, then the profit-indiffer-

ence curves (showing identical aggregate profits) will be convex from below for the seller, with upward rising indifference levels, and they will be concave from below for the buyer, with downward rising indifference levels. The contract curve connecting the points of tangency contains all points which express maximum joint profits and which in Figure 15 are derived not by this method but from the intersection of marginal cost with marginal-value product. In Figure 15 the locus of all points showing prices between AC and AVC for the joint-profit-maximizing output (Qc) corresponds to the contract curve. Shifting from an agreement by which joint profits are *not* maximized to an agreement by which they *are* maximized always makes possible an increase in the profits of *each* participant. Therefore, a tendency towards joint-profit maximization should be expected here as under oligopoly. The analytical transition from the "reaction-functions approach" to joint-profit maximization is here analogous to the transition described in Chapter IV for oligopoly (except that in bilateral monopoly we start from the supply and demand functions of page 241 rather than from the "classical" oligopoly reaction functions of Chapter II). In bilateral monopoly, as in oligopoly, the "pure theory" analysis leads to the conclusion that the joint profit will be maximized and that it will be divided in accordance with the forces discussed in Chapter I (pages 24–9).

The tendency toward joint-profit maximization will, however, be counteracted by certain circumstances not habitually taken into account in the "pure" varieties of economic theory. In reality, joint-profit maximization applies with qualifications here as under oligopoly.

The preceding discussion contains two chapters on qualifications of the profit-maximization postulate. The qualifications considered in the first of these two chapters were said to apply to monopoly as well as to oligopoly, although not necessarily in the same degree. Here it should be added that these qualifications apply also to the bilateral-monopoly problem. In other words, the statement that in bilateral monopoly the joint profit will be maximized should be interpreted with all the qualifications considered in Chapter V. These are connected with the attempt of firms to secure safety margins against outcomes which are less favorable than those appearing most probable; with long-run objectives of firms; and with the existence of controlling groups in enterprises.

In the second of the two chapters dealing with qualifications we turned to those applying to the oligopoly problem specifically. These are concerned with (1) the adoption of cutthroat policies or the desire to avoid them, (2) the incompleteness of co-ordination concerning technological changes and product variation as well as advertising, and (3) cost differences and product differentiation. The first of these is valid as a qualifying factor also in relation to profit maximization under bilateral monopoly. The second and the third have no counterpart here. They apply, as qualifying circumstances, to the relationship between rival firms, not to the relationship between buyer and seller.

The meaning of cutthroat policies is somewhat different in oligopoly, on the one hand, and bilateral monopoly, on the other. This again is a consequence of the fact that in the one case we are dealing with relationships between rivals, in the other with buyer-seller relationships. In oligopoly, *actual* cutthroat policies express themselves in cutthroat *competition*, aimed at harming the competitor with the intent of forcing him to agree on terms which otherwise he might not be willing to accept. Such cutthroat competition frequently characterizes phases of oligopolistic relations during which relative strength is tested. The desire to *avoid* cutthroat competition provides a qualification to joint-profit maximization because the firms possess imperfect information of each other's probability judgments concerning what constitutes profit maximization,[5] and therefore a "correct" move [6] may not be undertaken because it might be interpreted as a move towards cutthroat competition. In bilateral monopoly, actual cutthroat policies express themselves in a refusal to conclude an agreement which is favorable to the other party, even if this refusal is temporarily harmful to both parties.[7] The ultimate objective here, too, is to force the other party later into sharing the maximized joint profit in proportions which he otherwise might not be willing to accept. In bilateral monopoly, as in oligopoly, such policies frequently are phases of strength testing. The desire to avoid cutthroat policies exerts an influence also in bilateral monopoly because, in the course of the negotiations, there always is doubt about what the other party has in mind. By making an offer, or by refusing one, he may be moving toward joint-profit maximization, or he may be moving toward cutthroat policies. His appraisal of joint-profit maximization, and his appraisal of the other party's appraisal, are not known to the other party. These can only be guessed, and the uncertainty attaching to these guesses may sometimes make it appear desirable to refrain from moves in the "correct" direction.

---

[5] I.e., "most probable" profit maximization.

[6] A move in the direction of joint-profit maximization on the basis of some "average" appraisal of the parties.

[7] The result may be that no agreement is concluded, i.e., that temporarily no business is done; or that an agreement is concluded which is harmful to both parties (or, at least, considerably less profitable than would be possible).

We have now discussed the analogies, in bilateral-monopoly theory, to the following concepts of oligopoly theory: intersection-point equilibria; leadership equilibria; the "analytical transition" from the traditional reaction-function approach to profit-maximizing agreements; and qualifications to joint-profit maximization. The analogy is not complete; the difference between rival relationships (in oligopoly) and buyer-seller relationships (in bilateral monopoly) make it necessary to reinterpret certain sections of the analysis when it is applied to the one rather than to the other problem. But so far as the foregoing concepts and arguments of oligopoly theory are concerned, the analogy is close, even though not perfect; and, in our judgment, the core of oligopoly theory and of bilateral-monopoly theory consists of just these concepts and arguments.

Our discussion has not attempted to establish an "analogy" for every phase of the preceding oligopoly analysis. We limited this discussion to those phases of oligopoly and bilateral-monopoly analysis which enter into our general conclusions. A reasonable analogy to all specific propositions in oligopoly theory does not exist. For example, in bilateral monopoly the identity of the seller's price with that of the buyer and the identity of the seller's sales with the buyer's purchases is a definitional property of the problem, while some of the suggested oligopoly equilibria become "determinate" by introducing a rule of the game by which prices will be held equal and (or) the volume of business will be divided according to some principle. This is connected with the fact that the difference between rival relationships and buyer-seller relationships *is* fundamental in certain respects.

Furthermore, reaction functions based on conjectural

variation have no close analogy in bilateral-monopoly theory. This also is a consequence of the fact that if the buyer buys at a certain price then the seller by definition sells at the same price, and *vice versa*, so that neither parties can believe that by buying (selling) at some price he induces the other to sell (buy) at a different price. The same is true of quantity as well as of price because the quantity sold also is definitionally identical with the quantity purchased. Of course, the parties involved in the bilateral-monopoly relationship may believe that by *offering* to buy or to sell some quantity at some price they induce the other party to *offer* to sell or to buy another quantity at another price. But this is the analogy to what happens in oligopoly during "testing" maneuvers preceding the conclusions of quasi-agreements. It is not the analogy of what is meant to be expressed by reaction functions based on conjectural variation.

CHAPTER TEN

The Element of Bilateral Monopoly in Labor-Management Relations

THE FRAMEWORK

THE specific properties of labor markets must be considered before the foregoing analysis can be extended to labor-management relations.

Under collective bargaining an element of bilateral monopoly is contained in the wage-determining mechanism. Labor representatives have some monopoly power because the trade agreements set the conditions on which labor may be employed by an enterprise or by a group of enterprises; and managements frequently have some monopsony power because employment by other enterprises is not typically a *perfect* substitute for the *given* employment, as viewed from the standpoint of the worker. It is true that while management is a buyer of services, unions cannot properly be considered selling agencies. But this can be taken into account by recognizing that the motives of unions on the supply side of the bilateral-monopoly relationship are different from the motives of firms functioning on the supply side of product markets. While they are not sellers, unions clearly operate on the supply side of a market.

In perfect competition[1] wages and employment would be determined by the intersection of labor-supply functions with demand functions (that is, with marginal-productivity functions). Involuntary unemployment could not exist. In merely pure competition (that is, in all-round atomistic competition with lagging adjustments to changes) the intersection of labor supply functions with demand functions would always determine the point toward which an adjustment may be said to take place but during the adjustment further shifts might occur and the intersection point might never be actually realized. This is true if the functions are interpreted as expressing what the individuals and institutions are planning to do within reasonable periods of time.

If the demand and supply functions are interpreted as indicating what will be done in the next moment, then even in pure (not only in perfect) competition the intersection point of supply and demand functions will always be realized. But this is not a very significant statement because these instantaneous functions may be based on entirely incorrect notions of demanders and suppliers concerning the consequences (implications) of their behavior on the market. For example, at the wage rate corresponding to the instantaneous intersection point, unemployed workers may voluntarily withhold their services,

---

[1] That is to say, pure (atomistic) competition plus instantaneous adjustments (perfect mobility).

that is, they may refrain from developing an excess supply and from accepting a specific, lower wage rate because they may believe that in some area of the economy they will shortly obtain employment at the going wage rate; yet the shrinkage of aggregate demand to which the wage-bill deflation contributes may produce a continuous downward shift of the labor demand function with the result that, by the time the workers make up their minds to accept the lower wage rate which was called for by the previous functions, an even lower wage rate would be required and unemployment would have increased. Subsequently, the same development may repeat itself. The statement that in competition that is pure but not perfect employment is determined by the intersection of *instantaneous* demand and supply functions is correct but not particularly significant. The statement that in competition that is pure but not perfect there would be a *tendency* toward the intersection points of demand and supply functions *such as express long-run plans and correct expectations* must be supplemented by the statement that this tendency may or may not become realized within reasonable periods of time. In perfect competition the tendency would become instantaneously realized, but this is merely a definitional proposition.

In conditions of collective bargaining the labor supply function does not play the role which can be attributed to it in perfect *or* in merely pure competition. This is a consequence of the bilateral-monopoly element. However, the specific characteristics of labor markets make it necessary to modify the preceding bilateral-monopoly analysis before attempting to apply it to labor markets.

The fundamental reason for modification is that unions

do not try to maximize the "satisfaction" of their membership in a sense analogous to that in which a monopolistic producer tries to maximize his profits. For producers, profit maximization means maximizing the difference between gross revenue and something in the nature of accounting costs. In regard to labor supply, accounting costs have no counterpart. In any individual industry, opportunity costs (wages in alternative occupations) may contribute to setting a level below which wages cannot fall. But for the labor supply there exists no cost concept which would be analogous to the accounting costs of producers. Psychological costs of individual workers cannot be made to serve as deductions from gross revenue for purposes of maximization (just as psychological costs of individual shareholders cannot), because it would be absurd to assume pooling of money incomes and redistribution of net gains over and above psychological costs. Hence, at least to the extent to which their objectives are "economic," unions try to get a high *gross* income per unit of time for their membership, or for a segment of their membership which is large enough to make the position of the leaders safe; and this gross income is at the same time regarded as the *net* income of labor because there are no accounting costs.

We conclude that, for the problem at hand, union preference functions (or indifference maps) take the place of cost functions. The indifference functions may be straight lines, as in Figure 16, expressing the assumption that the satisfaction of the union increases with rising money wage rates, regardless of the amount of employment; or they may be concave from above, as in Figure 17, expressing the assumption that, from the standpoint of the union, more employment and higher wage rates are imperfect substitutes for each other.[2] Furthermore, even if the indifference map is linear (Figure 16), the level of satisfaction need not rise indefinitely as we move upward along

FIG. 16

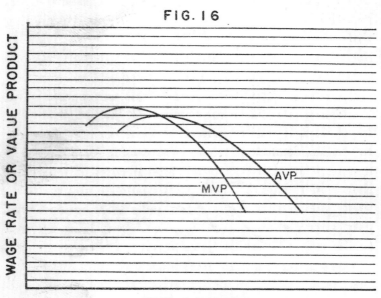

the ordinate. The level of satisfaction may rise to some point on the ordinate, and from there on it may decline. The leadership may have no desire to reach a wage level so high that it would be distinctly harmful to its public relations and its relations with the management when the membership exerts no effective pressure for such a wage level. Consequently, even if the union indifference map is linear, the utility indexes attached to the various lines in

---

[2] So that the union is as well satisfied with somewhat lower wage rates and somewhat higher employment as with somewhat higher wage rates and somewhat lower employment.

Figure 16 may rise to some height on the ordinate and from there on they *may* fall.

The *MVP* functions of the diagrams express the net marginal value product functions of labor for the enter-

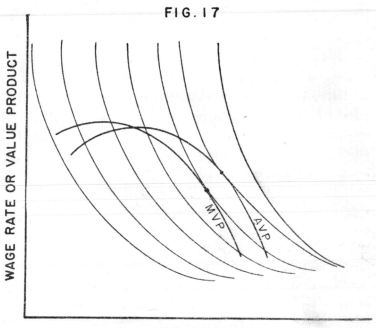

FIG. 17

prise; the *AVP* functions express net average-value product. If the union possessed *all the* "*bargaining power*"—that is, if it could set the conditions unilaterally—then one of the following possibilities would materialize.

With linear indifference maps and with ever-increasing utility indexes along the ordinate, the wage line would be chosen which is tangential to *AVP*.

With linear indifference maps and with utility indexes which first rise and then decline as we move upward along the ordinate, the same wage rate would be chosen, provided the line to which the maximum utility index is attached lies above the line which is tangential to *AVP*. Yet if the line with the highest utility lies below this tangent, the line with the highest index expresses the wage rate which will be chosen.

With concave indifference maps, the wage line would be chosen which goes through the point of tangency of the *MVP* function with an indifference curve, provided the enterprise is allowed to choose the amount of employment unilaterally, that is, provided no all-or-none clause (employment guarantee) is included in the contract. In this case, as in all previous cases, the enterprise will choose the employment corresponding to the intersection of the horizontal wage line chosen with the *MVP* curve. Considering this, the union will aim at the horizontal wage line going through the tangency in question. This proposition, however, is subject to the qualification that if the tangency in question should lie above the AVP function, then the horizontal wage line tangent to AVP will be chosen.

With concave indifference maps and all-or-none clauses (employment guarantees), the union will choose the wage rate corresponding to the tangency of *AVP* with an indifference curve, and it will insist on the employment expressed by the abscissa of this tangency.

The union indifference map may, of course, consist of a combination of these possibilities and it may be different in different regions.

It seems realistic to assume that the actual indifference maps are linear whenever the union does not feel that more employment would compensate it for a wage loss. In these cases, which might well be more typical than those to which concave maps apply, there usually will be a wage line up to which the utility indexes rise and beyond

which they fall. For the leadership usually is not interested
in obtaining a wage rate which is clearly beyond the expectation of the membership and which at the same time
has a distinctly harmful effect on relations of the union
with other agencies. But the wage line with the highest
utility index may frequently lie above the wage line which
is tangent to the AVP curve, and in this case the outcome
of the analysis is precisely such as it would be if the utility
indexes were ever increasing along the ordinate.

Concave indifference maps may be rare when a union
faces a single firm. But to assume concavity may be realistic when a union is faced with an industry, that is to say,
with firms operating along different cost functions. The
AVP and MVP functions will then have to express the
value product for the industry as a whole. The union will
usually have to take into account the fact that uniform
wage rates for the industry affect the various firms differently, and that wage rates which can be paid by certain
firms will result in closing down others. The "level of satisfaction" of a union may not be affected appreciably by
changes in the amount of employment in a single firm, and
consequently the indifference maps may typically be linear
when a single firm is faced. But the level of satisfaction
can hardly remain unaffected by the unemployment of
workers of whole establishments, because the group whose
interests are hurt in this event is an articulate organizational unit within the union. Therefore, concave indifference maps may be very much less uncommon in industry-
wide bargaining, and, generally speaking, in bargaining
between a union and a group of plants (which may be
owned by a single firm). However, if the industry-wide
bargaining establishes different wage rates for the different plants or for different firms, then, from the present

point of view, the situation is more like single-plant bargaining.

So far, we have been concerned with the upper limit of the bargaining range, that is to say, with the wages which the union would set if it were in a position to determine the conditions of employment unilaterally. The maximum bargaining power of the employer would establish a wage rate lying on the lowest indifference curve which is still acceptable to the union. For the economy as a whole, this lowest possible indifference level can, of course, not be lower than the "classical" level interpreted as a subsistence level; and in single occupations it cannot be lower than the level which will keep the workers in the given occupation. But even the lowest acceptable level may be considerably higher than these "classical" limits. The leaders of a union cannot afford to move below the limit at which the employed part of the membership still feels that it profits from the existence of the specific union in question as compared with other potential forms of organization, and at which it feels that it profits considerably from not being unorganized. The lower limit is a somewhat vague concept. But the actual outcome of the bargain—between the lower and the upper limit—usually is sufficiently far removed from the limits that the fine points connected with the concept of these limits lose much of their significance. The bargain expresses a way of dividing the gains in accordance with forces (a), (b), (c), and (d) on pages 24–9.

In the absence of all-or-none clauses (employment guarantees), the profit-maximization postulate requires that, given the wage rate, the management employ the number of workers whose net marginal-value product equals the wage rate. Trade agreements usually establish a structure of wage rates for services of different kinds, rather than a single wage rate. The net value product function of each kind of service depends on the wage rate established for the other services.[3] Given the *general* level of "the" wage rate —that is, of the entire wage structure—there usually exists a variety of specific structures (relative rates) which would correspond to the same bargaining strength of the union in relation to the management. In choosing between these it must, of course, be taken into account that workers cannot be kept in a specific job if *available* alternative jobs possess net advantages for them. But the significance of this consideration is reduced by the circumstance that under bilateral monopoly alternative jobs may become unavailable even if they have net advantages. Consequently, in the framework of given wage structures certain jobs may well be overpaid compared with others. Existing wage *structures* are largely determined by the influence of various groups of workers within a given union, which depends partly on their ability to seek alternative forms of organization in the event of discontent. Wage structures also depend on the relative influence of different unions (craft unions), which depends partly on how much harm they can do to management and to the other workers by not co-operating, that is, on what alternatives are available to management and to the other workers if they should not co-operate. But it remains a requirement of profit maximization that, given *all* wage rates, the amount of employment of all kinds of labor should equate the net marginal-value product of that kind of service to the corresponding wage rate, provided the management is free to determine the amount of employment. The management *is* free to do this. Arrangements

---

[3] Because in calculating the net value product, the costs of all co-operating services must be deducted.

in the nature of employment guarantees are exceedingly rare. The bearing of this on the principle of qualified joint maximization is discussed in Appendix 1 of this chapter.

SHORTAGES

In the foregoing exposition it was assumed that, at each wage rate, the labor force required for equating the marginal-value product with the wage rate is available. This need not always be true. If fewer workers are available, the competitive labor supply function becomes a significant notion. In the graphic presentation (Figure 16) [4] this expresses itself in the following manner: If at the wage rate which results from the negotiations, the competitive supply function is located to the right of the intersection point of *MVP* with the wage line, then the supply function plays no role in the determination of the amount of employment. If at that wage rate the supply function is located to the left of the intersection point of *MVP* with the wage line in question, then the amount of employment will be determined by the intersection of the wage line with the supply function (rather than with the *MVP* functions). [5]

For an industry possessing substantial monopsony

---

[4] Figure 17 is not relevant because in the event of shortages the union does not have a concave indifference map.

[5] The firm will not tend to overbid the established wage rate in order to get more workers than indicated by the supply curve because even in the limiting case in which the wage rate in question is the monopsony wage rate (i.e., the lowest wage rate which the firm would like to establish), the marginal cost of hiring additional workers along the competitive supply curve exceeds the marginal-value product. This follows directly from the definition of the monopsony wage rate.

power, the supply function may be upward sloping or backward rising (downward sloping) in the relevant range depending on circumstances similar to those discussed in Professor Robbins' well-known article.[6] The usual argument concerning the possibility of a backward rise (downward slope) relates primarily to the labor supply functions of individual workers but a *significantly* monopsonistic employer unit may in practice be faced with a given number of individuals, some of whom may be less willing to work if a wagè raise makes it possible for them and for their families to earn higher incomes even if they work less. Substantial monopsony power requires, however, that the employment offered by the industry should be *significantly* different, from the workers' point of view, from alternative employments. A single firm is scarcely ever in such a position; entire industries may or may not be. If the employer who negotiates with the union does not have substantial monopsony power, then—in any possible range of shortages—he is almost certain to face an upward-sloping supply curve. The fact that at a higher wage the same labor force may be less willing to work is almost certain to be outweighed by the circumstance that the higher wage rate attracts workers from other occupations. Regardless of whether the competitive supply function is upward sloping or backward rising at the wage rate actually established by the negotiations, only the number of workers indicated by the supply function will be employed, provided this number is smaller than that corresponding to the intersection of *MVP* with the wage line, that is, provided there is a "shortage" in this region.

---

[6] Lionel Robbins, "On the Elasticity of the Demand for Income in Terms of Effort," *Economica*, June 1930, reprinted in *Readings in the Theory of Income Distribution* (Philadelphia and Toronto, 1946).

If not only the wage rate actually established but also the limits of the bargaining range fall in the range in which not enough workers are available to equate the *MVP* with the wage rate, then the theory of the bargaining ranges must also be reconsidered. In fact this is true even if only one of the two bargaining limits falls in the region of shortage in this sense. For the views on the bargaining limits which were presented on pages 257ff., assume that there is no such shortage. The amendments pertaining to this case can also be expressed briefly. At an upper limit falling in the region of shortage, wage and employment will be determined by the intersection of the competitive supply curve with *AVP*. At a lower limit falling in the region of shortage, wage and employment will be determined in the manner expressed by the theory of monopsony.[7] The monopsony power of the firm may be small, in which event the supply curve is nearly horizontal, and the monopsony wage rate and employment are nearly the same as would be the case at the lower limit with no shortage. If the monopsony power is zero, and the supply curve literally horizontal, the analysis of shortages becomes irrelevant because down to the lower limit there can be no shortage.

It should be added that with an upward-sloping supply curve both the upper and the lower limit of the bargaining range *may* fall in the region of shortage. With a downward-sloping supply function the upper limit may fall in that region, but the lower limit may not. It follows from

---

[7] That is to say, the firm will find the most profitable point along the supply curve by equating the marginal function corresponding to the supply curve with the *MVP* function and by selecting the point of the supply function which lies vertically above this marginal intersection point.

the theory of monopsony that it always would pay the firm to lower the wage rate below the region of shortage.

INTERACTIONS BETWEEN SUPPLY AND DEMAND

A further complicating factor is introduced if we recognize that there may be interactions between the supply side and the demand side of labor markets. Of the various possible interactions two will be here considered.

(a) Rising wage rates may increase the efficiency of labor and, therefore, they may raise the marginal value product functions. This, of course, is more likely to be the case in low than in high regions of the wage-rate axis (Figure 16). The technical analysis of the preceding pages still holds but—if such interactions occur—a different value product function corresponds to each wage line. Consequently, the propositions relating to the union indifference map, on the one hand, and to *the* average or marginal value product function, on the other, should be reworded so as to apply to the union indifference map, on the one hand, and to a *family* of value product functions, on the other, where the label of each value product function indicates *with which wage line it is legitimate to pair it in the analysis*. Any proposition relating to the intersection of a wage line with the *MVP* functions should now be interpreted to relate to the intersection with the *corresponding MVP* function.

However, the supply-demand interaction may be largely unpredictable, and, therefore, in the setting of wage rates it may be left completely out of account. Even

in this case it will affect wages and employment gradually
(with a lag) because the shifts in the value product functions, which follow wage changes, will be noticed. Yet such
a lag would mean that, *at any moment of time*, the determinants of the bargaining limits and the determinants of
employment for alternative wage rates are unaffected by
the interactions by which they will actually be accompanied. They are affected merely by past interactions.
This is quite likely to be the case not only because of the
unpredictable character of these interactions but also because they are partly (largely) in the nature of "external
economies." Many advantages of higher wages depend on
change in the "way of living" of the worker which in turn
depends largely on what workers *in general* earn (that is,
on the environment in which the individual worker lives).

(b) In the event of general wage changes another "interaction" also develops between the supply side and the
demand side. Overall changes in money wage rates are
associated with changes in the demand for goods and,
therefore, of the value product functions. We have at
present no reasonably general theory of this interaction.
On the one hand we have the so-called orthodox tendency
toward disregarding the interaction in question, on the
other hand the Keynesian tendency toward assuming that
effective demand and the value product functions *adjust*
to general wage changes so as to leave real wage rate and
employment unaffected.[8] Neither of these extreme assumptions seems satisfactory. However, it is obvious that in a
theory of general wage changes the effect on the demand
side must not be left out of account.

---

[8] That is, so as to change merely the price level. However, all Keynesians would add that changes in money wage rates do change the demand for liquidity and, therefore, the interest rate. Via this repercus-
sion a purely monetary effect on employment is admitted.

We should like to repeat a suggestion from other writings on this problem.[9] The following two questions may be asked: (1) In what way are general changes in money wage rates associated with changes in real wage rates? (2) In what way are general changes in real wage rates associated with change in real output and employment?

As for the first question, we suggest that the effect of money wage changes on real wages depends on whether businessmen will undertake, after the change, *more, the same amount, or less investment per unit of simultaneous consumer demand.* If they undertake the same amount, real wage rates will remain unchanged. Both the demand for consumer goods and the demand for investment goods will adjust to the change in money wage rates. Prices will adjust completely.[10] If a rise in money rates reduces the amount of investment which producers are willing to undertake per unit of simultaneous consumer demand (and if a wage cut increases this amount), changes in money wage rates will be associated with changes in real wage rates in the same direction. Investment demand will not adjust completely to the change in money wage rates. Therefore, effective demand as a whole will adjust incompletely and so will prices.[11] If a rise in money wage rates

---

[9] Cf. the present writer's *Monetary Policies and Full Employment* (2nd ed.; Berkeley, 1947), chap. iii.

[10] Any change in real wage rates would have to be associated with a change in the propensity to consume. Postulating that the ratio of investment to consumption remains unchanged means postulating that no such change occurs (aside from incorrect expectations which we assume here will tend to become corrected).

[11] Assume that a rise in money wage rates reduces the amount of investment which producers are willing to undertake per unit of simultaneous consumer demand. This means that investment tends to become smaller in relation to the wage bill (because the propensity to consume out of wage income is higher than out of non-wage income). This in turn means that the sum total of producers' expenditures (i.e.,

increases the amount of investment which producers are willing to undertake per unit of simultaneous consumer demand (and a fall reduces this amount), then investment adjusts "more than completely," that is, price outweighs the wage changes with the result that money and real wages move in opposite directions. We are assuming here that after the wage change wage rates are expected to remain at their new level. Also, we are disregarding changes in productivity (man-hour output) which would call for expressing the argument in terms of unit labor cost instead of real wage rates.[12]

Some plausibility attaches to the assumption that a *rise* in money wage rates tends to *reduce* the amount of investment which producers are willing to undertake per unit of simultaneous consumer demand (and that a fall in money wage rates increases this amount). This would mean that changes in money wage rates tend to be associated with changes in real wage rates in the same direction. This seems a rather plausible assumption because wages are costs as well as direct demand-influencing factors for the consumer-goods industries, while the same is not true of *all* investment activity. Part of the investment

the sum of incomes) becomes smaller in relation to wage incomes. Given the man-hour output, real wage rates must rise. The analogous assumptions lead to the conclusion that a fall in money wage rates is associated with a fall in real wage rates *if* the fall in money wage rates increases the amount of investment which producers are willing to undertake per unit of simultaneous consumer demand.

[12] Changes in man-hour output need not be consequences of the setting up of new production functions. They may be consequences of changing unit costs, along given functions, as output changes. Strictly speaking, the argument of the text (and of footnote 1) shows that *unit labor cost* tends to rise or to fall, whenever we say that the real wage rate tends to rise or to fall. For producers' profit considerations as well as for the "propensity-to-consume" considerations it is the unit labor cost that matters!

activity of any period produces additional investment goods which subsequently will again be producing additional investment goods and so on, and this proposition remains true *ad infinitum*, as long as the marginal propensity to consume is smaller than one. For this kind of investment activity wages are costs but not demand-influencing factors in any direct sense. Therefore, we may assume that investment demand as a whole adjusts incompletely to money wage changes, which in turn creates a presumption that real wage rates tend to move in the same direction. If, on the other hand, we assume that the amount of investment per unit of simultaneous consumer demand remains unchanged, general changes in money wage rates will tend to be associated with no change in real wage rates.

We may now turn to the second question raised on page 267. In what way do changes in real wage rates (unit labor costs) [13] affect the level of real output and of employment? The answer depends on whether the change in the average and the marginal propensity to consume does or does not affect the uncertainty attaching to profit expectations. If it does not, a rise in real wage rates tends to reduce employment (and *vice versa*). If, however, the uncertainty attaching to profit expectations falls with rising propensity to consume (and *vice versa*), then the outcome depends on *how strong* this effect on uncertainty is. It *may* be strong enough to lead to increased output *in spite of* the rise in other costs, and to reduced output *in spite of* the lowering of other costs. Or it may provide merely an incomplete offset to the change in other costs. For a change in uncertainty is tantamount to a change in one cost item, namely, in the necessary profit included in the cost curves. Consequently, if a fall in money wage rates re-

---

[13] Cf. footnote 12, p. 268.

sults in increased investment per unit of simultaneous consumer demand and therefore in lower real wages (page 267), and, if without the increase in uncertainty [14] this would result in an increase of output from O to O_1, then the uncertainty effect will actually lead to an output O_2 which is lower than O_1. Whether O_2 is also lower than the original output (O) depends on whether the adverse effect of uncertainty and the required increase of the "necessary profit" is greater or smaller than the lowering of unit wage costs. It may be argued with a great deal of *a priori* plausibility that a fall in the average propensity to consume increases uncertainty because consumer demand is more stable, more "dependable" (and is *known* to be more so) than the demand for producers' goods.[15] But no general conclusion is suggested on whether—in the event of

---

[14] Which attends the fall in the propensity to consume.

[15] Logically, there is no more inherent difficulty in describing a full-employment economy with an average and marginal propensity to consume of 0.1 than in visualizing a full-employment economy in which these propensities are 0.9. But the uncertainty attaching to business expectations would be very much greater if the propensity to consume were very low because in these circumstances the functioning of the economy would depend *almost entirely* on producers' expectations *concerning each other's* expectations. Uncertainty would be so high that an economy of this kind presumably would never start functioning properly. The demand for consumer goods is known to be more stable because much of it is based on rather rigid institutional factors (habits, customs), and in part even on biological properties of mankind. Furthermore, in a full-employment economy with a very low propensity to consume, the ratio of capital stock to output might have to rise considerably all the time. We may take it for granted that filling a very high savings gap (which corresponds to a low propensity to consume) would require *more* capital formation than is compatible with an unchanging capital-output ratio. Technological uncertainty may be higher if constantly changing capital-output ratios (methods of production) are required which are *not* induced by inventions or by preceding shifts in buyers' preferences but have to develop through spontaneous investment activity. In summary, *full employment with extremely low average and marginal propensities to consume is "logically conceivable"* but it would be associated with exceedingly high uncertainty.

moderate wage reductions—the stimulating effect of fall-ing wage costs is stronger or weaker than the adverse effect of the rising uncertainty which is associated with the fall in the propensity to consume. In the event of *extreme* wage reductions the propensity to consume would fall, and the degree of uncertainty would rise, out of proportion to any favorable effect of rising profit margins. A zero-consump-tion economy is an absurdity, and, at the other end, a zero-profit private-enterprise economy also is. Hence, in conditions characterized by low profit margins and a high propensity to consume, a fall in wage rates is likely to exert, on balance, an expansionary influence,[16] while with high profit margins and with a low propensity to consume, rising wage rates may provide a stimulus.[17] But at present we have no definite criteria by which we could tell whether, in a given set of circumstances, these magnitudes are "high" or "low" in the foregoing sense. All we can main-tain with assurance is that it is possible to describe wage rates which are too low for full utilization, just as it is possible to describe wage rates which are too high.

In summary we may conclude that *general* changes in money wage rates cannot be analyzed along given mar-ginal value product functions because these changes tend to shift the product functions. It was suggested that a theory of these interactions should be concerned with the effect of money wage changes on the amount of investment which producers are willing to undertake per unit of simultaneous consumer demand, *and* with the effect of

[16] Because uncertainty is comparatively small *but not zero* if the pro-pensity to consume is high. Therefore, profit margins may be too low to compensate for uncertainty, even if the propensity to consume *is* high, and an increase in profit margins may provide a stimulus even if it oc-curs "at the expense" of the propensity to consume.

[17] Because the uncertainty created by a very low propensity to con-sume may be in excess of what the high profit margins can compensate.

changes in real wage rates on the propensity to consume (thereby also on uncertainty). The first of these effects must be explored in order to find out how the money wage change will be connected with real wage changes. The second effect must be known before a judgment is made on the probable consequences of real wage changes for aggregate employment.

These views imply that, aside from uncertainty, a high investment ratio in relation to total output (low propensity to consume) would do no harm because investment opportunities would be practically inexhaustible. In fact, there are strong *a priori* reasons to assume that an increase in physical product could always be obtained by increased application of capital. This does not exclude zero *net* marginal productivity if factor services are monopolistically overpriced "in just the right way" to produce this result. But in the circumstances here considered this would be most unlikely (aside from uncertainty). For we are concerned with the consequences of a low propensity to consume brought about by low real wage rates, rather than with the overpricing of labor services. As for the possibility of high material prices, these alone are unlikely to exert a general contractionary effect because the materials of one industry are the finished products of others. High prices of materials may, of course, give rise to cyclical depressions via partial overproduction and immobility. But this is another question.

RANGES OF INDETERMINATENESS

Discontinuities—that is, ranges of indeterminateness—may be carried over into the marginal value product functions either from the production functions or from the marginal-revenue functions. Production functions become discontinuous in certain ranges if factor proportions cannot be varied continuously. There is no reason to assume that this should be the case in the long run, in *any* range. But in the short run, factor proportions may be fixed (constant) in a great many plants. In these plants, in the short run, only a bundle of several factors possesses "productivity" but it becomes meaningless to speak of the productivity of the constituent factors individually. Yet, even in the short run, this difficulty is less severe than might appear to be the case at first sight, considering that the proportions in which the factors are combined in different industries are not identical. Over the economy as a whole ("cross-sectionwise") proportions are variable even in the short run: they can be varied by producing more goods in certain plants and less in others. This would eliminate the discontinuities if the plants and industries of an economy represented a continuous array of all conceivable factor proportions. Only to the extent that this is not the case does the marginal-value product of the single factors remain indeterminate in certain ranges.

We may now turn to the discontinuities which are carried over into the marginal value product functions from the marginal-revenue functions (rather than from the technological functions). Aside from the oligopoly problem these might merely justify the general comment that economic theory represents all functions as being smoother than they actually are. The nature and the consequences of these simplifying assumptions are rarely misunderstood. But the oligopoly problem gives rise to a fundamental difficulty.[18]

---

[18] The same difficulty exists if the firm buying or hiring the factors in question sells its product under bilateral monopoly.

Under oligopoly no firm is in a position to estimate the marginal-value product of a factor unless it can make a guess concerning rival reaction to changing individual outputs and prices. This difficulty is merely a reflection of the central problem of oligopoly theory. Consequently, any theory of oligopoly deals indirectly with this difficulty as well as (directly) with the central problem of price and output determination on oligopolistic markets. The views concerning oligopoly expressed in this volume lead to the conclusion that under quasi-agreements the individual marginal value product functions should be defined in view of what behavior must be expected of rivals, on the basis of the quasi-agreement, when the individual firm hires a greater or smaller quantity of a factor and thereby produces more or less output. For changes in input such as comply with quasi-agreements, the value product functions become determinate because the movements of the rival firms are known and so is the effect of these movements on the conditions in which the firm operates. For retaliation and cutthroat competition or unpredictable retaliation the concept of the individual marginal value product function loses its usefulness just as do the individual demand functions. In the absence of quasi-agreements, all these functions shift depending on how the individual firms move along them and depending on the impact under which they move.

WHAT IS INCLUDED IN LONG-RUN ECONOMIC OBJECTIVES

Not all union policies are aimed at securing high wages for the membership or for part of the membership. Certain

economic advantages, while not accruing in the form of
wage payments, can be easily interpreted as the equivalents of wage payments but neither the union nor the firm
may be indifferent as between these various "equivalents."
It might, of course, be maintained that the choice depends
on assumed long-run *economic* consequences, and that,
therefore, we are not here faced with extra-economic
preferences. The same may be maintained concerning all
problems encountered in labor-management relations
which do not fit into the short-run maximization framework. One might argue that the long-run qualification,
which was emphasized in the previous analysis, "takes
care of" all these problems without lifting them out of the
context of economic maximization. Ultimately, one might
argue, firms are interested in maximizing "net-worth"
values for owners, and unions are interested in economic
advantages for members (although the interests of some
owners and of some members may be weighted more
heavily than those of others). We do not consider this a
satisfactory way of looking at *all* objectives by which
persons and institutions are led in their activities pertaining to economic matters. It is a satisfactory way of looking
at a great many of these objectives; a great many are
economic in the long run even if not in the short run. But
persons and institutions may also subordinate certain
economic interests to considerations of a genuinely different sort which cannot properly be regarded as economic
in the long run. Power and prestige, for example, are
partly complementary to economic advantage, but they
may be partly competitive with it, especially if we compare
the power and the prestige of leadership or of influential
groups with the economic advantage of the rank-and-file
member or shareholder. In Chapter V this was discussed

briefly in relation to profit-maximizing units in the usual sense. The same point applies, of course, also to unions, and it may even have a particularly high degree of validity in relation to some. The reason for not going into this matter at greater length is methodological. These aspects of social and economic behavior require a different type of analysis.

APPENDIX ONE

Employment Guarantees and Limited Joint Maximization

The (practical) insignificance of employment guarantees does not require much explanation if we assume that union indifference maps are linear (Figure 16). The equilibrium actually established is marked by the intersection of a wage line with MVP; moving to another point along the same wage line would be harmful to the firm without giving the union additional satisfaction. Neither side is interested in an employment guarantee. The locus of the intersection points of MVP with the wage lines is the contract curve in Edgeworth's sense because it is impossible to move away from this locus curve without harming at least one of the two parties, and it is always possible to give a benefit to one party without harming the other by moving onto this locus curve. It could, of course, not be maintained that the input and the output are of the "ideal," that is, of the "competitive," size: the preferences of the union do not coincide with the marginal preferences of the *labor force*.[1] But neither the firm nor the *union* could gain from an employment guarantee.

However, if the union indifference map is concave (Figure 17), the failure to adopt all-or-none clauses (employment guarantees) does require special explanation. In the absence of such clauses the equilibrium will again be marked by the intersection of a

_____

[1] They are more nearly like *weighted averages* of the preferences of the employed membership (or conceivably of the entire membership).

horizontal wage line with the *MVP* function. Yet the model seems
to indicate that movement away from such an equilibrium *is* possible with benefit to both parties. In Figure 17 an all-or-none
clause *is* required to achieve an equilibrium point that for the
firm is the most favorable point along the union indifference curve
on which it lies, and that for the union is the most favorable point
for the amount of aggregate profit which the firm actually earns.
Without all-or-none clauses the equilibrium is determined by the
intersection of a horizontal wage line with *MVP*. Such an equilibrium point, of course, lies on *some* union indifference curve.
But this is not the firm's most favorable point *along that union
indifference curve*. It is not that point of the union indifference
curve which lies on the contract curve. The firm's most favorable
point along *any* union indifference curve is found by considering
the indifference curve in question, a supply curve, that is to say,
by drawing a marginal curve to the indifference curve and then
finding the intersection point of that marginal curve with the
MVP curve and finally finding that point on the indifference curve
itself which lies vertically above the marginal intersection.[2] This
is a point on the contract curve. It is that point of the contract
curve which lies on the union indifference curve in question. If the
indifference curves are concave, such a point cannot be established
without all-or-none clauses because the intersection point of a
horizontal wage line with *MVP* is *not* such a point along the
MVP curve in question. But if the union indifference maps are
horizontal (Figure 16), the firm's optimal points along any given
union indifference curve become established without all-or-none
clauses because the marginal curve to a horizontal indifference
curve (or, in this case, the marginal curve to a horizontal wage

---

[2] This is completely analogous to monopsony equilibrium. Finding
the firm's most favorable point on a union indifference curve means
making the assumption that the union is willing to stay on the curve as
if it were a supply curve, and then letting the firm choose (cf. the
present writer's *op. cit.*, *Quarterly Journal of Economics*, August 1947).
All points of the contract curve can be found by applying the foregoing
"marginal-intersection method"—or monopsony-equilibrium method—
to the successive union indifference curves. Alternatively, the contract
curve can be found by drawing profit-indifference curves for the firm
(expressing the wage rate—employment combinations yielding equal
aggregate profits) and by connecting the points of tangency of these
curves with the union indifference curves. Cf. Wassily Leontief, "Pure
Theory of the Guaranteed Annual Wage Contract," *Journal of Political
Economy*, February 1946.

line) is the wage line *itself*. Consequently, the method by which the firm's most favorable point along a given indifference curve is found yields in this case the intersection point of a wage line with MVP.

In reality, arrangements in the nature of employment guarantees (all-or-none clauses) are very rare, in spite of the fact that concave union indifference maps may be less rare (cf. page 259). The reason is that firms and unions would find it most difficult to agree on the likelihood of adverse shifts of the value product functions during the lifetime of wage agreements, and, therefore, firms would presumably always insist on an uncertainty discount which exceeds the amount which unions would be willing to "pay" in the form of wage allowances. The guarantee would, of course, have to be unilateral because unions are not sellers in the ordinary sense. If on the level of pure theory we postulate that the bargain will always lie on the contract curve—and this is here the closest analogy to the postulate of joint maximization on product markets —then the unwillingness of firms to guarantee the size of the market for an extended period of time makes for deviations from the postulate. *The outcome will be determined by the intersection of a horizontal wage line with MVP, and—if union indifference maps are concave—this is not on the contract curve.* This qualification of joint maximization applies to labor-management relations specifically. It has no close analogy for oligopoly or for bilateral monopoly on product markets because in these market-structures joint maximization does not require that one participant should unilaterally guarantee the market of the other. The other qualifications of joint maximization to be here considered are analogous to those discussed in connection with bilateral monopoly on product markets (pp. 248). These qualifications arise because (1) firms usually are not interested in the maximization of most probable profits alone but in some compromise between this objective and the maximization of safety margins; [3] (2) firms take long-run considerations into account which cannot be conveniently expressed by the usual functions of value theory, and the analogous statement may in many cases be true of unions; [4] (3) both firms and unions may be "maximizing" pri-

---

[3] Maximization of safety margins against parallel downward shifts of the value product functions would require maximizing the excess of average value product over average wage cost, rather than equating the marginal-value product to the marginal-wage cost.

[4] In other words, the maximum point of the N function in Figure 13

marily for specific groups of owners or members, and while for unions this may already be expressed by the shapes of the union indifference maps themselves, the value product functions apply to firms as a whole, so that the outcome of the analysis may have to be qualified on this account; [5] (4) periods of cutthroat policy create obvious deviations from joint maximization and the desire to avoid cutthroat policies may have the same effect because it may prevent "correct" moves for fear they might be misinterpreted as moves towards cutthroat policies. These qualifications are analogous to those applying to bilateral monopoly on product markets.

APPENDIX TWO

Overtime Work

The model of pages 255ff. was developed on the assumption that the amount of employment (which is measured along the abscissa of Figures 16 and 17) is the same thing as the number of workers employed, that is, that working hours are given. Unless we are willing to make a drastic simplifying assumption, it is impossible to define a single union indifference map for rising wage rates versus rising employment in *both* senses of the term "rising employment." Indifference maps for higher wages versus more workers (given hours) were expressed in Figures 16 and 17. These cannot be expected to have the same shape as the indifference maps for increasing wages versus rising hours (given number of workers). For increasing wages (measured along the ordinate) versus rising hours and given number of workers (measured along the abscissa) the indifference *curves* decline to the right to some "normal" number of hours and beyond this point they rise. This defines the attitude of unions on what may be called the "abnormal-hours market." The preceding sections of

becomes relevant instead of a compromise point between most-probable profit maximization and the maximization of safety margins. Cf. p. 223.

[5] In other words, the N function of Figure 13 should express *effective* ownership interests.

this chapter pertain to the determination of wages and employment on the "normal-hours market." Firms and unions usually
reach wage agreements for both kinds of market. Employment
will be forthcoming on the abnormal-hours market only if some
(marginal) amount of labor is more expensive on the normal-
hours market. Can this be the case, in spite of the fact that the
shape of the union indifference curves on the abnormal-hours
market makes it certain that one and the same worker must be
paid a higher hourly rate for abnormal hours?

The answer is in the affirmative, for two distinct reasons. In
the first place, the indivisibilities of equipment may require that
(say) eight extra hours should be performed on eight different
pieces of equipment rather than eight hours by one extra worker
on one piece of equipment. Secondly, shortages may exist on the
normal-hours market. In other words, at the ruling wage rate,
the labor supply curve of the normal-hours market (Figure 16)
may intersect with the wage line in question to the left of the
intersection point of the wage line with the MVP function (cf.
page 262). In this event the firm cannot hire on the normal-hours
market more workers than the number indicated by the supply
curve for the ruling wage rate. It will not be profitable for the
firm to move to higher wages along the supply curve *of the
normal-hours market* because it must be assumed that the established wage line is higher than the monopsony wage rate,[1] and
at the monopsony wage rate the firm would be hiring a number
of workers for which the marginal labor cost equals MVP. Any
further increase in wage rates along the supply curve would give
rise to marginal labor costs that exceed the marginal-value product. This is true even if we start from the monopsony wage rate,
and it is true *a fortiori* if the established wage rate exceeds the
monopsony rate. Therefore, if shortages exist in the sense that
at the established wage rate the supply curve of the normal-
hours market indicates a smaller number of workers than the
number which the employers would like to hire at that wage rate,
they will not bid up the wage rate along the supply curve of the
normal-hours market. They will hire the available number at the
going wage rate. The slope of the supply curve of the normal-
hours market is too high to induce them to bid up the wage rate,
and, therefore, it is also too high to destroy their resistance
against union claims to raise the level of the established wage

---

[1] Or that in the limiting case it *is* the monopsony wage rate.

rate. The slope of the supply curve of the normal-hours market depends, of course, on the raise it takes to attract workers from other occupations or from idleness. However, while in these circumstances it is too expensive to attract workers from elsewhere, it may not be too expensive to hire the "own" labor force for more hours. The upward slope of the union indifference curves for a given number of workers and for rising hours may be smaller than the upward slope of the competitive labor supply curve for normal hours.

Earlier we saw that in certain ranges the labor supply curve of the normal-hours market may be backward rising. However, in the contemporary institutional setting the significance of supply curves is reduced to particular instances of shortage. Here it should be emphasized that the basic psychological assumptions, which on the normal-hours market may express themselves in a backward-rising supply curve, find a somewhat different expression on the overtime market. The indifference curves for rising wages versus rising hours (given number of workers) slopes downward up to some normal number of hours and turns up thereafter. The minimum point of the various indifference curves is likely to lie the more to the left, the higher we move up along the ordinate (wage-rate axis). In other words, the length of the "normal" working week becomes shorter as wage incomes rise. The reasons are similar to those which may produce backward-sloping supply functions on the normal-hours market.

CHAPTER ELEVEN

Problems of Appraisal and Policy

THIS concluding chapter is concerned with some consequences of fewness and with problems of policy. We
shall first consider oligopoly and then turn to the bilateral-monopoly relationships involved in collective bargaining.

THE STATIC AND THE DYNAMIC
VIEWPOINT

The broadening of oligopolistic market structures,
that is, increasing the number of competitors in oligopolistic industries, would in certain instances be associated with a real-cost disadvantage on a static level, while
in others it would not be. It would be associated with a
real (social) cost disadvantage in Case 1a (production
costs) and Case 1b (selling costs), as defined on pages 44–
9. Even in cases where a real-cost disadvantage would

develop on a static level, such broadening might be socially desirable, provided the real-cost disadvantage is not very substantial, and especially if the disadvantage expresses itself more in the relationship of selling cost to obtainable revenue than in production cost. This is because the broadening of oligopolistic structures and the loosening of oligopolistic co-ordination is likely to increase the incompleteness of quasi-agreements concerning technological progress and product variation. It is likely to result in more non-price competition, and hence in more rapid progress. In some cases it might also result in more price competition.

That forced broadening of market structures—that is, increased competition—*may* go with real-cost disadvantages is a consequence of the fact that the reduction of the number of firms (reduced competition) is associated with the growth of individual firms and hence with more complete exploitation of intra-plant economies as well as of inter-plant economies. The intra-plant economies are those obtainable along cost functions applying to individual plants when managed separately; the inter-plant economies are those obtainable when an increasing number of plants becomes included under the same unit of management. However, the broadening of oligopolistic structures *need not* be associated with real-cost disadvantages because the reduction of the number of firms (reduced competition) may also be accompanied by intra-plant and inter-plant diseconomies, as the size of the individual firms grows. These diseconomies may outweigh the economies obtainable by reducing the number of firms. If this is the case, the broadening of the market structures (increased competition) will go with real-cost advantages. Nevertheless, such broadening may not materialize automati-

cally because the existing oligopolistic firms may find
it profitable not to reduce their size, owing to non-real-cost
advantages accruing from the exploitation of oligopoly
power or oligopsony power, or owing to specific advantages which may accrue to controlling groups from size.
The financial superiority of the existing large firms or
certain exclusive rights (discriminatory treatment) which
they enjoy may keep out potential entrants of smaller
size who would have *real* (social) cost advantages over
them.

We shall first argue that the broadening of market
structures (increased competition) might be justifiable
even in cases where it would result in some real-cost disadvantage on a static level. However, such a policy would
have to adopt arbitrary, *ad hoc* criteria of weighing real-
cost disadvantages against other advantages of increased
competition. This is a substantial drawback. It may,
therefore, be desirable to concentrate *mainly* on the broadening of market structures where such broadening does not
go with real-cost disadvantages on a static level. To try
to atomize oligopolistic industries, that is, to try to eliminate oligopoly regardless of real costs, is not a well-chosen
policy objective in the given institutional and technological
setting.

Let us now turn to the reasons why the broadening of
market structures might be considered socially desirable
even where it would be associated with real-cost disadvantages on a static level, provided these would not be very
substantial. As was said before, the real-cost disadvantages
may be outweighed by the social advantages of increased
competition in technological change and product variation.
For the same reason the further narrowing of market
structures may be undesirable even where it would be

accompanied by real-cost advantages on the static level.

We have reasons to believe [1] that in the American economy, during the inter-war period, output per man-hour rose at an average yearly compound rate of between 2 and 3 per cent. This is not a precise measure of the consequences of technological and organizational change because movements along given production functions may also bring changes in man-hour output and, on the other hand, improvement does not express itself in changing man-hour output alone. But that the change in man-hour output is more intimately connected with improvement than with any other factor is highly probable. A substantial reduction of the rate of technological and organizational improvement would slow down significantly the rate of increase in man-hour output. Productivity (output per unit of input) did not rise at equal rates in the various past periods that we can distinguish, and extrapolating into the future is always a doubtful procedure. But it is legitimate to argue that, in the industrialized economies of our civilization, productivity has consistently risen at a very significant rate, and that the doubling of productivity within considerably less than the lifetime of a generation has probably been quite common. The signifi-

---

[1] E. E. Hagen and Mrs. N. B. Kirkpatrick (*American Economic Review*, September 1944) arrived at a 34 per cent total increase for real output *per worker*, for the period 1923–40. The increase *per man-hour*, which must have been in excess of the foregoing rise, was not estimated by these authors for the economy as a whole but only for a segment of the economy consisting of manufacturing, mining, railway transportation, electric power and gas utilities, and construction. They arrived at a 78 per cent increase for the seventeen years considered. Morris Livingston in *Markets After the War* (Washington, D. C., 1943) estimated the overall increase in man-hour output in the American economy at a yearly compound rate of 2.5 per cent, for the period 1929–41. He added that "there is ample evidence of about the same rate of gain during the preceding thirty years."

cance of this phenomenon outweighs the importance of a great many that can be observed on a static level of analysis.

When we stress the dynamic aspects of the problem, the general case against monopoly appears to be stronger than the case against oligopoly, and the case against narrower oligopoly stronger than against broader oligopoly, except when the static cost disadvantage is *substantial* and except when even that amount of uncertainty which goes with increased oligopolistic competition is considered excessive. It seems reasonable to maintain as a general proposition that a market structure compares favorably with another if it brings *somewhat* worse allocation of resources on a "static" level but, at the same time, markedly speeds up technological advance, especially if it also improves the distribution of income. Undoubtedly, a broadening of industrial structures would frequently stimulate progress and a further narrowing of market structures would impede it. The looser the co-operation with respect to technological change in general and product variation in particular, the more of it is there likely to be. The more incomplete the co-ordination of business policies with respect to these variables, the more likely does it become that firms introduce changes which are partly at the expense of competitors rather than merely the changes which a monopolist would also adopt. In loosely co-operating oligopoly a change may be introduced because it increases the bargaining strength of a firm in the group, or because it improves the profitability of a firm and worsens that of the others even without changing relative bargaining strength (as would be the case if, with given relative strength, the ruling market price always lay midway between the price which is in the best interest of A and that which is in the best interest of B).

The narrower the group, the tighter the co-ordination of policies is likely to be, and the more will change be limited to the merely monopolistic rate. In completely co-ordinated oligopoly only "monopolistic" changes would be introduced, that is, changes at a rate justified by the increase in the joint profit, on the basis of a calculation in which all past fixed costs are valued at zero. In loosely co-operating oligopoly the rate of progress is greater because the individual net profit may rise by further innovating activity even if the joint profit does not.[2] Part of the so-called progress calls forth adverse value judgments from the majority of reasonable persons. The market does not distinguish between the desirable kind of product variation (product improvement), and the illusory kind; it does not distinguish between the informative kind of advertising and the "superfluous" or the misleading kind. Progress in the true sense is accompanied by "progress" in the sense of creating and of satisfying bad taste and bad judgment, and by charging the costs of this to the buyer

---

[2] However, in deciding on the profitability of an innovation the oligopolist will tend to value his fixed cost at zero, and entrants (if entry is possible) will know that the existing firms will base their defensive moves on such a calculation. In pure competition the rate of progress would be increased by the fact that innovating entrants take the ruling price as given and the price expresses the *total* cost, not merely the *variable* cost, of the existing firms. In other words, in pure competition, an innovation will be introduced if the new total cost is smaller than the old total cost and the old firms will have to adjust their prices to those of the innovating entrants (whose number is determined by the elasticity of the market-demand). Under monopoly the new total cost must fall short of the old variable cost before the new process is introduced or affects the price, because the old fixed cost is disregarded. In loosely colluding oligopoly, the new total cost *minus the gains at the expense of rivals* must fall short of the old variable cost. One might conclude from this that progress is fastest under atomistic competition. This, however, must be qualified by the statement that in the absence of the research facilities of large-scale enterprise, inventions might be forthcoming at a considerably slower rate. Furthermore, in some cases uncertainty might be very high and this impedes progress through excessive charges for obsolescence.

as though they were the costs of producing a superior commodity. But promoting monopolization and the narrowing of market structures is no way of improving the ideals of Western society. Monopolization impedes not only the "spurious" varieties of progress; it impedes progress in general.

Owing to the incompleteness of oligopolistic co-ordination, there is more uncertainty under oligopoly than under monopoly, and more uncertainty in broader than in narrower oligopoly. The profit expectations of the oligopolist are subject to the uncertainities which attach to the expectations of the monopolist plus the uncertainties deriving from the incompleteness of co-ordination and from the increased rate of change. But to reduce uncertainty by promoting monopoly would mean seeking the kind of certainty which is incompatible with progress. Avoidance of excessive price fluidity that makes it difficult to "calculate" should surely not stand in the way of broadening oligopolistic structures.

The appraisal of atomistic competition is a different matter. An attempt to transform oligopolistic structures into atomistic ones would not go with "some" real-cost disadvantage on the static level but usually with a prohibitive disadvantage. Furthermore, such an attempt might frequently create a degree of uncertainty which impedes adjustments and progress. Pure competition (atomistic but not "perfect" competition) automatically becomes approximated in certain segments of the economy although even these segments do not fully satisfy the conditions of pure competition. The mere fact that in many periods quasi-chronic difficulties have arisen in connection with the industries most closely approximating pure competition does not prove that competition is excessive in these industries. In the first place, the coexistence of highly competitive industries with very imperfectly competitive ones raises problems which need not arise in an all-round highly competitive economy. Secondly, the extent to which the difficulties of an industry are emphasized and the extent to which government intervention is forthcoming depend largely on the distribution of political power in the community rather than on more purely economic circumstances. But, while experience has not established the proposition that pure competition is bad if it tends to develop automatically along the most efficient cost functions, it has also not established the proposition that all-round atomistic competition would be desirable. We do not know what an all-round purely competitive world would look like. Even if it did tend to develop automatically along the cheapest available cost functions, there might conceivably be an "excessive" amount of change in such a world—an "excessive" degree of price fluidity and of shifts in demand and production functions, in consequence of which adjustments might all the time be so far from being "completed" that serious trouble might become perennial. *If* this were so, long-run trends might also suffer from the stability.[3] Furthermore, the fact is obvious that all-round atomistic competition does not tend to develop automatically along the cheapest available cost functions and that the real costs of enforcing such a state of affairs would be exceedingly high.

All this is recognized by those who, in recent years, developed the concept of "workable" rather than "pure" competition, that is, particularly by Professor J. M. Clark and Professor Howard S. Ellis.[4] The main implica-

---

[3] As for the rate of technological progress, cf. footnote on p. 287.

[4] Of the extended literature pertaining to this problem, cf. mainly

tion of a program of workable competition is to decide, on
the basis of the specific information available for individual industries, what degree of competition is obtainable
by methods of practical policy without substantial loss
of technological efficiency at the time when the policy is
adopted, and does not presumably create a degree of
uncertainty such as would offset the advantages. What is
obtainable by method of practical policy is an involved
question about which a specialist in politics is likely to
know more than most economists. As for the maximum
degree of competition which is compatible with efficient
methods of production and does not create "excessive"
uncertainty, it is very likely that this is considerably
higher than the competition which becomes automatically
established in oligopolistic industries. The degree of competition which oligopolistic firms consider to be desirable
from their own point of view is likely to fall short of the
social optimum by a considerable margin. Conceivably,
in some of the atomistic industries there is "too much"
competition. But in oligopolistic industries a considerably
higher degree of competition than that which exists would
usually be quite "workable."

The gradual narrowing of oligopoly into monopoly is

J. M. Clark, "Toward a Concept of Workable Competition," *American
Economic Review*, June 1940, and Howard S. Ellis, "Economic Expansion through Competitive Markets" in *Financing American Prosperity* (Twentieth Century Fund, 1945). Also an earlier article by Paul
T. Homan, discussing the bearing of this general problem on anti-trust
policy, "Notes on the Anti-Trust Law Policy," reprinted from the 1939
volume of the *Quarterly Journal of Economics* in *Readings in the Social
Control of Industry* (Philadelphia and Toronto, 1942). A highly interesting discussion of these problems is contained in Corwin D. Edwards,
Maintaining Competition (New York, 1949) which unfortunately ap-
peared too late for thorough perusal for the present volume.

justifiable in those exceptional cases where the technical economies of monopolistic concentration are substantial up to the extreme degree of concentration and where the avoidance of uncertainty is so important that even "oligopolistic uncertainty" is excessive. Where these circumstances seem to outweigh the disadvantage of slower progress, narrower oligopoly may be superior to the broader, and monopoly may be superior to oligopoly. The deliberate establishment of government-supervised monopolies in certain areas (utilities, communication, and so forth) should presumably be attributed to the conviction that, in the areas in question, these conditions are satisfied. Where these conditions are not satisfied, monopoly is inferior to oligopoly, from the social point of view, and narrow oligopoly (which approximates monopoly more closely) is inferior to broader oligopoly (in which the competitive element is likely to be stronger). Usually the static real-cost advantages of high concentration must be significant to justify it from the general economic point of view. They must outweigh the dynamic disadvantages.

It also follows that restricting atomistic competition (that is, restricting pure but not perfect competition) where it tends to develop automatically is justified only in the cases where a combination of uncertainty and of immobility creates conditions under which a reasonable development of the areas in question is seriously hampered. Such areas may very well exist. The writer would be unwilling to argue that they exist in no branch of farming or of retail trade or of the service industries. But great caution is required here because organized attempts to secure restriction are far more frequent than are the instances in which "Case 3 restriction" is justified.

ANTI-TRUST POLICY

Let us now turn more specifically to the policy problems to which "Case 1a," "Case 1b," and "Case 2" oligopoly give rise (cf. pages 44–9).

In case 1a oligopoly, competition could be increased only by forcing the firms onto more expensive cost-of-production functions.[5] Such intervention could be justified in cases where the real-cost disadvantage of broadening the market structure is not so substantial as to outweigh the advantages of increased competition and progress. This may frequently be true, but it must be admitted that vague and arbitrary criteria would have to be applied in most individual instances.

In Case 1b oligopoly competition could be broadened by prohibiting certain sales techniques which bring increasing returns over a wide range of individual output. This may be feasible and highly desirable in some instances. More vigorous action against misrepresentation would certainly be justified.[6] But whether substantial

---

[5] The size of the firms would have to be reduced by limiting their activities (by "dissolving" large units), and this would result in higher costs.

[6] It is sometimes maintained that this kind of policy problem calls for consumer representation in policy formation. What consumer representation means is not obvious, considering that practically all persons have producer's interests as well as consumer's interests. In other words it is not obvious what is meant beyond the statement that public-minded persons should have an influence on policy formation. (Cf. Ben W. Lewis, "The 'Consumer' and 'Public' Interests under Public Regulation," reprinted from the 1938 volume of the *Journal of Political Economy* in *Readings in the Social Control of Industry*.) Advocates of "consumer representation" probably are led by the desire to see persons represented who have good reasons to assume that the specific policy measures in question have a comparatively small effect on their money income and a comparatively great effect on their well-being via prices

reduction of Case 1b oligopoly could be accomplished along these lines is doubtful because the sales techniques resulting in oligopoly may be simple techniques of calling attention to the existence of a brand. They need not include misrepresentation or even debatable assertions. Publicizing the fact that someone is selling a specific brand of a commodity can scarcely be made punishable; yet such publicity alone can bring increasing returns over a wide range and it may give rise to 1b oligopoly. Misrepresentation is a substantial evil in itself. But the oligopoly-creating effect of sales techniques need not mainly (or even largely) stem from "misrepresentation." False statements favor something that is worse than is pretended, potentially at the expense of something that is better. They may in some cases also favor the big at the expense of the small but it is not clear that they do this regularly on a major scale. Publicity in general does tend to favor the big at the expense of the small but publicity in general cannot be made a violation.

In Case 2 oligopoly the big firms have no real-cost advantage over smaller entrants. Competition can be broadened by forcing the firms to divest themselves of exclusive rights (discriminatory advantages) and by preventing the use of financial superiority for beating down entrants. For, in Case 2 oligopoly potential entrants are being kept out by these discriminatory or predatory practices. In the hybrid forms of Case 1 and Case 2, where

---

and product quality. It is not desirable that policy decisions should be made on the assumption that they affect prices and product quality greatly without affecting money incomes. But it may be argued that influential producer groups have good reasons to assume that the policy measures in which they take an interest have a comparatively great effect on their money incomes and a comparatively small effect on their well-being via the prices and the quality of the products they consume. Consequently "consumer representation" may tend to create an offset.

the real-cost advantage of big firms results in oligopoly, but further concentration develops from financial superiority or from exclusive rights, the policies appropriate to Case 2 can be used to broaden the oligopoly. Such broadening may be expected to make the oligopolistic co-ordination of business policies less tight, especially with respect to the dynamic variables (technological progress, product variation, and so forth). These policies appropriate to Case 2, and to the hybrid forms of Case 1 and Case 2, consists of forcing oligopolists to sell part of their property in those natural resources that they own exclusively; or of forcing the owners of patents or the producers of the raw-material-producing industry,[7] or the unions of the oligopolistic industry itself, or the producers of the finished-product-purchasing industry,[8] or the firms of the transporting industry [9] to deal with outsiders on the same terms as with the oligopolistic group in question; or, if these producers of the other industries are the same firms as those constituting the oligopolistic group in question,[10] of forcing these firms to deal with outsiders on fair terms. *All these are methods of forcing firms to divest themselves of exclusive rights (discriminatory advantages).* However, Case 2 oligopoly—or the "Case 2" element in the hybrid forms of Case 1 and Case 2 oligopoly —may be the consequence of the misuse of financial superiority as well as of the existence of exclusive rights. The methods available for *preventing the beating down of*

---

[7] The industry from which the oligopolistic group buys its raw materials.

[8] The industry which purchases the goods produced by the oligopoly.

[9] The industry which transports the raw materials or the finished goods of the oligopolistic industry.

[10] That is, if the oligopolistic group in question dominates one of the industries described in the preceding three footnotes.

entrants by the misuse of financial superiority range from punishing those applying cutthroat tactics against technically efficient entrants to directly supporting technically efficient entrants by means of credit policy. Cutthroat tactics against entrants express themselves in different policies when entry threatens than when it does not.

If these policies could be carried out fully and with complete precision, the prevention of mergers and the dissolution of giant units would not be required to prevent concentration that is "unjustified" in terms of real costs. Direct interference with size would not be required to prevent Case 2 oligopoly or the Case 2 element in hybrid forms of Case 1 and Case 2 oligopoly. It would not be required to prevent concentration that is not justified by real-cost advantages. This is because the Case 2 element— the element not justified by real-cost advantages—would always be eliminated by the competition of entrants. Direct interference with size might still be justified in certain Case 1 instances, namely in those in which the broadening of the market structure is associated with real-cost disadvantages, but these are not great enough to offset the prospective social gains of broadening (in view of the expected loosening of co-operation, especially with respect to non-price variables). Aside from these instances, direct interference with size would not be justified if the policies of the preceding paragraph could be fully realized. But these policies cannot be fully realized in practice, and consequently the prevention of mergers that are not justified by real economies would be a desirable supplementary policy in any event.

One of the disconcerting circumstances attending antitrust policy is the lack of definiteness of the criteria on which it is compelled to proceed. It is therefore desirable to emphasize primarily the policies which can be based on comparatively "definite" criteria, or at least on criteria which are less vague than those underlying some of the alternative policies. *On the whole it seems that suppression of the Case 2 element in oligopoly structures can be based on comparatively articulate criteria.* Generally speaking this is much less true of policies which aim at the broadening of some market structure in spite of the real-cost advantages of concentration (Case 1 oligopoly). Here usually the criteria on which individual instances would have to be decided become distinctly vaguer, although this may not be true of special instances where "reason" clearly indicates that small *static* advantages of concentration are outweighed by *substantial* dynamic disadvantages.[11] Most oligopolistic structures seem to be hybrid forms of Case 1 and Case 2 oligopoly, and the Case 2 element seems to be considerable.[12] The foregoing considerations favor placing the emphasis *primarly* on reducing and, if possible, eliminating the Case 2 element, except for that amount of "artificial exclusion" through patent and trade-mark protection which is deemed necessary to stimulate inventive activity.[13] As a rule it is too difficult to

---

[11] Also, suppression of Case 1b oligopoly is clearly desirable whenever it rests on misrepresentation.

[12] Cf. Howard S. Ellis, Financing American Prosperity (*op. cit.*) p. 179.

[13] That oligopoly is partly a consequence not of real-cost advantages but of the possession of certain high-grade resources and of exclusive rights (or special treatment) obtained from other industries or from other stages in the structure of production has been shown in various studies pertaining to the history of specific industries (petroleum, moving pictures, aluminum, etc.). In addition TNEC monograph No. 13, U. S. Federal Trade Commission, *Relative Efficiency of Large, Medium-Sized and Small Business* (Washington, D. C., 1941), submits data which point to the likelihood that in a great many industries the biggest firms may not be those operating at the lowest real cost. An interesting discussion of recent data pertaining to this problem is found in John M. Blair, "Technology and Size," *American Economic Review*,

distinguish those "Case 1a" instances in which action is justified from those in which it is not. Energetic action against misrepresentation in advertising would undoubtedly be justified. This might automatically reduce 1b oligopoly to some extent but to what extent is questionable.

An anti-trust policy which tries to avoid significant real-cost disadvantages may result in a considerable broad-

---

Papers and Proceedings, May 1947. This paper also contains some discussion of earlier findings, e.g., of those of A. S. Dewing in *Quarterly Journal of Economics*, November 1921, which focused attention on these matters. It is not even obvious that the real-cost disadvantage of size (whenever such disadvantage exists) is outweighed by other (oligopolistic or oligopsonistic) exploitative advantages for the firm as a whole. Incentives to maintain excessive size may result from specific gains accruing to controlling groups—managerial or financial groups. Excessive size may also be the result of misjudgment. In this connection it is interesting to note that for the years 1931–36 Professor Crum has found a general tendency for the rate of earnings of corporations to rise with the size of assets but this tendency becomes *very much* weaker in the high-asset classes than in the lower classes. For some years and some industries the tendency is even *reversed* for the high-asset classes (i.e., for a transition from high to even higher classes). The "over 100 million dollars" class could be examined separately only for 1936, since for the earlier years the data of this group are merged with the other "over 50 millions" corporations. For 1936 the rate of earnings of the aggregate of "all corporations," not merely that of specific subgroups, *falls* for the transition from the next-to-highest class (over 50 millions) to the highest class (over 100 millions), although it rises up to the next-to-highest class. Superficial inspection of data pertaining to later years makes the present writer suspect that this behavior is rather generally characteristic of the transition from the "over 50 millions" class to the "over 100 millions" class. Moreover, Crum found a *general* tendency for the rate of earnings to *fall* with increasing assets when he examined merely those corporations which made positive profits, that is, when he excluded deficit corporations. Cf. William Leonard Crum, *Corporate Size and Earning Power* (Cambridge, Mass., 1939). This raises the question whether the tendency of the rate of earnings to fall with increasing assets is not *generally* characteristic of the economy in periods in which the weight attaching to deficit corporations is smaller than was the case during the period 1931–36. At least in two years during the nineteen-twenties this actually seems to have been the case (cf. Ralph C. Epstein, *Industrial Profits in the United States* New York, 1934).

ening of oligopolistic structures, but it cannot result in
their elimination. In pure instances of Case 2 oligopoly,
atomistic competition may be approximated by such a
policy, but this would undoubtedly be exceptional. However, the broadening of oligopolistic structures up to the
point where the policy runs into appreciable real-cost disadvantages is a highly desirable objective, mainly because
the spontaneous co-ordination of business policies in general, and especially co-operation with respect to the
dynamic variables (pertaining to progress) is likely to be
looser under the broader types of oligopoly.

The question arises here whether the discrimination involved in freight absorption and phantom-freight charges
falls under the same heading as the kind of discrimination
or special treatment (exclusive rights) which creates Case
2 oligopoly. The answer is in the negative. Special treatment or discrimination *is* involved in the basing-point
system because various customers are not treated identically in terms of the costs to which they give rise but there
is no presumption that better treatment of distant customers coupled with worse treatment of nearby customers
fosters monopoly among buyers more than does contrary
treatment of these classes of customers. Freight absorption merely *reshuffles* the monopoly element inherent in
space, it does not *create* this monopoly element, while
discrimination in other respects tends to create monopoly
or oligopoly. Therefore, the discrimination involved in
freight absorption is a distinct problem.

This problem would arise even if the number of firms
was large and if there was no co-operation between the
firms because the spatial monopoly element would still
make it possible for each firm to discriminate in the mill-
net equivalent of its various sales. Each firm would favor

distant customers who are nearer its competitor and this amounts to freight absorption. However, pricing formulae based on co-ordinated action result in *systematic* freight-absorption, and sometimes in phantom-freight charges. For example, the hotly contested basing-point system expresses itself in charging to each customer the freight *from* the "basing point" nearest to him *to* the destination. This is a systematic method of setting delivered prices in accordance with relative strength. It leads to freight absorption on all deliveries going to destinations which are nearer to some basing point than to the mill which makes the delivery. Furthermore, the basing point system leads to charging phantom-freight (fictitious freight) whenever not all mills are located in basing points. If we were faced with independent, non-collusive local monopolies, they would presumably charge no phantom-freight. But, as we have seen, they would absorb freight in some unpredictable fashion. Their policies would be as unpredictable as are generally those of a fighting, differentiated oligopoly. They would not charge uniform mill-net prices to each customer of a mill. Uniform mill pricing would emerge automatically only if there were a great many mills in each center of production. This would result not merely in uniform mill pricing but in pricing at the competitive level.

Abolition of the basing-point system coupled with enforcement of f.o.b. mill pricing, would tend to result in the expansion of output in certain areas and contraction in others. Output would tend to expand in the basing-point neighborhoods which were locally undersupplied under the basing-point system (importing neighborhoods) and it would tend to contract in the neighborhoods of local excess. Each firm would reach out less far if distant sales necessitated price reductions in its vicinity. Under the constraint introduced by the abolition of the basing-point system, the desirable (and therefore the actual) relative share of certain firms would become smaller. This may increase or decrease unit social production costs (real costs),[14] or it may leave them approximately unchanged. It is obvious that no generally valid statement can be made on whether unit production costs (real costs) will rise or fall or whether they will remain unchanged. This depends on the cost conditions under which the specific firms of the various areas operate. In the expanding areas old firms may increase their output or new firms may enter but even entry leaves the question open whether unit production costs for the industry as a whole will rise or fall. The likelihood of entry is the greater the greater the number of basing-point neighborhoods which are characterized by very small output or zero output. The policy of nationally uniform delivered prices is, for example, the equivalent of a basing-point system with a practically infinite number of zero-output basing points because each buyer is by definition located in a basing point. The policy of establishing one or more basing points in centers of production, and nowhere else, differs from this in that none of the importing basing-point neighborhoods is characterized by zero (or small) output and consequently the *a priori* presumption for new entries in the event of f.o.b. mill pricing is weaker because, in the previously importing neighborhoods, old firms may expand their output when the output of other areas contracts. But this alone does

---

[14] By using the phrase "real costs" we mean to say that cost changes resulting from a changing degree of oligoposonistic exploitation should be disregarded.

not *decide* whether new entries will or will not occur, and
the occurrence of new entries does not decide whether unit
production costs in the industry will or will not occur. It
should be obvious what kind of specific information would
be required for predicting the effect on production costs.
If new entries do occur, the chances that unit production
costs for the industry will not rise, or will fall, are the
better the stronger the Case 2 element in the original
(spatially differentiated) oligopoly is. But the effect on
production costs *may* be unfavorable even if we are faced
with a pure instance of Case 2 oligopoly because, while in
this event the *appropriate* new entries would not raise production costs, entries *in the specific areas* into which they
are induced by f.o.b. mill pricing may raise production
costs.

On the other hand, the effect on unit *transportation cost*
is predictable. F.o.b. mill pricing should be expected to
reduce transportation costs for the output of the industry
in question, since importing areas will tend to expand and
exporting areas to contract. Transportation costs for the
raw materials of the industry may fall or rise but this is a
different problem because these enter into the *production
costs* which were previously considered.

If under f.o.b. mill pricing the freight saving is precisely offset by a rise in social production costs, then f.o.b.
mill pricing *may* still be socially preferable because it
eliminates the price discrimination. *Given the total unit
cost* this discrimination raises profits and hence reduces
buyers' advantages in each deal. But it is not generally
advisable to build policy on this consideration alone because it is uncertain whether, with given unit cost, price
discrimination increases or reduces output. This depends

on circumstances which probably cannot be appraised in advance with sufficient accuracy in any real situation.[15] If, given the total unit cost, price discrimination increases output, the social advantages of this increase for the economy as a whole should be set against the disadvantage of higher profits at the expense of buyers, and it would be difficult to arrive at general conclusions in this respect.

We conclude that there exists a case for the abolition of the basing-point system or its equivalents (for example, uniform delivered prices), and for the enforcement of f.o.b. mill pricing if the regional adjustments of output, to which f.o.b. mill pricing leads, are unlikely to result in appreciably higher real (social) production costs and if transportation costs are significant for the commodity in question.[16] Furthermore, there exists a case for the abolition of the basing point system and for letting producers substitute some other method of freight-absorption for it, if this is likely to reduce social cost and increase output. Otherwise there does not seem to be much point in proceeding against the basing point system, unless the problem possesses certain particular characteristics in some industry (unless, for example, the basing-point system is

---

[15] Cf. Joan Robinson, *The Economics of Imperfect Competition* (London, 1933), Book V. The answer depends on the relationship between the elasticity and the concavity of the various demand curves into which the discriminating monopolies divide the market-demand curve. If higher elasticity goes with greater concavity then this tends to increase the output under discrimination beyond what it would be in the absence of discrimination.

[16] Even in this event it is not *certain* that f.o.b. mill pricing raises output because *aside from the saving in total cost*, the abandonment of discrimination *might* reduce output. Moreover, in a period of private rationing (when prices may be kept below industry-optimum owing to political or other long-run considerations), producers may make use of the change for raising their mill-net prices beyond the previous mill-net equivalent of their delivered prices. This may of course offset or outweigh any advantages in the short-run.

operated in such a way as to secure special treatment to a monopolistic or oligopolistic group in another industry while the regional price differences under f.o.b. pricing would not happen to have this effect). The general argument that the basing-point system is bad because it is a typically non-competitive feature is unconvincing. In an industry consisting of local monopolies, competitive pricing could be enforced only by prescribing the methods of pricing, not by prohibiting a specific method of charging freight. Local monopolies with overlapping territories tend to absorb freight and, even if they are forced to charge uniform mill-net prices to their customers, they tend to develop spontaneous co-ordination in the setting of their prices. Competitive pricing could be enforced only by prescribing the level of specific prices in accordance with competitive norms. This of course we are not prepared to do.

A similar dilemma develops not only in connection with freight problems but with respect to anti-trust policy in general. The anti-trust acts make all monopolization, any attempt at monopolization, and all combination in restraint of trade illegal, except of course for such organized restrictions which have been made legal by subsequent legislative action.[17] The philosophy of the acts is obviously too broad to be fully applicable. This was recognized by the courts and they have interpreted the acts as applying

---

[17] Applying mainly to farmers, workers, retailers. The regulation of the bituminous coal industry also falls in this category. Organized restriction in the service industries is not usually a problem of interstate commerce and hence it is subject to state legislation. All these are instances of Case 3 restriction. Cf. Ewald T. Grether, *Price Control Under Fair Trade Legislation* (New York, 1939); W. F. Brown and R. Casady, "Guild Pricing in the Service Industries," *Quarterly Journal of Economics* (February 1947); cf. also TNEC monograph No. 21. (Clair Wilcox, *op. cit.*).

merely to *unreasonable* restraints of trade.[18] What would
be the economically desirable interpretation of "unreasonable restraints," and what has legal practice actually
included?

Except for the necessary degree of patent protection
and the like, Case 2 oligopoly and the corresponding
monopoly cases should clearly be included (cf. page
293). Legal practice agrees with this, except that it has not
always been vigorous. The legal term corresponding to
Case 2 oligopoly is artificial exclusion of competitors or
of potential competitors, by means of discriminatory or
predatory practices. If there were no artificial exclusion,
there would be no Case 2 oligopoly. Truly complete elimination of artifical exclusion would do away with all
oligopoly elements except those based on real-cost advantages (some of which may be "suspect" selling advantages,
but preventing unfair sales techniques is presumably a
distinct task of policy). The remaining oligopoly power
could not be exploited beyond limits set by the real-cost
advantages of the oligopolists because at those limits new
entrants would appear. Beating them down by temporary

---

[18] For a discussion of legal *practice* in these matters, cf. Milton Hand-
ler, *A Study of Construction and Enforcement of the Federal Anti-trust
Laws*, TNEC monograph 38; and Corwin D. Edwards, *Maintaining
Competition* (New York, 1949); also the papers of Wendell Berge and
Estes Kefauver in *The American Economic Review, Papers and Proceed-
ing*, May 1948. For a discussion of early judicial interpretation and
trust history, cf. also Henry R. Seager and Charles A. Gulick, Jr.,
Trust and Corporation Problems (New York, 1929); M. W. Watkins,
Industrial Combinations and Public Policy (New York, 1927); Joe S.
Bain, "Industrial Concentration and Government Anti-trust Policy,"
in *The Growth of American Economy*, ed. Harold F. Williamson (New
York, 1944). For a discussion of important recent decisions, and for
specific references to these, cf. M. A. Adelman's article in the September 1948 issue of the *Harvard Law Review* and Eugene Rostow's
article in the January-February 1949 issue of the *Illinois Law Review*.

cutthroat tactics is of course artificial exclusion by a predatory practice.

The courts have always considered artifical exclusion an unreasonable restraint of trade. While in several cases successful action was forthcoming against artifical exclusion,[19] past enforcement was frequently lax. It seems to be becoming more vigorous at present. This expresses itself mostly in interference with discriminatory practices of vertically integrated firms *in favor of their own subsidiaries*.[20] Thorough coverage of the area of artificial exclusion would be a great accomplishment. In principle this alone could eliminate all Case 2 oligopoly, that is, all oligopoly not based on real-cost advantages. In practice it would be desirable to supplement such a policy with the power to prevent large mergers and new acquisitions such as are not justified in terms of real cost. This, however, would presumably require new legislation.[21]

---

[19] The dissolution of the oil and the tobacco trust in 1911 was based largely on the finding relating to such practices. The dissolutions were successful in the sense that no firm, or even interest group, possesses a market-share comparable to those of the trusts dissolved. But oligopoly power has of course not been eliminated from these markets. Artificial exclusion was charged also in the International Harvester case, in which the corporation agreed to reduce its activities and its relative market-share before a court decision was reached. More recently, in the Alcoa case, the court held that the corporation would violate the Sherman Act if after the World War II it restored its prewar market-share by buying up war-time government facilities. As we have seen, the corporation has not done so (cf. footnote 1, page 18). The court has found no artificial exclusion, yet it maintained that the corporation was not merely a passive recipient of monopoly power. The monopoly was not merely the result of superior efficiency. It was not thrust upon the corporation. It is not easy to see what this distinction means.

[20] For example in the Yellow Cab case, in the Pullman case, in the motion picture cases. For detailed references, cf. the last two items in footnote 18, page 304.

[21] The Clayton Act prohibits the acquistion of stock in competing

So far the legal concept of unreasonable restraint and the economic concept of "oligopoly not stemming from real-cost advantage" move together. Here, however, legal and economic thinking part company. The economist would have to say that an anti-trust measure which is not directed at eliminating Case 2 oligopoly (not directed at artificial exclusion in the broad sense) is good or bad, depending on its effects on social cost, output, and pricing. Preventing the growth of Case 1 oligopoly power by direct interference with "Case 1" mergers or acquisitions may sometimes be a good measure because the static cost-advantage of concentration may be outweighed by the dynamic disadvantage of slower progress under tighter oligopoly. In this respect, the criteria are rather indefinite, as we have seen, except perhaps in "strong cases" where a small static disadvantage is obviously outweighed by a significant dynamic advantage. In addition, interfering with certain manifestations of oligopolistic co-ordination is a good measure *if* there exists a presumption that they will give way to less undesirable manifestations of oligopolistic co-ordination. The previous discussion of freight-absorption illustrates this proposition. But legal practice is not usually led by this type of consideration. In periods of laxity it was lax in relation to artifical exclusion and it went beyond concerning itself with artificial exclusion only in condemning price-fixing or market-sharing based on explicit agreement. In periods of vigorous activity (as at present) legal practice is stricter with artificial exclu-

---

enterprise, when this lessens competition materially. But it does not prohibit the acquisition of real assets. It is true that the general provisions of the Sherman Act could in principle be interpreted to prohibit everything except pure competition. But we have seen that they are not so interpreted and could of course not be so interpreted. This is the reason why such further legislation as is contained in the Clayton Act, Robinson -Patman Act, etc. was adopted.

sion and it goes beyond the area of artificial exclusion in an economically haphazard way. This is the point where the clash between legal and economic thinking is most apparent.[22]

Haphazard expressions of the intention to cover more than artificial exclusion by the concept of unreasonable restraint have recently become numerous. Basing point systems were outlawed (cement and steel conduit cases) because they were said to prove the existence of explicit agreement *or of the spontaneous co-ordination of business policies*. Yet freight-absorption in general was not outlawed, apparently with the idea that somewhat unsystematic freight-absorption is good because it is reminiscent of competitive flexibility. In the Alcoa case a very high market-share was declared a violation because the corporation sought rather than merely received a monopolistic position. According to the court the monopoly was assuredly not thrust upon the corporation by its superior skill, yet at the same time it was said (possibly) not to have practiced artificial exclusion.[23] The objectionable market-share was stated as 90%. No one knows at what percentage figure the market-share becomes objectionable per se and what it means to be a passive recipient of monopoly power. In other cases the ability to exclude was held to be a violation, regardless of whether exclusion was, or was not, practiced (tobacco case). This should mean that oligopoly in general is a violation, although obviously

---

[22] The attention of economists and of lawyers was called to this conflict very effectively by Professor E. S. Mason, "Monopoly in Law and Economics," reprinted from the 1937 volume of the *Yale Review*, in *Readings in the Social Control of Industry*, Philadelphia, 1947.

[23] Cf. footnote 19, page 305. This really means interpreting artificial exclusion narrowly instead of broadly and then basing an adverse decision on something else.

no one contemplates atomizing the American industry, without regard to real costs. It should be added that in most cases where these general condemnations were made, something more specific also was present. This may even be true of all cases. Frequently the courts could have found artificial exclusion in the broad sense and in some cases they actually did find it, in addition to expressing these general condemnations. But the philosophy underlying the present legal practice is not clear in terms of economics.

The concept of artificial exclusion should be applied to all oligopoly not based on real-cost advantages. The area of artificial exclusion in this broad sense should be covered thoroughly. As for further measures, these should be justifiable by showing that the alternatives which they implicitly favor are economically superior. Otherwise they are likely to do more harm than good. *Suppressing certain manifestations of oligopolistic co-ordination means favoring other manifestations.* To rule against correct anticipation of rival reaction is a confused objective.

Government regulations of prices on the basis of competitive norms would not be a confused objective in the same sense. Yet there are at least three difficulties connected with such a program, and each of these is substantial. It is inconceivable that the authority should have objective information about cost functions and demand conditions in all industries such as would be required for setting relative prices correctly in accordance with competitive norms. Secondly, it is inconceivable that the authority should be capable of calculating the probable effects of uncertainty. In fact, there is no well-defined welfare criterion for the weight that should be attached to uncertainty; the propositions concerning competitive al-

location are established for models in which there is no
uncertainty concerning the shapes of the relevant functions. Thirdly, even if these difficulties were insignificant,
there still would be an overwhelming sentiment against
permanent and all-pervading price control in democratic
countries. Rightly so, because for efficient handling of such
a system by any authority, that authority would have to
be independent of all political and economic power groups
in a degree in which only the agencies of a totalitarian
government can be independent.

The establishment of government plants for setting the
prices of oligopolistic industries at a socially desirable
level gives rise to the difficulty that the conditions under
which government enterprise operates cannot be interpreted as duplicates of the conditions surrounding a private firm. Few persons will deny that government enterprise has a "rightful place" where the profit motive
cannot be made a sufficient incentive for calling forth a
clearly desirable economic activity. This, of course, is a
matter of degree. Where it is impossible to bring prices
down to a reasonable level in a private industry, the output
is insufficient and the case differs only in degree from those
in which private output is not forthcoming at all and
hence government production is justified. However, here
again one is building on vague criteria. When are prices
high enough to justify establishing an enterprise which
operates under very different circumstances? In "strong
cases" such action may be clearly justified. But the establishment of government plants in an otherwise privately
operated industry cannot be satisfactory as a *standard
weapon* of anti-trust policy.

To legislate against oligopoly and against quasi-
agreements is less promising than some optimists may have

believed. Not much is gained by trying to force a group
of oligopolists to behave as if they were not aware of their
individual influence on each other's policies. Trying to enforce certain superficial symptoms of price fluidity merely
because they are vaguely reminiscent of competitive price
behavior does not solve the problem. The enforcement of
competitive norms of pricing and of allocation throughout
the economy is clearly an impractical objective. Yet the
anti-trust agencies may contribute importantly to the
achievement of socially more desirable market results. In
the foregoing pages the opinion was expressed that public
policy may make its main contribution by interpreting
the time-honored concept of artificial exclusion very
broadly, as applying to all cases where oligopoly develops
from sources other than economic superiority; and by enforcing the law against artificial exclusion vigorously and
consistently. The general character of measures of this
sort was discussed on pages 294–5. Low cost entrants
could be given effective protection, and oligopolistic markets could be broadened. Even where entry does not materialize, the threat of entry at the cost-of-production price
of potential rivals would set narrower limits to the exploitation of oligopoly power. The effectiveness of such a policy
could be increased by the power to prevent large mergers
and new acquisitions such as are not justified in terms of
real cost. That such a policy would disorganize markets
by creating excessive uncertainty seems highly improb-
able. The obstacles standing in the way of competing with
well-established firms remain substantial and frequently
formidable. It is difficult enough to prevent these barriers
from becoming entirely prohibitive.

In most European countries it has been the practice

either to tolerate explicit cartel agreements without making them enforceable by the courts, or to give legal sanction to cartel agreements, but to require cartels to submit to certain controls. It seems to us that the advantages of control are usually outweighed by adverse effects on progress, owing to tighter co-operation in the handling of the market variables on which technological and organizational progress depends. For the effective limits of co-operation are set by the danger that fighting might recur and by the desire to stay armed in case a fight breaks out. The possibility of legal recourse against violators reduces this danger. In many cases even the mere existence of legally tolerated explicit agreements might reduce this danger, regardless of the possibility of legal recourse.

COLLECTIVE BARGAINING

On the "traditional" assumptions of economic theory (now frequently termed "orthodox" assumptions) unionization and the resulting collective bargaining leads to a rise in money and real wage rates and thereby to reduced employment. This conclusion may or may not be valid in different sets of circumstances. The outcome depends on considerations to which we shall now turn.

(1) *The possibility that neither money nor real wage rates are affected appreciably:* Money wage rates probably are higher with than without collective bargaining, assuming identical circumstances in every other respect. However, the difference may be smaller than is commonly thought. So-called unorganized labor differs from organized labor more in degree than in kind. Employers face

groups and not individuals even if labor is technically unorganized. The wage policy must be acceptable to the group with which it is necessary to get along. If an individual worker is willing to work for less than the wage which is acceptable to the group, this does not usually make it possible to cut his wage, and if unemployed workers are willing to replace employed workers of a plant at lower wages, this does not usually make it possible to fire the old workers and to replace them by outsiders. The wage structure of a plant always rests on an implicit agreement (or "bargain") with groups, although a technically unorganized group is more nearly comparable to an "inefficient" union than to a union of average efficiency. However, it is not easy to arrive at general conclusions concerning the magnitude of the difference between money wages under efficient and inefficient unions, respectively.

The resistance against wage reductions in depressions may be great even if labor is technically unorganized, and this resistance is far from absolute (or "prohibitive") under collective bargaining. In periods of full employment the upward pressure on money wage rates is considerable even if labor is unorganized, and it is not unlimited under collective bargaining. For example, in the period from 1945 to 1948 it was not obvious from common observation whether a relatively "free" national labor market would bring smaller or greater wage increases than those actually occurring. During the "stagnant thirties" unionization produced money wage increases which presumably would not have taken place without collective bargaining because at that time there was substantial unemployment (even though the business cycle was on the upgrade). Wage increases during periods of unemployment may more or less regularly express a distinctive feature of wage behavior under collective bargaining, but the experience of the nineteen-thirties is inconclusive because this was the period in which unionization was spreading rapidly and, therefore, produced an initial effect.

An initial effect of unionization on money wage rates should be anticipated, regardless of the existence or of the magnitude of long-run effects. It is obvious from the analysis of Chapter X that the level of the actual wage rate between the upper and the lower limits of the bargaining range depends on relative bargaining power, and it also is obvious that unionization brings increased bargaining power for labor in relation to management. The question is whether given the "new" level of the bargaining power of labor in relation to management, money wage rates increase faster or at the same rate secularly. It is quite conceivable that the secular increase in *real* wage rates proceeds approximately in proportion to the increase in man-hour output, regardless of unionization. In fact, this would be in accordance with somewhat sporadic (and certainly incomplete) indications that over a period of many decades the relative share of labor in national income has not changed much in some of the industrially advanced economies, aside from cyclical variations. One possible explanation is that the long-run increase in *money* wage rates is not affected substantially by unionization, and that this long-run increase proceeds at a rate consistent with a long-run rise in *real* wage rates corresponding to rising man-hour output (and, therefore, to a stable share of labor).

This is a necessary conclusion *neither* from the "facts" (indicating some degree of long-run stability in the share of labor), *nor* from the analytical framework of Chapter

X. There are other possible explanations of the stability in labor's share. But we should not take it for granted that unionization brings a significantly different secular rate of increase in money wage rates, because, once the "new" distribution of bargaining power is established by the initial impact, the further rise may very well be determined by productivity considerations, that is, by the upward shift in the value product functions. In fact, this is one way of defining an unchanging relative bargaining power, after the initial increase produced by unionization. As for the initial impact, this might not stand out significantly in the materials from which the long-run trends are reconstructed because an average yearly rate of increase of 2 to 3 per cent during a decade (and a considerably higher increase in the manufacturing industries considered by themselves) may make it difficult to discern an extra increase of a few per cent which occurred sometime in the course of the decade in question. Also, while the available data give the general impression of reasonable long-run stability in labor's share in alternative income concepts, a slight increase does appear to have taken place from the late nineteen-twenties to the present. For example, the compensation of employees [24] as a percentage of privately produced national income rose from 56 to 58 per cent. In this period union membership rose from an insignificant figure to about one-half of the manual workers. However, there also was a significant fall in interest rates during these two decades and a considerable shift toward self-

---

[24] In addition to the compensation of employees, the income of owners of unincorporated business (including farmers) and professional income contain a considerable labor-income constituent. The total net income of these groups corresponds to roughly 20 per cent of national income. On the other hand, "salaries" probably contain non-wage elements.

financing which must have reduced the gross interest burden in favor of other distributive shares. Furthermore, there is a secular trend toward a higher percentage of employees in the labor force which might explain an automatic rise in their income share, except that the rise in the income share was at the expense of the profit-plus-interest share while the relative increase in numbers was at the expense of individual owners whose relative income share also *rose*. At any rate, the rise in the relative share seems to have been insignificant. The real hourly earnings of workers in the manufacturing industries rose by about 65 per cent during this period. Such a rise was compatible with a very small change in the relative share of labor because output per man-hour rose very significantly.

Approximate long-run stability of the share of labor points to a long-run increase in *real* wages which is roughly in proportion to rising man-hour output; [25] and one possible explanation of such trends is that in the long run money wage rates rise *because*, and to the extent to which, the value product functions shift upward. Real wage rates rise whenever the value product functions rise more than would correspond to price increase, that is, when productivity rises. The extra increase attributable to increasing relative strength in some periods may not affect the long-run picture very much. The problem here raised cannot be decided by the sole means of investigating

---

[25] If real output per man-hour changes in a different proportion from that in which real labor earnings per man-hour change, then the share of labor cannot remain unchanged. This assumes that the number of employees does not change in relation to the number of other members of the labor force. Hence the statement possesses merely qualified validity. But, as was argued above, shifts in the labor force could scarcely be used to explain share-stability if the assumption were made that wages did *not* rise in proportion to productivity.

whether union money and real wage rates have been rising more rapidly than non-union rates. They may well have.[26] But it is possible that productivity has risen more rapidly in unionized than in the non-unionized industries. At any rate, in the period of most rapid unionization (in the middle nineteen-thirties) wage rates seem to have *been higher* in the American industries which were being unionized than in the others,[27] and this may mean that these were comparatively high-productivity industries (therefore *possibly* also industries with rapidly rising productivity).

(2) *The possibility that money wage rates are affected but real wage rates are not*:   Yet it is possible that under collective bargaining money wage rates rise not only in response to shifts in the value product functions but in consequence of union pressure which might tend to bring about fairly continuously a more favorable division (from labor's point of view) of the margin between the upper and the lower limit of the bargaining range. In other words, money wage rates may be affected significantly by the bargaining strength of labor, but this effect may be offset by price adjustments, due to which the value product functions in monetary terms follow suit. For general wage increases this would be the outcome if the demand for goods and services adjusted consistently to changes in money wage rates. In this event prices might adjust completely, and real wage rates remain unaffected. This is essentially the "Keynesian" position to which, however, Lord Keynes himself did not adhere very rigidly. The present writer does not believe in the complete adjustment

---

[26] Cf. Arthur M. Ross, "The Influence of Unionism Upon Earnings," *Quarterly Journal of Economics*, February 1948.

[27] Cf. ibid.

of prices, as a general proposition, because investment demand is not geared completely to consumer demand, and there is no reason to believe that a rise (fall) in money wage rates will lead to a *corresponding*, proportionate rise (fall) in investment expenditures. But it is very likely that autonomous money wage changes—which are not responses to shifts in the value product functions—are *partly* (perhaps largely) offset by changes in expenditures and thereby by price changes and by shifts in the value product functions as expressed in monetary terms. This means that money wage changes may be associated with *very much smaller* real wage changes, and collective bargaining bears directly on money wages not on real wages.

(3) *The possibility that money and real wages are affected but the share of labor is not*: So far we have been concerned with the question whether collective bargaining does or does not affect real wage rates substantially. We have not excluded the possibility that it does. But we pointed out that it is equally possible to interpret the observed facts on the assumption that the effect of collective bargaining on money wage rates is limited to an initial impact, and that, for the rest, money wage rates change in response to shifts in the value product functions. Aside from this possibility, there is a presumption that autonomous changes in money wage rates are associated with much smaller changes in real wage rates. Keynesians have even argued that they do not tend to be associated with any "real" change at all. In this event real wage rates would merely respond to rising productivity. In other words, what was said under (1) (page 311) *or* under (2) (page 316) might explain why the share of labor has not

changed much, that is, why, aside from cyclical variations, wage rates change mainly *in response to changes in labor productivity* rather than in response to changes in bargaining strength.

In fact, this might seem to be a convincing explanation of the observed tendency toward a comparatively stable long-run share of labor. However, the argument is consistent only if we assume that the productivity of labor—that is, the value product function for labor input—rises in the same proportion as man-hour output. *For stability in the relative share of labor means directly (that is, without further assumptions) that real wage rates rise in proportion to rising man-hour output,*[28] *not in proportion to marginal value product functions of labor.* To maintain that the rise in real wage rates is in proportion to the rise in the value product functions of *labor* is to imply that the value product functions of labor rise in the same proportion as man-hour output. As Professor Hicks has shown,[29] this is plausible only if it is assumed that a rise in labor costs in relation to other costs induces labor-saving innovations, that is, innovations which increase the productivity of capital in a higher proportion than that of labor. It would also have to be assumed that a rise in non-labor costs in relation to labor costs induces capital-saving innovations, that is, innovations which increase the productivity of capital more than that of labor. Otherwise, if the secular accumulation of capital far exceeds the secular increase in the labor force—as was the case in many past periods—a more rapid increase in the productivity of labor than in that of capital would have to

---

[28] Cf. footnote 25, p. 315.
[29] J. R. Hicks, *The Theory of Wages* (London, 1932), chap. **vi**.

result, and hence the rise in the productivity of labor would considerably exceed the rise in man-hour output.[30] If the long-run increase in the labor force exceeds the rate of capital accumulation—as may have been the case during the last two decades—the rise in the productivity of labor would fall short of the rise in man-hour output. Consequently, the view that real wages rise in proportion to *labor productivity* and that relative shares remain stable for this reason implies that a rise in labor costs in relation to other costs induces labor-saving innovations with the result that labor costs do not remain high in relation to other costs. If this were not so, a change in labor productivity would not be the same thing as a change in man-hour output, and what we know by observation is that real wage rates rise roughly in proportion to man-hour output. If and only if we make the assumption that a rise in labor costs relative to other costs tends to call forth labor-saving innovations can the observed secular stability in labor's share—that is, the observed tendency of real wage rates to move in proportion to *man-hour output*—be explained by the theory that trends in real wage rates are determined by trends in *labor productivity*. Yet in this event it is also possible to reverse the causal sequence. Conceivably, unions *do* produce autonomous increases in money wage rates and these *are* associated with increases in real wage rates which also are autonomous in the sense of not being induced by rising productivity; yet the ensuing rise in labor costs relative to other costs may call forth (may "induce") innovations due to which the value

---

[30] The elasticity of substitution of capital for labor would have to fall below unity and—in the absence of labor-saving innovations—the share of labor would have to increase.

product functions of labor and man-hour output rise sufficiently to keep the share of labor approximately stable in the long run.

(4) *The possibility that money and real wages and the share of labor rise, but output does not contract*: Finally, we should not take it for granted that a rise in money and real wage rates, that is *not* matched by productivity increases, *always* results in the contraction of output. The conclusion that it does follows from a model in which uncertainty is disregarded, but the same conclusion does not follow *necessarily* if uncertainty is taken into account. An economy in which the average and the marginal propensity to consume is high is a more stable economy because consumer demand is a more stable, more dependable constituent of aggregate demand than is the demand for investment goods. This is true because consumer demand stems from deep-rooted habits and partly also from biological characteristics of mankind, while investment demand is more easily influenced by purely psychological factors. In other words, investment demand is even more sensitive to "expectations" than is the demand for consumer goods, and this is known to producers. Consequently, the uncertainty attaching to business expectations is greater if the propensity to consume is low than if it is high. In certain ranges lower profit margins coupled with reduced uncertainty is likely to exert, on balance, a favorable influence on the willingness to invest and on aggregate output. A rise in real wage rates tends to produce these two "coupled" effects. A favorable influence is almost certain to develop in conditions characterized by very low real wages and a very low propensity to consume, while an unfavorable influence may be taken

for granted at the opposite end of the range (that is, for very low profit margins and a high propensity to consume). Close-to-zero propensities to consume on the one hand, and close-to-zero profit margins on the other are prohibitive circumstances if high output is the objective. If aggregate demand consisted almost exclusively of the volatile investment demand, uncertainty would prevent aggregate demand from ever reaching a high level regardless of how high profits would be if it did reach a high level (although, of course, *logically* it is possible to describe a full-employment economy in which the average and marginal propensity to consume is, say, 1 per cent). At the other end of the range, if profit margins were close to zero, high output would not be forthcoming, regardless of how high the propensity to consume might be, because while a high propensity to consume diminishes uncertainty, it does not reduce it to the neighborhood of zero. Somewhere between these extremes there must be an optimum or there might be several. The available information does not make it possible to locate these, but we should not take it for granted that a general rise in real wage rates such as cuts into profit margins *always* tends to reduce output and employment.

CONSEQUENCES

To assure collective bargaining means institutionalizing and strengthening an element of labor monopoly in labor-management relations. Even in the absence of "collective bargaining" these relations would not be purely competitive, or atomistic, on the supply side because employers are always facing groups of workers rather than individuals. On the demand side these relations typically contain an element of monopsony in consequence of incomplete labor mobility. The effect of collective bargaining is to strengthen the monopoly element on the supply side. This is accomplished by what in Chapter I was termed Case 8 restriction. The Case 3 variety of restriction expresses itself in the legal enforcement of trade agreements.

While the "traditional" consequences of monopoly may develop from the trend toward unionization and collective bargaining, this need not always be true. In the first place, it is not obvious to what extent money wage rates are affected (pages 311–16). Secondly, for the economy as a whole, it is not obvious whether real wage rates move significantly when money wage rates do (pages 316–17). Thirdly, it is not obvious whether the share of labor, and labor costs in relation to aggregate revenue change significantly if both money wage rates and real wage rates do (pages 317–20). Fourthly, it is not always true that output is affected adversely by a rise in labor costs relative to aggregate revenue (pages 320–21). If all these qualifying circumstances possess partial validity, they add up to a significant qualification. The indications that the relative share of labor has not changed much in the long run (that is, over a period of several decades, aside from cyclical fluctuations) would seem to point to the likelihood that these qualifications do possess at least partial validity.[81] The standard of living of workers has been scarcely

---

[81] The approximate stability of labor's share does not really *prove* this. It is *conceivable* that in the thirties and in the forties labor's share would have been smaller than was the case earlier, had it not been for unionization and collective bargaining. However, Professor Kuznets's estimates for the nineteen-twenties point to approximate stability of labor's share even in that period of low unionization.

affected by changing relative shares, but it has been very greatly affected by rising productivity (cf. page 315).

Of course these various qualifications "mean very different things," so to speak. To the extent that money wage rates remain unaffected, unionization is ineffective on the wage front (but not necessarily in other respects). To the extent that money wage rates are affected but real wages are not, we are faced with an inflationary force. If money *and* real wage rates are affected, but this is matched by induced changes in labor productivity, we are faced with a force which produces labor-saving innovations. If money and real wage rates are affected, and if at the same time change is not matched by rising productivity and if, in spite of this, the "traditional" contractionary effect does not develop, we presumably happen to move in a range in which the uncertainty-diminishing effect of the rising propensity to consume outweighs the cost-raising effect of the rising real wage rates. All these are possible qualifications of the traditional line of reasoning. Some or all may possess more or less validity in different circumstances. Their implications, however, are quite different. Only factual inquiry can help in forming a judgment on the probable significance of these alternative possibilities. Without forming a judgment of this, it is difficult to make categoric statements concerning the economic effect of unionism.

The problem clearly involves choices between different distribution patterns as well as the weighing of productivity considerations against equity considerations. Economic analysis can call attention to the elements which an intelligent person may try to understand *before* arriving at value judgments. Making ultimate judgments is not a "professional" matter. This is true of value judgments

concerning oligopolistic concentration as well as those relating to the increasing power of unions. However, if we
wish to continue under the present type of political institutions and with an economy based mainly on private enterprise, then the broadening of oligopolistic market-
structures is a highly desirable objective. Significant further concentration would probably destroy these institutions. If such tendencies should be produced by truly economic (real-cost) factors, then they presumably could not
be suppressed because, in the long run, communities are
scarcely capable of organizing their activities with *deliberate* inefficiency. But we have no compelling reason to
anticipate such tendencies from real cost factors alone.
The present degree of concentration is partly—possibly
largely—a product of artificial exclusion in the broad
sense.

Atomizing the labor supply is neither desirable nor
practical. Yet the growth of unionism is also an aspect
of the problem of economic concentration and it should be
remembered that the preservation of the present type of
political system becomes impossible if the concentration of
economic power develops beyond certain limits. Economic
power groups are manageable by democratic methods only
if there is a variety of them and if their activities at least
partly neutralize rather than reinforce one another.

In every phase of the conflict of interests between labor
(or labor organizations) and employers (or their institutions) much depends on the attitude of the government.
This is true not only of the general government attitude
but also of the specific attitudes, as they develop in particular instances in relation to specific conflicts. In democratic countries, governments cannot afford to disregard

the "labor vote," nor can they afford to disregard employers' interests. This has its good side which expresses itself perhaps most clearly in the fact that union men are usually convinced of the potency of the reactionary pressures under which governments operate, while the other side is just as sincerely convinced that legislators and government officials are sacrificing the legitimate interests of management in order to capture the votes of the poor and envious. The kind of shifting and oscillating "equilibrium" which emerges in such circumstances has bad as well as good sides because it favors the well organized—and, within their ranks, the most powerful sub-groups—as against the comparatively unorganized.

A significant problem in connection with which some of the disadvantages become particularly apparent is the problem of full-employment policies. The fact that organized groups are capable of generating substantial inflationary tendencies at high levels of employment—even without pre-existing excess of demand over supply at given prices—creates the most important single difficulty with which a consistent full-employment policy would be faced. In the long run, this difficulty forces compromise solutions between the objective of constant full employment and price-stability objectives.

Adopting thorough-going and comprehensive government controls could not solve difficulties of this sort in the democratic framework. The absolute (general) price and wage level cannot be controlled without setting and controlling relative prices and wages. Setting and maintaining relative prices and wages more or less arbitrarily must necessarily impede adjustments. Such a policy cannot help sharing important features with the so-called parity-price

policy for agricultural products. Furthermore, even in
relation to the general price and wage level, total controls
could be handled effectively only by a government which
itself is independent of the various groups in the community. They could be handled effectively only by a
totalitarian government.—Total economic control tends to
be associated with total political control not merely because the one cannot be exercised effectively without the
other but also because it is impossible to become organized
successfully against the group on which everyone's job,
wages, and working conditions depend. In the economically
and politically successful communities few persons would
want to substitute a single, all-powerful group for the
variety of more or less organized groups with which we are
faced. The "radical" enthusiasm for this extreme degree of
concentration rests on utopian stories about the characteristics of the group which would take over. These are in
the nature of fairy tales. Aside from the political implications of such a change, it is highly questionable whether
anything like the present rate of technological and organizational progress could be maintained in such circumstances. The best we can do is to maintain a workable
equilibrium between the groups that have emerged and to
protect the individual within them as well as this can be
done without sacrificing too much of the efficiency of his
group in relation to others. Democratic government can
promote such equilibria, and it can provide considerable
protection to the individual in his relations to organized
groups. But it cannot shape things at will because, by its
very nature, it is a mediator who is recalled if he does not
satisfy all parties to some extent, or if he consistently dis-
appoints some parties very much more than the others.
This sets limits to how good these equilibria can be; it also

sets limits to how bad they can be. The second half of this statement is infinitely more important than the first. Recent world history has shown this clearly enough.

An irreparable accentuation of the conflict between organized groups is unlikely to occur as long as legislators and executives are forced to rely on groups of different kinds, located on opposite sides of the fence. This is true unless one side has the will and the power to force an ultimate showdown. It takes a great deal of desperation, and also of irresponsibility, to have the will; and as long as we are faced with a multiplicity of groups whose efforts at least partly offset one another, no organization has the power.

The present social order of the Western democracies depends on the multiplicity of influential groups which limits their power in relation to the individual and enables government to promote workable equilibria. It is, of course, possible to be pessimistic concerning the future of these systems. Technology *may* develop in such a way as to produce further significant concentration; and, as Marxians among others maintain, further concentration through the artificial exclusion of competitors *may* prove to be just as much a part of the "process" as technology itself. Also, the political obstacles standing in the way of successful business cycle policy *may* be insurmountable. However, the only way of testing these pessimistic views is to proceed consistently and vigorously on the assumption that they are wrong. At present it is impossible to base a convincing forecast on the past record.[32] But this surely does not mean that pessimistic guesses are just as good as confident ones. The acceptance of pessimistic predictions decides an otherwise undecided issue unfavorably. If tech-

---

[32] Cf. footnote 4, page 22.

nological trends, or artificial methods of exclusion, or the ineptness of monetary and fiscal stabilization policy should render democratic institutions unworkable, and if a combination of these factors should produce the extreme degree of economic and political concentration, then thousands of pages will be written to explain why the attempt to prevent this was hopeless from the outset. Presumably, it would also be explained how desirable the characteristics of the new, supreme power group are as compared to those of its relatively minor predecessors. Yet at present the only fruitful assumption is that the existing institutions are capable of being further developed and of being continuously adapted to the changing requirements of the times.

A NOTE ON THE TYPE

The text of this book is set in Scotch, *a type-face that has been in continuous service for more than one hundred years. It is usually considered that the style of "modern face" followed in our present-day cuttings of Scotch was developed in the foundry of Alexander Wilson and Sons of Glasgow early in the nineteenth century. The new Wilson patterns were made to meet the requirements of the new fashion in printing that had been set going at the beginning of the century by the "modern" types of Didot in France and of Bodoni in Italy. It is to be observed that the* modern *in these matters is a modernity of* A.D. *1800, not of today.*

The book was manufactured by Kingsport Press, Inc., Kingsport, Tennessee.